THIS IS YOUR SONG TOO

DIMYONOT דמיונות
Jews and the Cultural Imagination

Samantha Baskind, General Editor

EDITORIAL BOARD

Judith Baskin, University of Oregon
David Biale, University of California, Davis
Kathryn Hellerstein, University of Pennsylvania
Katrin Kogman-Appel, University of Münster
Laura Levitt, Temple University
Ilan Stavans, Amherst College
David Stern, Harvard University

Volumes in the Dimyonot series explore the intersections, and interstices, of Jewish experience and culture. These projects emerge from many disciplines— including art, history, language, literature, music, religion, philosophy, and cultural studies—and diverse chronological and geographical locations. Each volume, however, interrogates the multiple and evolving representations of Judaism and Jewishness, by both Jews and non-Jews, over time and place.

OTHER TITLES IN THE SERIES:

David Stern, Christoph Markschies, and Sarit Shalev-Eyni, eds., *The Monk's Haggadah: A Fifteenth-Century Illuminated Codex from the Monastery of Tegernsee, with a Prologue by Friar Erhard von Pappenheim*

Ranen Omer-Sherman, *Imagining the Kibbutz: Visions of Utopia in Literature and Film*

Jordan D. Finkin, *An Inch or Two of Time: Time and Space in Jewish Modernisms*

Ilan Stavans and Marcelo Brodsky, *Once@9:53am: Terror in Buenos Aires*

Ben Schachter, *Image, Action, and Idea in Contemporary Jewish Art*

Heinrich Heine, *Hebrew Melodies*, trans. Stephen Mitchell and Jack Prelutsky, illus. Mark Podwal

Irene Eber, *Jews in China: Cultural Conversations, Changing Perspectives*

Jonathan K. Crane, ed., *Judaism, Race, and Ethics: Conversations and Questions*

Yael Halevi-Wise, *The Multilayered Imagination of A. B. Yehoshua*

David S. Herrstrom and Andrew D. Scrimgeour, *The Prophetic Quest: The Windows of Jacob Landau, Reform Congregation Keneseth Israel, Elkins Park, Pennsylvania*

Laura Levitt, *The Objects That Remain*

Lawrence Fine, ed., *Friendship in Jewish History, Religion, and Culture*

Hassan Sarbakhshian, Lior B. Sternfeld, and Parvaneh Vahidmanesh, *Jews of Iran: A Photographic Chronicle*

J. H. Chajes, *The Kabbalistic Tree /* ילבקה וליאה

Alan Mintz, edited by Beverly Bailis and David Stern, *American Hebraist: Essays on Agnon and Modern Jewish Literature*

THIS IS YOUR SONG TOO

EDITED BY OREN KROLL-ZELDIN AND ARIELLA WERDEN-GREENFIELD

PHISH AND CONTEMPORARY JEWISH IDENTITY

THE PENNSYLVANIA STATE UNIVERSITY PRESS | UNIVERSITY PARK, PENNSYLVANIA

Library of Congress Cataloging-in-Publication Data

Names: Kroll-Zeldin, Oren, editor. | Werden-
    Greenfield, Ariella, editor.
Title: This is your song too : Phish and contemporary
    Jewish identity / edited by Oren Kroll-Zeldin
    and Ariella Werden-Greenfield.
Other titles: Dimyonot (University Park, Pa.)
Description: University Park, Pennsylvania : The
    Pennsylvania State University Press, [2023] |
    Series: Dimyonot : Jews and the cultural
    imagination | Includes bibliographical references
    and index.
Summary: "An exploration of Jewishness among the
    fan base of the band Phish, and how spirituality,
    ritual, and identity function in the world of rock
    and roll"—Provided by publisher.
Identifiers: LCCN 2023009761 | ISBN 9780271095660
    (hardback)
Subjects: LCSH: Phish (Musical group) | Jews—
    United States—Identity. | Rock music—Religious
    aspects—Judaism. | Rock music fans—United
    States.
Classification: LCC ML421.P565 T45 2023 | DDC
    782.42166092/2—dc23/eng/20230313
LC record available at https://lccn.loc.gov/2023009761

Copyright © 2023 The Pennsylvania State University
All rights reserved
Printed in the United States of America
Published by The Pennsylvania State University Press,
University Park, PA 16802-1003

The Pennsylvania State University Press is a member
of the Association of University Presses.

It is the policy of The Pennsylvania State University
Press to use acid-free paper. Publications on uncoated
stock satisfy the minimum requirements of American
National Standard for Information Sciences—
Permanence of Paper for Printed Library Material,
ANSI Z39.48-1992.

To our Little Ragers—Stav and Ido, Siona and Maya.
May they read Icculus when they come of age.

THE SET LIST

CONTENTS

ILLUSTRATIONS

FIGURES

ACKNOWLEDGMENTS

The task of compiling this book was complicated by a global pandemic and a consequent live music drought. And yet, we found ourselves surrounded by support, from both the Phish and academic communities, as we brought together the voices contained within these pages. We would like to thank many companions for coming along on this ride.

We offer our gratitude to Stephanie Jenkins, who, as the organizer of the Phish Studies Colloquium at The Gorge in 2018, planted the seed for this book and paved the way for thinking about Phish in a scholarly manner. She, too, deserves our gratitude for organizing the Phish Studies Conference at Oregon State University in May 2019, which jump-started this project. Thanks also to the Program Committee of the Phish Studies Conference, including Christina Allaback, Jnan Blau, Jacob Cohen, Natalie Dollar, Paul Jakus, and Elizabeth Yeager for recognizing that a panel on Phish and Jews was a worthy contribution to the proceedings.

We would like to thank all the contributors to this book for offering their perspectives on the myriad connections between Phish and Judaism. An extra special thanks to Mike Gordon for adding his unique perspective to the conversation. We also want to express our deep gratitude to Jason Colton of Red Light Management for his thoughtful consideration of this project and his support throughout the editorial process.

We are grateful to our many colleagues who read drafts, engaged us in conversation about the book, and encouraged us to explore this material in innovative ways. Thanks to Aaron Hahn Tapper, Camille Angel, Shaina Hammerman, Lila Corwin Berman, Terry Rey, and Laura Levitt. Phil Getz, too, offered important feedback and encouragement in the early stages of this work.

Many friends also helped us shape this project. Michael Beck, Taylor Ellis, Paul Goldberg, Dave Levin, Ian Schneider, Jason Ticus, Mike Greenhaus, Jen Lieberman, Eryc Klein, and Juli and Rick Palmon provided constant and instant feedback on ideas, gave valuable insight into Phish, and most importantly were a constant source of humor throughout the writing of this book. And many thanks to Andrea Nusinov for allowing us to use her remarkable photographs, which truly capture the essence of what it is like to be at a Phish show. We are additionally grateful to the many people who submitted photographs for use in this volume.

ACKNOWLEDGMENTS

Thank you to our editor, Patrick Alexander, and to the entire brilliant and visionary team at Penn State University Press for believing in this book and for shepherding us through the publication process.

Lastly, we would like to thank our families. None of this would be possible without their support. To Mike and Noga, we are eternally grateful for your love and support.

INTRODUCTION

The People of the Helping Friendly Book

Oren Kroll-Zeldin and Ariella Werden-Greenfield

A massive kosher hot dog hovers over the atrium of the Rock and Roll Hall of Fame in Cleveland, Ohio, greeting visitors to the building's central lobby. The airborne frankfurter, topped by classic yellow mustard and relish, earned its place in rock and roll history on New Year's Eve 1994 (fig. 0.1). As midnight loomed, Phish glided around the Boston Garden atop the formidable wiener in an iconic gag that stands out amid the band's storied tradition of annual New Year's Eve antics.

In the days leading up to the concert, bassist Mike Gordon invited a rabbi to bless the now famed hot dog, thus making it proverbially kosher.[1] The blessed, encased meat that soared above the crowd was not the only perceivably "Jewish" element of the Phish show that New Year's Eve; in the second set the band played a rendition of "Yerushalayim Shel Zahav," a popular Hebrew folk song.[2] Though most of Phish's listeners are likely unaware that the hot dog is kosher, the band's ride above the Boston Garden is part of their fans' lexicon. Since then, the hot dog has also become a relic of rock and roll, one that offers a taste of Phish's unique balance of humor and musical expertise and of the complex relationship between the band Phish, the live Phish experience, and contemporary American Jewish identities.

FIG. 0.1 Phish's infamous hot dog now hangs in the atrium of the Rock and Roll Hall of Fame. Photo: Hwy61Revisited.

Years later at Phish's New Year's Eve concert at Madison Square Garden in 2017, observant Jewish fans gathered during a set break for evening prayers, as they often do, most frequently at venues along the Eastern Seaboard. After the "set break minyan" concluded, the group danced and sang upbeat and joyous Hebrew songs, filling the lower-level concourse of MSG with sounds and movements associated with synagogues, not concert venues.[3] While the initial group who gathered for prayer was small, their song and dance captivated Jews and non-Jews alike who happened to walk by. Word of the gathering spread around the arena, drawing a crowd of participants and observers. On that particular New Year's Eve, fans carried a profoundly Jewish encounter with them as they headed back to their seats for Phish's next set.[4]

Phish is wild, wacky, and incredibly innovative. Although they infuse each show with a touch of theatrical absurdity, it is on New Year's Eve that the band most fully embraces playfulness through extravagant gags. Indeed, exactly twenty-three years after riding through the Boston Garden on a flying hot dog, the band's passion for theatricality emerged in a particularly elaborate visual display. As the clock approached midnight, Phish transformed Madison Square Garden's stage into an immense pirate ship as the band belted out heartfelt lyrics to a new song called "Soul Planet": "Everyone is together in this great big ocean / And the ocean is love."[5] Attendees enjoyed a graphic depiction of the high seas (plate 1). Yet it was the band's message of togetherness that made this New Year's Eve particularly meaningful. As fan reflections on this New Year's out-at-sea reveal, the Phish experience is fun, but it can also be emotive, love-filled, and personally transformative for those in the crowd.[6] As 2018 arrived and fans danced in the "ocean of love," the stage crew loaded cannons with blinking disco ball bombs, which exploded above the crowd in a confetti-filled countdown to 2018.

Phish does not limit their use of outlandish props or goofy hijinks to New Year's Eve. Drummer Jonathan Fishman wears a blue and red donut-patterned muumuu whenever playing with the band. He also occasionally solos on the Electrolux vacuum. Bassist Mike Gordon and guitarist Trey Anastasio jump on trampolines and perform elaborately choreographed dances from time to time. Such moments exemplify the band's whimsical persona, one that has endeared them to fans since 1983.

Live Phish

Though listening to a recording or reading about the band can provide a window into the world of Phish, the best way to fully understand the Phish phenomenon is through the live experience. A Phish show is more than a concert; it is a performative spectacle, one that invites attendees to become participants. Phish shows provide an opportunity not only to see and hear a talented rock band play exceptional music, but also to immerse oneself in a carnivalesque atmosphere that eschews the normalcy of everyday life. Some fans dress in elaborate costumes and some paint their faces. Others wear their most sparkly attire. Some sport dreadlocks and patchwork clothing, though admittedly less frequently today than in the 1990s when the band experienced a stratospheric rise to fame. Instead of strapping on high heels or loafers, fans don their favorite "kicks" for a night of dancing. Even those who wear street clothes to shows might opt to add an element of festive attire before heading to a concert. Others are gifted flair midshow from people they have never met. Fans bestow strangers with gifts of decorated Uno cards, homemade stickers, and pins as they pass joints and vape pens. Concertgoers share glowsticks and bags of white powder with friends old and new in an environment where excess is the dominant mode of being.

The visual impact of the crowds and their embellished outfits is enhanced by the smells of a Phish show. Cannabis smoke fills the air and comingles with the scent of sweaty, gyrating fans, many of whom wear patchouli oil or natural deodorant, if any at all. The prevalence of mind-altering substances is in and of itself jarring. Drug and alcohol use are rampant at Phish shows, as many fans indulge to enhance their musical and bodily experience. People move in uninhibited ways, twirling and bopping in freeform step. For such fans, drugs encourage such release. Others need no chemical encouragement to shed the expectations of general society and join the Phish experience.

FIG. 0.2 Shakedown at the Gorge Amphitheatre, George, Washington, July 2016. Photo: Carley Lauren Eiten.

The carnivalesque essence of a Phish show extends beyond the walls of a concert venue. In the parking lot before and after, fans sell everything from T-shirts to grilled cheese sandwiches and veggie burritos along "Shakedown," the main thoroughfare of "the lot."[7] Colorful tie-dye banners draw customers to makeshift booths where vendors, who travel from show to show to sell their wares, peddle handblown glass jewelry, fan concert art, and vegan *bánh mì* (fig. 0.2). You might hear calls of "Molly!" and "Doses!" resound through the busy marketplace as dealers promote their goods in a shockingly public way.[8] After a show concludes, such calls are drowned out by the hiss of nitrous tanks filling up balloons. The party doesn't stop when "the lot" is shut down. You just need to know which hotel lobby or campsite to visit.

Phish regularly turns cities and small towns across America into music-loving utopias and havens of countercultural activity. Hotels accustomed to hosting staid business luncheons during working hours become late-night discos. Attendants at gas stations for miles around are left wondering about the people inundating their usually quiet businesses. Even after fans leave the concert venue or festival field, their presence reverberates through communities who benefit from the financial boon of Phish's presence while recoiling from the fans themselves, who are often judged too liberal, too hairy, and too smelly. Undeniably, sometimes Phish and their throngs of fans wear out their welcome, as they did in 1996 in Morrison, Colorado, home of the famed Red Rocks Amphitheatre. The band returned only in 2009 after a thirteen-year ban due to fans' unruly behavior. While admittedly boisterous, Phish concerts are unique ephemeral spaces wherein enjoyment, freedom, and connection reign. Coupled with fans' deep love for the music itself, the visual, olfactory, and auditory experience draws fans to the band, helping to establish their incredibly large and loyal following.

"We Are Everywhere"

In the 2002 *Simpsons* episode "Weekend at Burnsie's," Homer is issued a medical marijuana card by his unnamed home state. He quickly becomes a pro-marijuana activist when his access to medicinal cannabis is put in jeopardy. Homer plans a rally to garner support for the cause and hires Phish to entertain the crowd. The band, who gladly guest-starred in the episode, plays "Run Like an Antelope" on a stage decorated with marijuana leaves, closing out their set with a bit of the secret language they developed with fans in the 1990s.[9] Anastasio plays a few measures of the series theme song, which cues fans in the audience, of whom there seem to be many, to shout in response Homer's catchphrase, "D'oh!" It is easy to miss this cartoon conversation between band and audience. Most viewers likely chuckle about the episode's prominent association of Phish with marijuana and recognize that the band plays *The Simpsons'* main title theme. But only Phish enthusiasts know the secret language for what it is: Phish having a private dialogue with their fan community. Though not the first time the cartoon referenced Phish, upon the episode's release fans were thrilled by the band's involvement and by their quiet nod.[10]

Phish's musical prowess and their ability to create a boisterous and free-spirited atmosphere that actively engages their audience has created a devoted fan base who use the band as a point of connection and community building. To this end, fans are delighted by references to the group. Similarly, they thrill in identifying other fans in contexts beyond Phish concerts. Though infrequently, Phish occasionally appears in major network programming, including on NBC's *Community* and Comedy Central's *South Park* and *Broad City*. Fans relish such instances, even those that poke fun at their favorite band. On occasion, parents watching *Sesame Street* with their children excitedly note a red-and-blue circle-patterned muumuu magnet hanging on Elmo's fridge, which they then mention on social media as proof of the band's ubiquitous albeit sometimes discreet presence.[11]

Enthusiasts react similarly when Phish's music plays during major sporting events as a transition to commercial breaks; they share the news eagerly via Facebook and Twitter, accompanying their announcement with the proclamation "We are everywhere!" borrowed from the dedicated fan base of the Grateful Dead. The phrase is not unique to jam-band fan bases, as it is often used by minority communities to indicate their integral presence in the American mainstream.[12] In noting the ubiquity of Phish enthusiasts in public spaces, the saying creates an insider-outsider dichotomy, enabling fans to feel as though they are in on an incredibly special joke and to connect with one another in meaningful ways.

Most sports viewers don't know that they are hearing Phish. But Phish fans celebrate the occasion as proof that they really are everywhere, even in the Fox TV production booth, where Phish fan Jake Jolivette programs music for live broadcasts.[13] MSNBC news correspondent Katy Tur is conceivably the most lauded publicly facing Phish fan, however. Her Phish references are blatant and her lyrical inclusions inconspicuous. During her final broadcast of 2020, Tur included lyrics from Phish's "Julius," "Sample in a Jar," and "Down with Disease" in her closing remarks, the latter of which was playing in the background as she spoke.[14] The average MSNBC viewer might likely find Tur's language poetic while missing the Phish references included in her end-of-year message. Tur's broadcast contained multiple levels of meaning, one of which is intelligible only to the Phish insider.

Fans, along with their beloved band, have fashioned a unique language all their own, one built on participation in the Phish cosmos. Individuals mark themselves as part of the in-group when they, like Tur, include lyrics in their speech or excitedly share her most recent Phish reference with friends. They mark themselves when they wear Phish-related clothing and when they adorn their vehicles with donut bumper stickers. They mark themselves as insiders when they join chat boards and social media groups focused on the talented foursome from Vermont. In defining themselves as fans, they declare their love for a band and also their participation in the accepting, debauchery-filled, and freeing world of Phish.[15]

Though Phish fans may be everywhere, the band is decidedly not for everyone. Their songs are lengthy, and many of them, especially the classics, boast nonsensical lyrics and exploratory improvisational sections that render them unfit for commercial radio play. Phish fans who try to hook others on the band are often rebuffed by hesitant or confused listeners turned off by a song's lengthy instrumental sections. A recent episode of FXX's hit show *Dave* involves such a scenario. In the episode, titled "Hypospadias," Mike, who is a major Phish fan, shares a live stream of a Phish concert and some marijuana with GaTa. GaTa, who has never heard the band, affirms that he likes what he is hearing before asking "But when they gonna stop warmin' up, though?" Even the most devoted Phish enthusiast can understand GaTa's confusion. Yet Phish fans enjoy the exploratory musicianship so deeply that the mere mention of the band's name evokes a palpable excitement that echoes the energy of the concert venue.

Jewish Identity and Phish

Over the past four decades, Phish has developed a diehard fan base with a voracious appetite for all things related to the band—concerts, musical recordings, films, articles, internet memes, books, and more.[16] It is not unusual to meet a fan, or "phan," who has attended hundreds of the band's concerts. And much like the followers of the Grateful Dead, a dedicated community of Phish enthusiasts follows the band around the country, attending *every* show. Even when fans can't attend shows in person, they often stream concerts through the band's LivePhish website, enjoying what they colloquially refer to as "couch tour" and the creature comforts that come with it. Though streaming a concert from the friendly confines of one's home is quite different from being at the venue, "couch tour" allows individuals to feel connected to the Phish community even when they cannot be physically present.

Despite the many benefits of a couch tour, fans generally do their best to make it to as many shows as possible. Some worry that if they skip even one, they could miss an elusive song (known among Phish fans as a "bust out"). People attending the Phish show at Alpine Valley in East Troy, Wisconsin, on July 14, 2019, were treated to one such track. The band played "Avenu Malkenu" for the first time in almost four years—a 147-show gap—proving the popular Phish fan adage "Never miss a Sunday show."

"Avenu Malkenu" is a classic Jewish prayer whose hauntingly beautiful melody and somber words express submission, service, and dedication to God. When Phish plays the prayer, they honor the composition's traditional melody and message while reshaping it with funky rhythms in an arena rock setting. Hearing Phish play "Avenu Malkenu" is exciting for most enthusiasts due to its rarity. But the experience can carry special significance for many Jewish fans; a Phish show momentarily transforms into a synagogue, a sanctuary filled with collective, joyous prayer. For some Jewish fans, the occurrence of catching "Avenu Malkenu" feels special and familiar, while for others it feels no different from hearing any other rare Phish song. But there are also those Jewish Phish fans who describe hearing Phish play the prayer as a powerful spiritual experience.

Beyond the band's performance of Jewish songs, there are numerous elements of the musical, communal, and sometimes transcendental world of Phish that can be interpreted through a Jewish framework and offer Jewish meaning. Two members—bassist Mike Gordon and Jon Fishman—were raised in Jewish households.

FIG. 0.3 The "Antelope Moses" design by Josh Brady and Andrew Luttrell has appeared on T-shirts and pins.

Jewish fans celebrate that heritage with great excitement. Phish concerts attract people from particularly privileged socioeconomic situations and geographic areas, a reality that encourages a Jewish presence at Phish concerts and increases the chances of Jews enjoying concerts in the company of other Jews.[17] At shows, Jewish fans engage in Jewish activities as varied as praying during set breaks, as at the 2017 New Year's Eve show, and donning shirts with "Phish" written in Hebrew script.

Although most Jewish fans do not wear Jewish- and Phish-themed clothing, nor do they pray while at shows, Phish has nonetheless amassed a considerable Jewish following over the course of their career. For some Jewish fans of the band, going to Phish shows is actually part and parcel of what it means to be an American Jew. While poet Andrew Lustig does not self-identify as a Phish fan despite having attended numerous shows, his notable poem "I Am Jewish" includes the line "I am going to all three Phish shows this weekend." Phish is an important aspect of the Jewishness of many in his community, and so Phish attendance is, for Lustig, a fundamental aspect of his American Jewish identity.[18]

To that end, this book asks a simple question: "What is the connection between Phish and Jewish identity?" Perhaps unsurprisingly, the answer is not so simple, as a complex mosaic of religious and cultural ties link the band's music with Jewishness. As evidenced by the chapters in this book, Phish shows are alternate sites of Jewish cultural production and religious connection. So too, Phish is one of many avenues through which Jews find Jewish cultural and spiritual fulfillment outside the confines of traditional and institutional Jewish life.[19] Put simply, in and through Phish, a multitude of Jews are creating innovative Jewish rituals, building Jewish community, and engaging with and producing Jewish culture. Phish fandom and the live Phish experience act as a microcosm through which we see American Jewish religious and cultural life manifest in unique and disparate spaces.

For much of the twentieth century, American Jewish life centered around institutions, including synagogues, federations, and community centers.[20] In recent decades these mainstays of Jewish institutional life have become less attractive, in particular to younger Jews. Today, fewer American Jews identify as "religious" than in decades past and fewer American Jews belong to synagogues. American Jews are increasingly choosing alternative Jewish spaces and seeking new and meaningful points of Jewish connection or eschewing Jewish connection altogether.[21] As a result, innovative and adaptive American Jews have created new models and organizations for engaging Jewishly. The past two decades have seen a proliferation of niche organizations offering opportunities to participate in Jewish life. Contemporary Jews have the freedom to choose from a wide tent of Jewish activities, institutions, and approaches, all of which offer Jewish cultural and/or religious connection.[22]

For example, Wilderness Torah and Hazon structure their environmental activism and outdoor education on a Jewish ethical foundation, while Be'chol Lashon and Jews in ALL Hues advocate for a full recognition of Jewishness that includes and celebrates Jews of Color. Organizations such as Moishe House and Tribe 12 offer social opportunities for Jews in their twenties and thirties as a means of fostering community and lifelong engagement. Even beyond these groups, American Jews craft Jewish experience in independent ways, carving out their own unique forms of Jewish expression. Younger Jews in particular are increasingly seeking out exciting and hip ways of being Jewish. Many want to connect to a Jewish past, to Jewish community, and even to Judaism and religious belief in ways that feel fitting and culturally relevant within their contemporary lives. They may embrace pickling, or perhaps they bake artisanal challah and post pictures on Instagram. They may be active in a Jewish a cappella group. They might meet weekly with their Jewish improv troupe, or monthly with their women's circle. Or maybe they gather with Jewish friends whenever they have the chance to see their favorite band. Though at first glance some of these activities might seem devoid of Jewish significance, for those engrossed in them, they represent methods of engaging with and performing Jewish identities in deep and meaningful ways.

These robust points of Jewish connection allow Jews to engage in Jewish life in ways that feel personally relevant. Indeed, there are myriad ways in which Jews live meaningful Jewish lives outside the auspices of Jewish legacy organizations and synagogues. Attending Phish concerts is one such method. As the relationships between Phish and Jews exemplify, younger generations of American Jews are connecting Jewishly in unexpected ways and in unexpected places, a reality that shapes the ways in which Jewish fans listen to and participate in the Phish experience.

Using a broad and inclusive understanding of Jewishness, this book counts all who identify as "Jewish" as Jews and all who identify as Phish fans as such. For some who identify as both, the experience of attending Phish shows feels distinctly Jewish, while for others it does not. Yet even Jewish fans who don't feel Jewishly inspired at Phish are often aware that Jewishness permeates the Phish experience for those who choose to seek it out. For many Jewish Phish fans, the band's music and the

surrounding scene serves as a space within which to connect with other Jews, celebrate tradition, and even engage in behaviors typically associated with the synagogue
setting.

In recent years, Jewish studies scholars have expanded understandings of American Jewish identity and religiosity, thereby providing a framework of analysis for
examining Phish shows as a site for cultural connection and religiosity.[23] As Rachel
Gross proposes, "American Jews participate in a broad array of ostensibly nonreligious activities . . . that are properly understood as religious."[24] According to Gross,
nostalgic activities that take place outside of traditional Jewish spaces like synagogues
and JCCs should be understood as religious endeavors. The appreciation of such
"unrecognized religious practices of American Jews," and the unexpected places in
which they can occur, such as Phish concerts, expands conceptions of what Jewishness looks like while "complicating notions of a divide between Judaism, the religion, and Jewishness, the culture."[25]

Our position is that religion and culture are inseparable from each other. As
such, this book offers an expansive and inclusive understanding of lived expressions
of Jewish religious and cultural identity in and through Phish. At the same time, we
recognize the value that Jewish Phish fans place on these categories, and thus we use
them as an analytical tool to understand the relationship between Phish and Jewishness. Phish concerts and the Phish scene offer opportunities for Jewish connection for those that seek it out while also functioning as an attractive and comfortable
space for nonaffiliated, unaffiliated, and self-identified "secular" Jews to connect both
Jewishly and in other ways. A point of connection with other Jews might not be a
driving force behind a fan's decision to attend a show, while for others it might, as
Phish is an intrinsic part of their relationship to and experience of Judaism.

When Jewish fans listen to Phish play "Avenu Malkenu" and then discuss their
feelings about the rendition outside of the concert setting, they reshape Jewish practice and identity. So too do the Jewish members of Phish when they play the prayer
at one of their concerts. Further, when Jewish Phish fans have Jewish experiences
at Phish shows, they define what Jewishness can look like, urging us to reconsider
how we understand contemporary American Jewish identities. Concert attendees
foster new forms of Jewishness at Phish shows, forms that feel authentic and that
match personal identifiers beyond just "Jewish."[26]

In his 1981 hit "You Can't Kill Rock and Roll," Ozzy Osbourne declares rock as
his religion.[27] Some Phish fans do the same, noting that their relationship with the
band fulfills that which childhood religious affiliation left wanting, a perspective that
confirms the power of fan communities while affirming the work of notable scholars of popular music.[28] Yet, for many Jewish fans, Phish is far from a surrogate for

traditional religious belonging. Instead, the band and the world surrounding it foster distinct Jewish meaning-making. For many, the Phish phenomenon amplifies and enhances Jewish identification and spirituality.

Origins and Intentions

In May 2019, just months before Phish played "Avenu Malkenu" in Alpine Valley, over three hundred people gathered at Oregon State University for a three-day multidisciplinary conference dedicated to the academic study of Phish. The brainchild of Stephanie Jenkins, it was the first academic conference to focus solely on the broad Phish ecosystem. The tremendously successful conference drew attention to the academic study of Phish and encouraged the inquiries included in this volume. This book is an extension of a conference panel titled "The People of the Helping Friendly Book: Jews, Judaism, and Phish," organized by Oren Kroll-Zeldin.

We intend for this book to give readers a window into the remarkable depth of Jewish themes within the Phish ecosystem. Bringing together notable Phish fans, academics, clergy, and journalists, *This Is Your Song Too: Phish and Contemporary Jewish Identity* provides an in-depth analysis of Jewishness in the Phish universe while also pursuing a deeper understanding of how spirituality, ritual, and identity function in the world of rock and roll fan communities more broadly. The title of this book, *This Is Your Song Too*, derives from the lyrics to Phish's "Joy," which invites listeners to embrace happiness as indicated through the band's direct appeal in the song's chorus, "We want you to be happy / Cause this is your song too."[29] The presence of the word "too" in the band's lyrics includes listeners as participants in collective delight. The presence of the word "too" in this book's title alludes to Jewish inclusion in a countercultural space. Indeed, this book is about finding a joyful source of Jewish connection.

The title of this introduction derives from the eponymous book in Phish's fictional "Gamehendge" saga and draws on the colloquial name of Jews as "the People of the Book." Phish's musical canon includes numerous tracks that playfully whisk listeners away to the mythical land of "Gamehendge," where the prophet Icculus wrote the "Helping Friendly Book," a sacred text that "contains the secrets of eternal joy and never-ending splendor."[30] Almost four decades after Anastasio wrote about the pursuit of happiness, Phish continues to sing about finding gratitude and bliss in "Joy." As this volume shows, many Jewish Phish fans locate a distinctly fun and spiritually significant Jewishness in and through the band.

This book contributes to the nascent academic field of Phish studies, a subject area that takes seriously the investigation and analysis of Phish's music and fan community.[31] It represents the first scholarly investigation of the wide-ranging connections between Judaism and Phish. As such, we anticipate that readers will come to understand some of the myriad ways that Phish can be understood, experienced, and analyzed through a Jewish framework. Jewish meaning-making occurs at Phish concerts and in the fan community, which, in turn, impacts the religious and cultural identities of Jewish fans.

Structure of the Book

This book's structure mirrors that of a Phish concert; it includes a first set, a second set, and an encore. The first set centers on Jewish culture, while the second focuses on religious identification. We recognize that religious and cultural categorizations are arbitrary, as is the dichotomy between cultural and religious behavior and belief. Nonetheless, Jewish fans making Jewish meaning at Phish generally identify their connection to Phish as cultural and/or religious in nature. As such, we embrace these dominant modes of identification as they provide a framework through which to explore how Jewish fans connect to Phish while demonstrating how permeable these categories can be. The first two sections are followed by an encore that features prominent members of the Phish scene who each provide valuable insight into the world of Phish. The sections of this book each incorporate unique voices, much like Trey Anastasio's set lists, which habitually include varying types of arrangements.[32] Our contributors come from diverse professional and personal backgrounds. And yet, a love for Phish and a fascination with the Phish phenomenon draws together a wide-ranging group of academics, rabbis, journalists, musicians, and music industry insiders who each offer their thoughts to this conversation about Jewish identity, music, and popular culture.

Set 1 introduces readers to the ways in which Phish concerts and Phish culture more broadly can foster Jewish cultural connection. Kroll-Zeldin begins the first set with an opener that traces Phish fans from Jewish summer camps to summer tours. He introduces five key factors that contribute to disproportionate numbers of Jewish Phish fans relative to the general population in the United States. Jacob Cohen then considers the fan experience of hearing Phish's rendition of "Avenu Malkenu" and the consequent sense of belonging it provides for Jewish audience members. In chapter 3, Evan Benn moves from the auditory world of Phish into the culinary realm with a personal reflection that navigates the relationship between Phish, food (and Phish Food), and Jewishness. Thereafter, Isaac Slone explores dance as a means of connection, offering powerful reflections on movement, queerness, and Jewish masculinity while problematizing the male-dominated nature of the Phish concert experience. In chapter 5, Caroline Rothstein negotiates troublesome elements of the Phish experience in her reflection on whiteness, Jewishness, and privilege at Phish shows. Rothstein wrestles with the tensions inherent in recognizing something problematic about a situation that serves you—or about a band that you love—while also celebrating the work being done by social activists in the Phish scene who work to make Phish shows a safe space for all. Finally, the set concludes with Ben David's personal reflection on the healing effects of Phish's music and the live Phish experience. Together, the chapters in set 1 demonstrate that Phish concerts, the surrounding Phish culture, and Phish's music itself offer multiple possibilities for Jewish connection, identification, and healing.

Between the first and second set, we invite the reader to wander around the "venue" of Phish fandom through a selection of poignant and playful images that summon readers further into the Phish cosmos to a vantage point from which meaningful Jewish experiences during the live experience make sense.

Imagine the lights dimming and a cacophony of cheers as you turn the page to begin the book's second set. The contributions to set 2 address some of the innumerable ways in which Jews connect and engage religiously through the live Phish experience and subculture. In the opener, Ariella Werden-Greenfield explores the religious roots of songs in Phish's repertoire and reflects on fan responses to their rehearsal. Werden-Greenfield reasons that the significance that Jewish fans assign to Phish's renditions of Hebrew songs is distinctive and demonstrative of a desire for societal acceptance and religious self-determination. Mike Greenhaus interrogates some of the ways in which Jewish faith and religious practice inform the lives of fans and the band itself. In Jessy Dressin's contribution, she compares the rituals and routines of a Phish show to those associated with the ancient Israelites' sacred pilgrimage to the Temple in Jerusalem. The second set continues with Josh Fleet's reflection on Shabbat observance, religious obligation, and the live Phish experience. While Fleet centers on halachic regulations and the logistics of attending shows as an observant Jew, Joshua Ladon considers how impactful the live Phish experience can be in the religious lives of ritually observant Jews. Ladon argues that such experiences can inform how Jewish religious and cultural leaders shape their own religious communities. Noah Munro Lehrman closes out the set with a poetic reflection on Phish tour and Torah, a piece in which he offers both textual exegesis and lyrical analysis.

Even after two sets of music, the crowd's anticipation builds as they wait impatiently for an encore, giddy with the promise of a favorite song or a rarely played tune. This volume's encore includes interviews with individuals worthy of similar excitement and anticipation. Shirley Halperin of *Variety* describes helping Phish learn "Yerushalayim Shel Zahav" and shares stories from her time in Israel with drummer

Jon Fishman; Rachel Loonin Steinerman discusses her love for Phish and the challenges and joys of attending shows as a religiously observant person; Marc Brownstein of the Disco Biscuits reflects on Phish's influence on him as a young musician; Jonathan Schwartz of SiriusXM shares insights about the music scene; and Mike Gordon, Phish's bass player, shares his thoughts about Phish, Jews, and Judaism in chapter 17. In the volume's afterword, Dean Budnick reflects on Jewish identity in the Phish ecosphere. Our inclusion of an afterword is an homage to the elusive second encore.

Some of the sentiments encountered in the following chapters may seem repetitive. Contributors to this book, much like other Jewish Phish fans, frequently cite their experiences with "Avenu Malkenu," discuss the Jewish identity of band members, and recount chilling, thrilling moments from concerts. These reflections and the voices of contributors echo one another, as they do the voices of other Phish fans, strengthening the claim that Jewish meaning-making in and through Phish is a significant form of contemporary Jewish practice. We anticipate that readers will approach this book in various ways. For that reason, this volume's contributions sometimes share thematic elements and are in conversation with one another. Some might read *This Is Your Song Too* cover to cover, while others will read chapters in a nonconsecutive order. Both approaches introduce readers to the phenomenon of Phish-infused contemporary Jewish identity.

Each chapter reveals Jewishness in and around Phish. Readers will encounter celebrations of the band's renditions of Jewish songs by Jewish fans as well as Jewish- and Phish-inspired merchandise available for purchase both outside of concert venues and online. From concertgoers gathering for prayer during set breaks to participating in Jewish fan groups on social media, Jewish fans are engaging in distinctly Jewish behavior as they celebrate their favorite band. The contributions to this volume individually and collectively explore Phish as a site for cultural connection and religiosity. Together, they beg you, our reader, to consider what Jewishness looks like, what constitutes religion, and how transformed we can be by rock and roll.

NOTES

1. Thompson, *Go Phish*.

2. Furthermore, in the third set, Gordon's maternal grandmother joined the band on stage.

3. Religious Jews pray three times a day in a minyan, or a quorum of ten people required for prayer.

4. Sylvan, *Traces of the Spirit*.

5. Phish lyrics included in this volume are based on those provided by Phish.net and verified by the band's management.

6. The contrast of the wackiness of riding on a flying hot dog in 1994 with the playful yet heartfelt "Soul Planet" in 2017 is

indicative of Phish's emotional growth over the span of their career and their remarkable musical and lyrical range.

7. This is a reference to the Grateful Dead song "Shakedown Street," track 3 on *Shakedown Street* (Arista, 1978).

8. "Molly" is a colloquial term for MDMA; "doses" refers to LSD.

9. Phish.net, "Secret Language Instructions," https://phish.net/song/secret-language-instructions/history.

10. The band appeared two years earlier in the episode "Lisa the Tree Hugger."

11. According to https://muppet.fandom.com/wiki/Phish, the magnet, which first appeared in 2018, can be attributed to set designer and Phish collaborator David Gallo.

12. Riemer and Brown, *We Are Everywhere*.

13. Orr, "Phish-and-Football Thursdays?"

14. Broerman, "MSNBC's Katy Tur."

15. Phish fans are not always accepting. Egos, attitudes, and prejudices surface in the Phish community, a reality addressed by several contributions to this volume. Nonetheless, love and acceptance reign as dominant ideas emanating from the Phish community.

16. In 2016, Phish ranked twenty-fourth in highest-grossing touring acts for the year, ahead of such famed groups as the Dave Matthews Band and Pearl Jam. Meyer, "Phish, Dead and Company."

17. See Oren Kroll-Zeldin's chapter in this volume.

18. Andrew Lustig, interview by Ariella Werden-Greenfield, March 12, 2021.

19. Gross, *Beyond the Synagogue*.

20. Pew Research Center, "Portrait of Jewish Americans."

21. Kosmin and Keysar, "American Jewish Secularism."

22. Alpert, *Whose Torah?*

23. Dash Moore, *American Jewish Identity Politics*; Hahn Tapper, *Judaisms*; Horowitz, "Reframing the Study"; Aviv and Shneer, *New Jews*; Levisohn and Kelman, *Beyond Jewish Identity*.

24. Gross, *Beyond the Synagogue*, 4.

25. Ibid., 5, 23.

26. Music is only one of many cultural pathways through which younger generations of American Jews are engaging Jewishly. The Jewish food renaissance, the recent rebirth of the American Jewish crafting movement, the celebratory resurgence of klezmer music, and the recent revivification of Yiddish theater are exemplary of such pathways. These cultural spaces are beacons of Jewish existence—and even observance—for Jews who identify as secular, and for others who are religiously observant. Gross, Myers, and Rosenblum, *Feasting and Fasting*; Eichler-Levine, *Painted Pomegranates*.

27. Ozzy Osbourne, "You Can't Kill Rock and Roll," track 3 on *Diary of a Madman* (Jet, 1981).

28. Till, *Pop Cult*; Hager, *Religion and Popular Music*.

29. Phish, "Joy," track 3 on *Joy* (JEMP, 2009).

30. Trey Anastasio, "The Lizards" track 3 on *The Man Who Stepped into Yesterday* (senior thesis, Goddard College, 1987).

31. Allaback, "Theater of Jambands"; Blau, "A Phan on Phish"; McClain, "Framing in Music Journalism"; Morris, "'Destroying America'"; Yeager, "Understanding 'It.'" A forthcoming special edition of the *Journal of Public Philosophy* is dedicated to scholarship on Phish. Additionally, an online Listserv of scholars called "University of Gamehendge" is dedicated to the exchange and circulation of scholarship about the band. Finally, Stephanie Jenkins, the organizer of the Phish Studies Conference and a pioneer in the field of Phish studies, teaches a course at

Oregon State University called "The Philosophy School of Phish."

32. Remarkably, Phish has never played the same set list twice.

REFERENCES

Allaback, Christina L. "Theater of Jambands: Performance of Resistance." PhD diss., University of Oregon, 2009.

Alpert, Rebecca. *Whose Torah? A Concise Guide to Progressive Judaism*. New York: The New Press, 2008.

Aviv, Caryn S., and David Shneer. *New Jews: The End of the Jewish Diaspora*. New York: New York University Press, 2005.

Blau, Jnan. "A Phan on Phish: Live Improvised Music in Five Performative Commitments." *Cultural Studies ↔ Critical Methodologies* 10, no. 4 (2010): 307–19.

Broerman, Michael. "MSNBC's Katy Tur Delivers Phish-Filled Farewell to the Year 2020." *Live for Live Music*, December 31, 2020. https://liveforlivemusic.com/news/katy-tur-phish-send off-2020.

Eichler-Levine, Jodi. *Painted Pomegranates and Needlepoint Rabbis: How Jews Craft Resilience and Create Community*. Chapel Hill: University of North Carolina Press, 2020.

Gross, Aaron S., Jody Myers, and Jordan D. Rosenblum, eds. *Feasting and Fasting: The History and Ethics of Jewish Food*. New York: New York University Press, 2020.

Gross, Rachel. *Beyond the Synagogue: Jewish Nostalgia as Religious Practice*. New York: New York University Press, 2021.

Häger, Andreas. *Religion and Popular Music: Artists, Fans, and Cultures*. New York: Bloomsbury Academic, 2018.

Hahn Tapper, Aaron. *Judaisms: A Twenty-First-Century Introduction to Jews and Jewish Identities*. Oakland: University of California Press, 2016.

Horowitz, Bethamie. "Reframing the Study of Contemporary American Jewish Identity." *Contemporary Jewry* 23, no. 1 (2002): 14–34.

Kosmin, Barry A., and Ariela Keysar. "American Jewish Secularism: Jewish Life Beyond the Synagogue." In *American Jewish Yearbook 2012*, edited by Arnold Dashefsky and Ira Sheskin, 3–54. Dordrecht: Springer, 2013.

Levisohn, Jon A., and Ari Y. Kelman, eds. *Beyond Jewish Identity: Rethinking Concepts and Imagining Alternatives*. Boston: Academic Studies Press, 2019.

McClain, Jordan. "Framing in Music Journalism: Making Sense of Phish's 'Left-Field Success Story.'" *Journal of Popular Culture* 49, no. 6 (2016): 1206–23.

Meyer, Chris. "Phish, Dead and Company, and DMB Among Top 50 Grossing Tours of 2016." *Live for Live Music*, January 12, 2017. https://liveforlivemusic.com/news/phish-dead-company -dmb-among-top-50-grossing-tours -2016.

Moore, Deborah Dash, ed. *American Jewish Identity Politics*. Ann Arbor: University of Michigan Press, 2009.

Morris, Edwin Kent. "'Destroying America': Phish, Music, and Spaces of Aesthetic and Social Exception." *International Review of the Aesthetics and Sociology of Music* 45, no. 1 (2014): 167–81.

Orr, Connor. "Phish-and-Football Thursdays? Credit (or Blame) This Guy." *Sports Illustrated*, December 17, 2020. https://www.si.com/nfl/2020/12/17/fox -producer-who-got-the-nfl-to-jam.

Pew Research Center. "A Portrait of Jewish Americans." October 1, 2013. https://www.pewforum.org/2013/10/01/jewish-american-beliefs-attitudes-culture-survey.

Riemer, Matthew, and Leighton Brown. *We Are Everywhere: Protest, Power, and Pride in the History of Queer Liberation.* Berkeley, CA: Ten Speed Press, 2019.

Sylvan, Robin. *Traces of the Spirit: The Religious Dimensions of Popular Music.* New York: New York University Press, 2002.

Thompson, Dave. *Go Phish.* New York: St. Martin's Press, 1997.

Till, Rupert. *Pop Cult: Religion and Popular Music.* New York: Continuum International, 2010.

Yeager, Elizabeth A. "Understanding 'It': Affective Authenticity, Space, and the Phish Scene." PhD diss., University of Kansas, 2011.

SET 1

"SHARING IN THE GROOVE"

Phish and Jewish Culture

1.

From Summer Camp to Summer Tour

PHISH AND THE CULTIVATION OF JEWISH CULTURAL IDENTITY

Oren Kroll-Zeldin

In the summer of 1994 I spent three weeks at Camp Swig, a Reform Jewish summer camp nestled in the Santa Cruz Mountains of Northern California. It was a beautiful place that smelled of redwood trees and was awash in the sounds of joyful children playing in the warm summer sun. Many of us lucky enough to spend the summers of our youth there understood it to be an extension of our souls. We deemed the space sacred and found tremendous meaning in its mere existence. It was where we returned, summer after summer, to reconnect with old friends, make new ones, and experience inexplicable magic.

One night that summer, our counselors organized a special evening activity. They had been talking about it for an entire day and we were eager with anticipation, likely thinking they were going to give us candy. Instead, they instructed us to sit on our beds as they took a CD out of its jewel box and popped it into the stereo. "This is 'Contact' by the band Phish," they said. "Listen to it carefully. When it finishes, we're going to talk about it."[1] In many ways, I haven't stopped talking about it since. I was transfixed by the whimsical lyrics, rhythmic complexity, and soaring jams that were unlike anything I had heard before.

That summer I found meaning not only in my Jewish camp experience but also in the vast Phish universe. Instead of seeking to relive the youthful magic of summer camp, which as an adult is rather difficult, I now desire to return time and again to Phish concerts, where I experience a different and similarly indescribable mystic enchantment. Even though I didn't know it at the time, that first encounter with Phish would springboard into a lifelong connection to the band, their music, the community that surrounds it, and, in unique and significant ways, to my Jewish identity. And now, more than a quarter century later, I still see Phish with friends I made at Camp Swig.

It is not a coincidence that I first learned about Phish at Jewish summer camp. As I came to understand in doing research for this chapter, the "Phish origin story," or the moment when people first encountered Phish, occurred for countless other fans at Jewish summer camp, particularly in the 1990s, in geographically diverse locations across the United States.[2] In fact, according to data from a survey compiled by Rabbi Josh Ladon that examines connections between Phish and Jewish identity, 32 percent of respondents said that they first encountered Phish at Jewish summer camp.[3] For those of us who first heard Phish within the context of this meaningful Jewish experience, it makes sense that our connections to Phish and Jewish identity would develop in tandem.

I consider parts of my Phish community to be an extension of the meaningful Jewish community I developed at camp. Conversely, going to Phish concerts and engaging with the band's music and the community that surrounds it helps connect me to my Jewish identity in particular ways. It would be a stretch to say that I perform my Jewish identity in and through Phish, meaning I don't do anything intentionally Jewish such as light Shabbat candles in the parking lot at a Friday-night concert or attend the set-break minyan where Jewish fans gather to pray (see fig. 11.1). But so much of the way that I experience Phish is through a lens of Jewish culture. In other words, Phish has helped me cultivate elements of my Jewish cultural identity because I approach the band, music, and community from a Jewish perspective.

As I thought about writing this chapter, I looked inward to try to understand why Phish is an avenue through which I cultivated a personal sense of a Jewish cultural identity. Sure, it could be that I first learned about the band at Jewish summer camp, or that many of the people with whom I regularly see Phish are Jewish. It could certainly be that as a cultural anthropologist who studies contemporary Jewish identity, I intentionally choose to see many things in the world and in my life through a Jewish lens. But as I researched and spoke with other people, I started to understand that this was not merely a personal experience. My experience reflected a widespread phenomenon. I heard countless stories from others who also felt deeply connected to their cultural Jewish identities in and through Phish. That led me to ask a much broader and more important question: why are there are so many Jewish Phish fans?

Though it is difficult to estimate exactly how many Jews there are in the Phish scene, there is little debate that Jews are disproportionately represented at Phish concerts, especially when we consider that Jews make up a mere 2 percent of the total US population.[4] A preliminary demographic study of the Phish fan community conducted in 2018 by musicologist Jacob A. Cohen confirms this, as roughly 26 percent of survey respondents reported growing up in a Jewish household.[5] Prior to Cohen's demographic survey, members of the fan community confidently stated that 30 percent of Phish fans are Jewish. This figure is anecdotal at best. Of the many fan blogs, articles, and comments in online chat rooms that reference this 30 percent figure, nearly all of them point to an article published in *The Forward* about Jews at Phish's music festival in Coventry, Vermont, in August 2004, which first deployed this statistic.[6] Interestingly, the anecdotal 30 percent figure supports the survey data showing that 26 percent of fans are Jewish, which reveals the fact that there is indeed a large Jewish presence in the Phish scene.

While Jewish summer overnight camp contributed to the development of a large Jewish fan base, it was not the only element that brought significant numbers of Jews to Phish. Through my research I discovered five key factors that explain the large Jewish fan base and Phish's appeal to Jews. A substantial Jewish fandom emerged as a direct outgrowth of multiple forces that converged, with Phish at the center. Phish was the axis mundi, the epicenter of various factors that drew Jews to the band and enabled Phish to be an important vehicle for them to connect to their Jewish identities. In addition to the significance of Jewish summer camps as sites that developed a large Jewish fan base, other factors include the rise of cultural Jewish identity in the 1980s and '90s, a Jewish affinity for countercultural movements, the socioeconomic class status of many American Jews, and the importance of humor to Jewish American cultural identity.[7] I interrogate each of these factors below in order to uncover why so many Phish fans are Jewish and why Phish serves as a radical conduit through which Jews in the United States perform and connect to their Jewishness.[8]

Summer Camp and Jewish Community

Numerous research studies point to the fact that attending a Jewish overnight summer camp dramatically increases the likelihood that an individual will have a strong Jewish identity as an adult.[9] These studies consider Jewish overnight summer camp to be one of the most important institutions to instill within young Jews a lifelong meaningful connection to their Jewishness. For many young Jews in America, summer camp is not only a center of joy in their lives, but also where they feel most comfortable as Jews in a safe and accepting Jewish space. Avi, who went to a Jewish summer camp in the Poconos, said, "Camp helped me understand the world through a Jewish lens. I kept going back year after year because it was fun and I liked hanging out with my friends there. But the most special thing about it was that it was the only place in my life where I was totally surrounded by other Jews, and it felt safe for me to explore what being Jewish meant to me."[10] Camp is a place where people create memorable experiences of singing songs, playing sports, dancing, and connecting with people who often become lifelong friends. According to Amy L. Sales and Leonard Saxe, camp is integral to the ways that many young Jews are socialized into what it means to be a Jew in the United States.[11] Through intentional educational programming in an isolated environment, camps provide a blueprint for how to live a Jewish life by teaching Jewish history, culture, and values to young campers.

Music itself is a big part of the camp experience and is integral to the intentional educational programming. At most Jewish camps, each meal ends with a song session, and the Shabbat song session on Friday night is often one of the most fun and memorable experiences of the summer for campers. Sometimes the song session may include popular American folk songs; other times they focus only on Jewish music. Regardless of the song selection, the joy of singing is central to infusing Jewish values and teaching into camp.[12] The songs come from Jewish sources as varied as the Torah, the Talmud, and the traditional prayer liturgy, thereby providing a venue through which one could claim, as one former camper and current rabbi did, that "all I really needed to know I learned in song session."[13]

The musical significance of camp transcends the teaching of Jewish values through song. Prior to the social media age, camp was a central place for people to share music with their friends and to be introduced to new music. Trading tapes and CDs was a common experience for many people at Jewish summer camps. Avi first learned about Phish from a counselor when he was a teenager, and a few years later when he himself was a counselor he introduced Phish to the kids in his bunk. He made an interesting point, telling me that "at camp we pass the music down from generation to generation, acting the way Jews are supposed to act when we pass down the teachings of the Torah from generation to generation." Phish's music sometimes acts as an auxiliary Torah; therefore, when I first encountered their music as a camper, it tied, consciously or subconsciously, into the intentional educational programming at camp, becoming the soundtrack of my Jewish education. Furthermore, Phish's music has been integrated into prayer services at some Reform Jewish

FIG. 1.1 Atlantic City Beach, Atlantic City, New Jersey, August 2021. Photo: Kory Brownlee.

summer camps, for example, by combining the melody of the Phish song "Wading in the Velvet Sea" with the prayer "Mi Chamocha."[14]

Since the "origin stories" of many Jewish Phish fans, especially in the 1990s, emerged from Jewish overnight camp, the meaningful Jewish experiences cultivated at camp often extended to the Phish experience. For many Jews who first encountered Phish at camp, their Phish crew grew out of the circle of friends from camp and extended from there. Of the people I interviewed for this project, many claimed that Phish shows act as camp reunions, while others noted that a shared love of Phish enabled them to build long-term sustainable friendships with people they first met at camp. Jon, for example, expressed that there was always an overlap between his friends from camp and his friends who loved Phish, which he says amplified his connection to both his Jewishness and his love of Phish. He "found his people" at camp based on their mutual interest in Phish. Jane expressed something similar. When she went to her first Phish show, she randomly bumped into friends from camp, including her former counselors, which made her feel included in something special that was bigger than herself. Since then, she frequently goes to Phish concerts with those camp friends she encountered at her first show.

Talia explained that one reason the connection between Jewish camp and Phish is so significant is that "they are both about *ruach*." *Ruach* is the Hebrew word for spirit. At camp, ruach is ubiquitous. From the raucous color wars to the sweaty folk dancing and energetic Shabbat song sessions, ruach infuses camp with an exciting energy. At its most stimulating and thrilling moments, the ruach at camp is at once palpable and indescribable. It is one of the feelings that people long for all year, eagerly anticipating the return to camp so they can experience and feel the ruach. There is a similarly indescribable yet palpable spirit at a Phish show. In the Phish universe fans often describe this spirit as "it" or "the vibe," and it is no different from the camp ruach.[15] Ruach is everywhere at Phish shows, from the anticipation before the show to the peaks of soaring and phrenetic musical jams and the moments in between. When fans could no longer experience the ruach from camp, they searched for, and found it, at Phish concerts.

The Rise of a Cultural Jewish Identity

Jewish identity is complex. In addition to being a religious identity, Jewishness is also a marker of cultural and sometimes ethnic identity. The 2013 Pew Survey "A Portrait of Jewish Americans" shows the changing nature of Jewish identity and the ways in which Jews are increasingly identifying with Judaism as their culture rather than their religion.[16] According to the survey, 26 percent of Jews born between 1965 and 1980 identify as culturally Jewish, whereas 32 percent of Jews born after 1980 surveyed say they identify as culturally Jewish.[17] Compared to older generations of Jews who identify in much higher numbers with Judaism as their religion, Gen X and millennial Jews are much more likely to have little or no affiliation with religious elements of Judaism. These trends encapsulate the main demographic of Phish fans.

Most Jewish Phish fans do not identify as religious, which is reflective of the overall Jewish population in the United States, where only 10 percent of Jews identify as religiously observant.[18] Not all Jewish Phish fans identify as culturally Jewish either. However, most Jewish fans skew secular; they are less connected to Judaism as a religion and are more inclined to the cultural aspects of the faith. Of those who identify as culturally Jewish, many believe that the traditional institutions of Jewish life do not provide the desired spiritual, religious, or even cultural fulfillment they may be seeking in their lives.

Among young adult Jews in the United States, synagogue membership and affiliation with other traditional forms of Jewish life, such as Jewish community centers and schools, has waned in the past few decades. There is tremendous fear among Jewish community leaders that this decreased participation in Jewish institutions will lead to a detachment from living a Jewish life and to the eschewal of Jewish identity altogether. According to one study, "The challenge of passing along Jewish connection and commitment to new generations has become the most important concern on the agenda of the American Jewish community."[19] As a result, people in the institutional Jewish world are devising creative ways to get Jews to engage with Jewish community. They have done so with varying success, as is evidenced by the popularity of international programs such as Taglit–Birthright Israel as well as more local initiatives such as Urban Adamah in California and Adamah in Connecticut, two organizations that use urban farming and outdoor education within a Jewish framework to connect Jews to their Jewish identities.[20] While these organizations foster intentional Jewish communities that draw on the intersectional identities and interests of Jews, Phish is part of society writ large and draws in a wider range of people. In other words, Phish is not an intentionally Jewish space, though many Jews are drawn into it.

While for some seeing Phish is akin to going to synagogue, for others Phish provides an alternative to the mainstream ways to be Jewish that are neither interesting nor meaningful.[21] Phish became one of the things that filled the void for those seeking meaningful Jewish community and didn't find it by engaging in more traditional forms of Jewish life. But perhaps more importantly, Phish satisfies these Jews' craving for spiritual and cultural fulfillment in ways that mainstream Jewish institutions never did. For example, Gabe told me in an interview that when he rejected Judaism religiously, he was still searching for community and spirituality, which he eventually found in the Phish scene because it fulfilled him in ways that traditional Jewish life and community didn't.

Through Phish fandom, some Jews tap into something that allows them to feel as though they are part of something significant and tribal that transcends the normal boundaries of everyday life and that has tremendous appeal. Noa says that she didn't connect deeply with Jewish life when she was younger but was seeking a meaningful Jewish connection nonetheless. "I found a meaningful place at live Phish shows that opened the door to the idea of God and Judaism being more than I knew," she says. "I started on a path to explore my Jewish identity as a result of being exposed to Phish." While many culturally identified Jews in America today are disengaged from the mainstream institutions commonly connected with Jewish identity, the Phish experience provides a site where fans can have meaningful Jewish experiences with others who are similarly seeking social, spiritual, and cultural fulfillment. Mark perfectly sums this up when he explains, "Phish brought me a step closer to the Jewish roots I shied away from as a youth by highlighting . . . the fact that you can have a strong Jewish identity while not practicing on a traditional level." Though seeing Phish may have been an important spiritual or religious experience for some, Phish shows also became, and remain, significant sites of alternative Jewish cultural production.

Affinity for Counterculture

Though Jews are a mere 2 percent of the population in the United States, they have an outsized presence in fields such as academia, politics, and popular culture. Yet despite their assimilation into mainstream American society, Jews remain a marginalized ethnic, cultural, and religious community.[22] While on the one hand, Ashkenazi Jews have successfully integrated into mainstream American life, they are also perennial outsiders who exist on the fringes of society and even today remain a targeted minority community that does not conform to the dominant white Christian American identity.[23] As a marginalized group, Jews often seek out spaces where they can be accepted as insiders, and Jews sometimes find that acceptance in countercultural movements, which tend to be more tolerant of difference than mainstream societal spaces. For example, Jews are disproportionately represented in new religious movements, which can be understood as countercultural since they characteristically eschew the values of mainstream religious and cultural life. Two possible explanations for this disproportionate representation of Jews is that "the major constituency of new religious movement members were 18–25 year old, middle-class, college educated youth, a community in which Jews were also disproportionately represented, and that the top three states where new religious movements flourished were California, New York, and Illinois, three states where approximately half of all U.S. Jews reside."[24] This might as well describe a major cohort of Phish fans in the 1990s.

Furthermore, many Jews were influenced by the phenomenon of new religious movements in the 1960s and created distinctly Jewish movements intended to spiritually reengage Jews in the traditions of their faith such as the Jewish Renewal movement, which is today a thriving religious and spiritual community. According to Yaakov Ariel, Jewish engagement in new religious movements since the 1960s helped expand the boundaries of Jewish life and showed that nontraditional affiliations and practices could be accepted in and by Jewish communities.[25] Some even consider the practice of Judaism in the United States to itself be a counterculture.[26] But perhaps the most relevant of the countercultural new religious movements to Phish fans, due to its physical and cultural proximity to the Grateful Dead, a band to which Phish is often compared, is the House of Love and Prayer, a radical Jewish experiment in the late 1960s and early 1970s. The House of Love and Prayer was a hugely popular hippie, neo-Hasidic, countercultural Jewish commune in San Francisco that successfully redefined methods of religious worship while revitalizing Jewish spiritual connections among detached and disaffiliated Jews at a time of great crisis in Jewish and American life. The individuals who lived at and created the House of Love and Prayer attempted to infuse greater Jewish spirituality and tradition into everyday experiences for those hippies who were searching for meaning, offering a uniquely Jewish alternative to the mostly secular counterculture. The House of Love and Prayer was attractive to those Jewish outsiders seeking spiritual fulfillment during the heyday of the 1960s countercultural revolution.[27] Phish offers something similar to culturally identified Jews seeking fulfillment outside of mainstream Jewish life today.

Phish allows some fans new and creative ways to connect to their Jewish identities. Avi's experience illustrates how this can manifest for individual fans. "My second Phish show took place on a Friday night," he said.

> I was 17 and it was my first time openly not keeping Shabbat. The show turned out to be one of the best shows of my life and opened me up to the possibility that I could encounter God outside the norms and social binds of my childhood. Later in life I would discover a whole community of Jews who had similar tendencies and for many of them, Phish was a core feature of their religious orientation. So, in a sense, Phish both helped me ease out of my given Jewish sociality and helped me find and create a new way of being Jewish.[28]

For Avi and others like him, it was easy to find Jewish nourishment through Phish in part because the community surrounding the band is open to ways of being outside the traditional norms of American life, and by extension to Jewish Americans. Phish is, after all, the quintessential countercultural outsider musical act in the United States and has been for the past three decades.

Phish exists on the fringes of popular music in America. Those unfamiliar with the Phish phenomenon are often baffled by their popularity, especially given the fact that their music is rarely played on the radio and they have never had a single or album climb to the top of the pop charts. Their firm entrenchment at the apex of countercultural musical acts in the United States is attractive to many young Jews who reject what they find to be uninteresting forms of Jewish life. The band and its community took hold as one of the countercultural spaces that attracted young Jews in the '90s and gave them the opportunity to become insiders despite being treated as outsiders by the general society. Within the Phish scene, fans can feel comfortable making the conscious choice to be Jewish, knowing that the band, their music, and the live concert experience help them connect to something greater than themselves. Though other musical acts could play the role that Phish does in cultivating cultural Jewish identity, it is certainly impactful that half of the band members were raised in Jewish homes and that they play Jewish and Israeli music as part of their expansive musical catalog.

Socioeconomics

After forming at the University of Vermont, Phish catapulted to fame by playing frequently in college towns throughout the Northeast. Relative to the general population, Jews represent a disproportionate percentage of students at institutions of higher education. Some estimate that the proportion of Jewish students at elite colleges and universities in the United States, particularly the esteemed private schools in the Northeast, was as high as 25 percent in the 1990s, just as Phish was rising to fame.[29] Since large numbers of Jews attended Phish's early concerts, and since many had the socioeconomic privilege that enabled them to see live music as high school and college students, many found the Phish scene to be an attractive alternative to the more mainstream institutions of their youth.

The socioeconomic class status of many Jews is integral to their ability to see Phish concerts. In the early years of the band's career, only those college students with disposable income or the class privilege to drive all over the Northeast were able to follow Phish and see shows night after night. The same continues to be true today, even as many fans are older and may need to cover the costs of a babysitter on top of ticket prices. Not all Jews enjoy this level of privilege.

Growing up in California I had fewer opportunities to see Phish than people who lived in the Northeast, where Phish played more frequently. Whenever Phish did play on the West Coast, I did everything I could to see them play. I remember traveling from my home in Los Angeles to Las Vegas in 1998 for the Halloween concerts and feeling so grateful for the opportunity to see those shows. I had worked the previous summer to make enough money to pay for the trip, yet the journey was only possible because my family helped support my travels. I saw many more Phish concerts as an undergraduate at Skidmore College in Saratoga Springs, New York, as the band played so frequently in the area. I also had the class privilege to be able to afford to see numerous concerts, even while I was in school. At nearly every show I went to while I was in college I bumped into other Skidmore students, many of whom were Jewish, including my classmates and friends Ariella Werden-Greenfield (coeditor of this book) and Mike Greenhaus (see chapter 8), whom I still see at Phish concerts two decades later! Phish was a big part of my college experience, and one of many reasons I decided to enroll at Skidmore was that I knew Phish was part of the campus culture. Phish shows have therefore become pseudo–college reunions in the same way that they are camp reunions. Still, not everyone has the financial ability to attend Jewish summer camp, a private liberal arts college, *and* numerous Phish concerts. The class privilege enjoyed by many Phish fans, including Jewish fans, is starker and more evident today than ever before, especially as ticket prices soar to stratospheric heights.

Another important marker of the privileged socioeconomic status of many Phish fans is the fact that so many people keep track of and tout the number of shows they have attended. Among Phish fans, the number of shows attended is often perceived as a hierarchical status of fandom; the more shows you have attended, the more devoted you are to the band. Given that concert tickets are expensive and that people often spend significant sums of money on travel, lodging, food, and other accoutrements such as drugs and alcohol to enhance the show experience, it can cost a startling sum of money to go on Phish tour.

Humor

According to the 2013 Pew Research Center survey on American Jews, 42 percent of Jews in the United States say that having a sense of humor is an important facet of their Jewish identity.[30] This is an astonishing figure that ranks equal to the percentage of Jews who say that caring about Israel is important to them as Jews; it is also significantly higher than the percentage of Jews who say that observing Jewish law is essential to what being Jewish means to them. Jews, who have long been targets of antisemitism, persecution, and oppression, often turn to humor in light of and despite their struggles. Many Jews use humor as a coping mechanism and strategy of survival, and humor was even critical to helping Jews survive the Holocaust.[31]

The 1942 film *To Be or Not to Be*, directed by Ernst Lubitsch and starring Jack Benny and Carole Lombard, provides a fascinating example of how Jews joked about the Holocaust in an effort to cope with the absurdities of what was happening to them. In the film, a group of actors performing a satirical play about the Nazis called *Gestapo* use their acting skills to fight Nazis through deceit. It is a slapstick masterpiece that allows the audience to laugh hysterically at the tragic situation during World War II. The film makes the point that it is acceptable to laugh at unthinkable tragedy, reinforcing the notion that Jews' humor is critical to their survival. Furthermore, the self-deprecating and inward-looking stand-up comedy of Lenny Bruce, Jerry Seinfeld, and Sarah Silverman, among other Jewish comics, often reflects on the Jewish condition, using humor to cope with the difficulties of being a misunderstood and sometimes maligned minority. But Jewish humor is not only about survival. Jeremy Dauber, author of *Jewish Comedy: A Serious History*, argues that Jewish humor is also about satirizing social and religious norms, the use of intellectual wit, and a key way to document the quotidian aspects of Jewish life, among other things.[32]

One of the major appeals of Phish for many people is that they infuse their music and the concert experience with humor. Aside from the absurdity of their songs' lyrics, the band is a group of jovial college friends who like to bring their fans on a whimsical journey each night. It is not insignificant that the ringleader of the band's humor is Jon Fishman, one of the two members with Jewish upbringings, whom many consider to be the heart of the band. Phish is named for him after all. According to band legend, Fishman ardently detests the song "Hold Your Head Up" by Argent.[33] Early in the band's career, as they would start rehearsing, the other three members of the band would start playing the song, just to annoy their drummer. While the three guys playing the song were laughing, Fishman would storm out of the practice room. Phish started to play a few bars of the song in concert, again to joke with Fishman, and now the song is a staple in their repertoire. Every time they play the introduction to the song, Fishman will get up from his drum kit, sing a song, and treat the crowd to a solo he plays on an Electrolux vacuum cleaner. Phish also has a secret language with their fans that is intended both to be funny and to confuse people in attendance not familiar with the cues. For example, if guitarist Trey Anastasio plays a specific pattern of four descending notes, the audience is supposed to fall to the floor in an act called "All Fall Down."

These are just two examples of the many ways the band uses humor in their live musical performances. Phish also loves trolling their fans. For example, in 2011 during their annual Labor Day shows at Dick's Sporting Goods Pavilion in Commerce City, Colorado, they played an entire show with songs whose titles started with the letter *S*. The next year at the same venue, they started a tradition to spell out a phrase with the first letter of the title of each song. At the end of the first set, the songs spelled out "Fuck You." By the end of the second set they finished spelling "Fuck Your Face," and then played their song with the same title. In 2013, the band played a set list that, when read backward, said "Most Shows Spell Something."

Perhaps their biggest prank of all took place on Halloween 2018, when they performed an entire set of music that they attributed to a fake Scandinavian band called Kasvot Vaxt, tricking fans with an elaborate "Phishbill" that detailed everything about this little-known prog rock band from the '80s. Fans were simultaneously confused and elated by the extravagant stunt, and Kasvot Vaxt is now an integral part of Phish's hijinks history. Countless examples of Phish's humorous and playful banter are now part of the band's lore and appeal.[34] Fans sometimes wait with eager anticipation for these whimsical moments, which allow for a playful interplay between band and audience, to the great delight of both. Since having a sense of humor is so central to the identity of many Jews in the United States, Phish was well positioned to take hold for Jewish music fans.

Conclusion

In this chapter I offered these five factors to help explain Phish's large Jewish fan base. These factors also serve as an important backdrop for my argument that Phish is a vehicle through which Jewish fans connect on a meaningful level with their cultural Jewish identity. Phish provides an alternative venue to build Jewish community, and Phish shows become a site where fans can have meaningful Jewish experiences outside the confines of traditional Jewish life. With the failure of mainstream Jewish institutions to fulfill such a large sector of Jewish Americans, it is significant that Phish shows, which are not in any way an intentionally Jewish space, are able to fill the void for so many.

Phish can be a vehicle for people to connect to their Jewish identities in unique and unconventional ways. Those who are seeking a connection to Judaism but find traditional forms of Jewish life to be uninspiring often find that Phish provides a meaningful outlet for community fulfillment. The moment the lights go down at a Phish concert, in the parking lot beforehand, and through the entire collective experience of the Phish community, the culturally Jewish fan becomes part of Phish's "spirit family." Eagerly anticipating the palpable ruach that emanates from the live music experience, the fan can set their soul free and perform their identity through a radical innovation in Jewish cultural life—a Phish concert.

NOTES

1. Phish, "Contact," track 11 on *Junta* (Elektra, 1992). My counselors were so inspired by the success of that evening's cabin activity that the next night we did the same thing with the song "Fee" (track 1). *Junta* was the unofficial soundtrack for our cabin that summer.

2. In my research I also discovered that this phenomenon is not unique to Jews or to Jewish summer camps and that many fans first learned about Phish at overnight summer camp.

3. Joshua S. Ladon, "Phish and Jewish Spirituality Survey." This survey is unpublished. Josh Ladon shared it with me in advance of the Phish Studies Conference in May 2019. See Ladon's chapter in this volume.

4. The total Jewish population in the United States is approximately 7.5 million people, based on 2018 survey data compiled by the American Jewish Population Project at Brandeis University, which can be accessed at https://ajpp.brandeis.edu/map.

5. Jacob A. Cohen shared the data from this unpublished survey with me in May 2019. See Cohen's chapter in this volume.

6. Tapper and Hahn, "Phish Phans Give Phinal Phreylach Pharewell."

7. While some may consider geography to be another significant factor, I reject this as a key reason for the large Jewish fan base. It is true that Phish became popular initially by playing concerts at small liberal arts colleges throughout the Northeast, an area of the country with a large Jewish population. But Phish enjoyed success and a Jewish fan base in geographically diverse locations early on in their career, not only in the Northeast. As early as 1988 Phish played in Colorado, developing a large fan base in the West, and the popularity of fans trading tapes of Phish concerts made it easy for people along the West Coast to access the band's music.

8. This research is based on an analysis of both survey and ethnographic data. I conducted in-depth ethnographic interviews with fourteen Jewish Phish fans, spoke with dozens of other fans in person and over email and social media, analyzed Phish fan chat groups, and read popular articles on the connection between Phish and Jews.

9. See Cohen et al., *Camp Works*; Wertheimer et al., *Generation of Change*.

10. All names are pseudonyms used to protect the identity of the person interviewed. Ladon, "Phish and Jewish Spirituality Survey."

11. Sales and Saxe, *"How Goodly Are Thy Tents."*

12. Kramarz, "Culture and Music."

13. Kipnes, "All I Really Needed to Know."

14. Phish, "Wading in the Velvet Sea," track 10 on *Story of the Ghost* (Elektra, 1998); Ladon, "Phish and Jewish Spirituality Survey."

15. Yeager, "Understanding 'It.'"

16. Pew Research Center, "Portrait of Jewish Americans."

17. Ibid.

18. Ibid.

19. Cohen et al., *Camp Works*.

20. See Hahn Tapper, *Judaisms*, 235–40.

21. Fleet, "Phish and Judaism."

22. Brodkin, *How Jews Became White Folks.*

23. For a discussion on how people experience this at Phish concerts, see Caroline Rothstein's chapter in this volume.

24. Tapper, "'Cult' of Aish Hatorah."

25. Ariel, "Jews and New Religious Movements."

26. Bush, "Judaism as a Counterculture."

27. Kroll-Zeldin, "House of Love and Prayer."

28. Ladon, "Phish and Jewish Spirituality Survey."

29. Aronson, "Princeton Puzzle"; Telushkin, "Vanishing Ivy League Jew."

30. Pew Research Center, "Portrait of Jewish Americans."

31. Slucki, Finder, and Patt, *Laughter After*; Carpenter, "Laughter in a Time of Tragedy"; Ostrower, "Humor as a Defense Mechanism."

32. Dauber, *Jewish Comedy.*

33. See Phish.net, "Hold Your Head Up," https://phish.net/song/hold-your-head-up

/history; Argent, "Hold Your Head Up," track 1 on *All Together Now* (Epic, 1972).

34. See Bernstein, "Phish Pranks Throughout the Years."

REFERENCES

Ariel, Yaakov. "Jews and New Religious Movements: An Introductory Essay." *Nova Religio: The Journal of Alternative and Emergent Religions* 15, no. 1 (2011): 5–21.

Aronson, Karen W. "Princeton Puzzle: Where Have Jewish Students Gone?" *New York Times*, June 2, 1999. https://www.nytimes.com/1999/06/02/nyregion/princeton-puzzle-where-have-jewish-students-gone.html.

Bernstein, Scott. "Phish Pranks Throughout the Years." *Jambase*, April 1, 2018. https://www.jambase.com/article/phish-pranks-throughout-years.

Brodkin, Karen. *How Jews Became White Folks and What That Says About Race in America*. New Brunswick, NJ: Rutgers University Press, 1998.

Bush, Lawrence. "Judaism as a Counterculture." *Jewish Currents*, October 1, 2007. https://jewishcurrents.org/judaism-as-a-counterculture.

Carpenter, Whitney. "Laughter in a Time of Tragedy: Examining Humor During the Holocaust." *Denison Journal of Religion* 9, no. 3 (2010): 12–25.

Cohen, Steven M., Ron Miller, Ira M. Sheskin, and Berna Torr. *Camp Works: The Long-Term Impact of Jewish Overnight Camp*. New York: Foundation for Jewish Camp, 2011.

Dauber, Jerry. *Jewish Comedy: A Serious History*. London: W. W. Norton, 2017.

Fleet, Josh. "Phish and Judaism: Going to Synagogue at Madison Square Garden." *Huffington Post*, December 6, 2017. https://www.huffpost.com/entry/the-phish-concert-as-a-je_b_826260.

Hahn Tapper, Aaron J. *Judaisms: A Twenty-First-Century Introduction to Jews and Jewish Identities*. Oakland: University of California Press, 2016.

Kipnes, Paul. "All I Really Needed to Know I Learned in Song Session." *eJewish Philanthropy*, July 3, 2015. https://ejewishphilanthropy.com/all-i-really-needed-to-know-i-learned-in-song-session.

Kramarz, Benjamin Max. "The Culture and Music of American-Jewish Summer Camp." Master's thesis, University of California, Berkeley, 2014.

Kroll-Zeldin, Oren. "The House of Love and Prayer: A Radical Jewish Experiment in San Francisco." Mapping Jewish San Francisco, n.d. http://scalar.usc.edu/works/the-house-of-love-and-prayer.

Ostrower, Chaya. "Humor as a Defense Mechanism During the Holocaust." *Interpretation: A Journal of Bible and Theology* 69, no. 2 (2015): 183–95.

Pew Research Center. "A Portrait of Jewish Americans: Findings from a Pew Research Center Survey of U.S. Jews." October 1, 2013. https://www.pewforum.org/2013/10/01/jewish-american-beliefs-attitudes-culture-survey.

Sales, Amy L., and Leonard Saxe. *"How Goodly Are Thy Tents": Summer Camps as Jewish Socializing Experiences*. Hanover, NH: University Press of New England, 2004.

Slucki, David, Gabriel N. Finder, and Avinoam Patt, eds. *Laughter After: Humor and the Holocaust*. Detroit: Wayne State University Press, 2020.

Tapper, Aaron J. "The 'Cult' of Aish Hatorah: Ba'alei Teshuva and the New Religious

Movement Phenomenon." *Jewish Journal of Sociology* 44, nos. 1–2 (2002): 5–29.

Tapper, Aaron J., and Laurie Hahn. "Phish Phans Give Phinal Phreylach Pharewell to Band." *The Forward*, August 20, 2004. https://forward.com/news/5160/phish-phans-give-phinal-phreylach-pharewell-to-ban.

Telushkin, Shira. "The Vanishing Ivy League Jew." *Tablet*, October 15, 2018. https://www.tabletmag.com/jewish-news-and-politics/272350/the-vanishing-ivy-league-jew.

Wertheimer, Jack, Sarah Bunin Benor, Steven M. Cohen, Sylvia Barack Fishman, Ari Y. Kelman, and Shaul Kelner. *Generation of Change: How Leaders in Their Twenties and Thirties Are Reshaping American Jewish Life.* New York: AVI Chai Foundation, 2010.

Yeager, Elizabeth A. "Understanding '*It*': Affective Authenticity, Space, and the Phish Scene." PhD diss., University of Kansas, 2011.

2.

Performing Jewish Identity and Community Through Phish's "Avenu Malkenu"

Jacob A. Cohen

On November 29, 1997, I was a sixteen-year-old kid from the Boston suburbs about to see my first Phish show at the Worcester Centrum.[1] I knew about two or three dozen Phish songs, and though I'd never heard the show opener, "The Wedge," I did recognize the two ensuing songs, "Foam" and "Simple."[2] Although I don't recall my reaction to hearing the gentle arpeggiated melody that began the next song, "The Man Who Stepped into Yesterday," I vividly remember the moment that followed: Phish launched into a Latin-jazz tinged, irregular meter and began singing the Jewish High Holy Day prayer "Avenu Malkenu."[3]

I was floored.

At the time, it seemed as though the band was directly acknowledging my presence in the venue. This was a melody that I had heard every year on Rosh Hashanah and Yom Kippur, the two holidays when even my secular, mostly nonobservant family attended synagogue. And I am not alone among American Jews who have felt a connection with the band through their performance of this song. Numerous fans growing up in Jewish households have admitted similar identifications of kinship with the band and their scene.[4]

How, then, do Jewish Phish fans experience the performance of "Avenu Malkenu," and how does this event figure into Jewish fans' performance of identity? Although individual fans may connect their Jewish identity to the band and concert experience in various ways, the band's performance of "Avenu Malkenu" is the most overtly Jewish moment associated with the generalized Phish phenomenon.[5] Based on ethnographic research as well as theories of identity and diaspora, I contend that Jewish Phish fans experience a double layering of "collective identity affirmation" when the band performs "Avenu Malkenu" in concert.[6] In contrast to W. E. B. Du Bois's concept of a "double-consciousness," which is a constant self-awareness of two identities (Black and American) in conflict with each other, this double layering is a brief episode during the performance of "Avenu Malkenu" when two identities (Phish fan and Jewish) complement and indeed reinforce and strengthen each other.[7]

At a Phish show, I feel connected to an idealized countercultural scene of outsiders, an authentic sense that I belong *here* in this venue just as many of my fellow showgoers belong *here*. Phish fans (or "phans") are a group that performs communal identity through a shared, spiritualized musical experience.[8] Performing communal identity in such a way opens up the concert site as a space where, as Elizabeth Yeager has called it, phans enact a "spatial articulation of affective authenticity," assigning meaning and investing importance into the musicalized concert space.[9] We phans often invest the concert experience and spaces with notions of home, family, and spirituality. Going to a Phish show often feels like a homecoming, a rush of familiar faces and sensory experience. Phish excels at improvising within a singularly focused, goal-oriented musical idiom, which allows for fans to have a numinous experience with the music. For example, in the song "Harry Hood," the musicians start the improvisation at an incredibly low dynamic, gently articulating the jam's basic chord progression of D major, A major, G major.[10] When Phish finally brings that jam to a climax around those chords anywhere from six to sixteen minutes later, the audience is enraptured in a state of blissful celebration.[11] Furthermore, the phenomenon of a Phish show spills out beyond the walls of the venue, encompassing many experiences and interactions with other phans surrounding the actual musical performance. All this allows for a Phish show to be a site of what anthropologist Victor Turner might call "communitas," a "generalized social bond" that obviates normative social structures.[12] This emplaced and embodied investment of meaning then becomes a way for us to construct identity and package it for consumption, or perform it, for both ourselves and others.

When Phish plays "Avenu Malkenu," a melody that is seemingly ubiquitous throughout American Jewry, I experience an additional layer of identity construction as I am reminded of my belonging to another subset of showgoers, a community of Jewish Phish fans, as a Jewish ritual musical performance is mediated through the secular, but still spiritualized, venue of the Phish show. The band's performance of "Avenu Malkenu" becomes the moment of double layering of identity, as multiple senses of group belonging—Jew and Phish fan—occur simultaneously and harmoniously. In an online survey I conducted as part of my research for this chapter, many Jewish Phish fans relayed feelings about the band's performance of "Avenu Malkenu" that corroborate this double layering of Jewish and phan identity.[13] As one Jewish fan put it in the survey, the band's choice to play "Avenu Malkenu" "confirms some aspect of my connection to Phish."[14] Ultimately, "Avenu Malkenu" allows Jewish fans to intensify their affective connection not only with the band but also with other Jewish fans, as well as their own Jewish identity.

Performing Identity

Sociologist Erving Goffman first proposed that we might think of identity as a kind of performance in his foundational 1959 book *The Presentation of Self in Everyday Life*.[15] Goffman concluded that individuals and groups function simultaneously as both performers and audience, always presenting their self-identity while functioning as audience for the identity performance of others. Cultural theorist Simon Frith extends this theory to popular music, thinking of "performance as an experience (or set of experiences) of sociability."[16]

Following this reasoning, it is natural to think of phan identity as a performance, one that is based on a set of socially mediated experiences of going to a Phish show, talking about it afterward, and thinking about the next show. Phan identity is both emplaced and embodied: it is performed within the physical space of the band's performance and is mediated through the body's presence within that space. Phan identity can also be performed in cybernetic space, since many fans watch these live performances on a web stream from their homes, affectionately known as "couch tour," which can foster a sense of connection and community mediated through social media. While it is different from physical presence at the show, I have still felt the same powerful sense of communal belonging with other phans as we tweet and text about hearing rarely played songs, creative set list choices, or unexpected improvisational explorations.[17]

Frith notes that audiences intuitively understand an onstage performance through "*their own experience of performance*," and indeed it is useful to think of phan identity as theatrical because of the homology between the Phish experience and the theater.[18] At a Phish concert, I embody certain practices of phandom—dancing, audience participation, writing the set list in my notebook as each song begins, talking with friends and strangers about the show—within the figurative stage of the concert space, even though I am literally watching the band on another, more literal stage. We also understand our phan identity via the communicative relationship between band and audience, engendering a phan ethos built around elements we see and hear on stage in the music: openness, freedom, personal expression, play, gratitude, and empathy. Performance studies scholar Jnan Blau summarizes this process of collaborative creation as Phish and their audience being "cosituated in the performance moment."[19] Even the preferred nomenclature phans use for an evening with Phish, "show" as opposed to "concert," suggests the performative, theatrical, and carnivalesque nature of the phan experience. Phans often dress up in outlandish psychedelic garb for shows and turn the parking lot outside the venue into a Bakhtinian carnival, a place that represents a separate, subversive reality to the normative and hierarchical ordering of society.[20] While there are multiple ways to perform phan identity, they mostly center on the communal, spiritualized experience of the music.

Following Frith, phans interpret Phish's rhetorical communication of meaning and identity through their own rhetorical communication of meaning and identity. By this logic, Jewish phans understand the performance of "Avenu Malkenu" through their own performance of Jewish identity. However, Jewish phans are not a homogeneous group and therefore perform their Jewish identity in myriad hidden and visible ways. Like most American Jews, Jewish Phish fans lean secular; still, a relatively small number of observant phans attend shows.[21] Observant Jews may perform their Jewish identity by wearing a kippah (head covering) or tzitzit (fringes) along with secular clothing, or refraining from attending Phish shows on Shabbat or other holidays. Hasidic phans even wear their customary traditional clothing to Phish shows and sometimes lead a prayer service at set break in the venue concourse, constituting a highly visible performance of religious Jewish identity.[22]

Less religious and secular phans may still visibly perform their Jewish identity through the wearing of clothing displaying Jewish or Israeli references, including shirts and stickers that combine Phish song titles or lyrics with Hebrew, Hebrew-styled lettering, or other Jewish references. During the November 2019 series of shows in Providence, Rhode Island, which coincided with the first nights of Hanukkah, someone gave me a "Treydel" sticker: a dreidel with Trey Anastasio's face replacing one of the Hebrew letters traditionally emblazoned on the side of the spinning top (plate 17).

For some Jewish phans, the choice of concert companions also becomes an opportunity for the performance of Jewish community identity. I was introduced to Phish at a Jewish summer camp and frequently see former campers and counselors at shows. I continue to see Phish with friends that I initially met over twenty years ago in USY (United Synagogue Youth), the main youth group of Conservative Judaism. While, for me, there is no religious aspect or conscious desire to create Jewish community behind my choice to attend shows with these friends, we nonetheless unintentionally replicate the initial Jewish connections that brought us together.

Despite all the practices and resonances with Jewish culture enumerated in the preceding paragraphs and elsewhere in this volume, there is no reason to assume that any Jewish phans in attendance will necessarily be cognizant of their performance of Jewish identity at a Phish show. As a mostly secular Jewish phan myself, I have attended plenty of Phish shows where my Jewish religion and culture never enter my mind, nor am I consciously aware of my performance of Jewish identity (which is not to say that this performance ceases to happen). Other than encounters with other attendees who are actively, and often visibly, performing Jewish identity, Jewish phans mainly can perform their own Jewish identity in situations where they are responding to a performance of that identity from the band. When the band engages Jewishness in some way, it constitutes a performative response from Jewish phans. The band seldom performs Jewishness explicitly on stage either through their visuals (neither Mike Gordon nor drummer Jon Fishman, the two Jewish members of the band, wear prominent references to their Judaism) or through spoken acknowledgment (if a Phish show occurs on a Jewish holiday, the event is seldom mentioned).[23]

Rather than visual or verbal, Phish's primary mode of communication with their audience is via their music and lyrics. This is true of all music, as performance studies scholar Jnan Blau notes: "Music thus becomes a form of social discourse; in short, a *communicative text*."[24] The band communicates to phans through music, and phans reciprocate with kinetic, embodied energy and voices. Blau argues that this commitment to reflexivity, to treating communication as not only crucial to the dynamic between band members but to the dynamic between band and audience, is a distinguishing feature of Phish's modus operandi: "A good deal of the impetus for Phish's sustained, ongoing reflexive work stems from their connection with, and care for, both each other's and their audience's *experiences*."[25] Phish's communicative relationship with their audience allows for the mutual opening up of a space for the enacting of phan culture, including not only the music but a phan ethos built around openness, freedom, personal expression, play, gratitude, and empathy. Blau summarizes this process of collaborative creation and highlights the homology between the band's improvisational approach to music and this cocreation of culture: "Every night that Phish take the stage is an exercise in improvising, together, what that night will come to mean."[26] This is the reason that phans see multiple shows in a row on a single tour, and hundreds of shows throughout their lives: each night is different not only in song choices but also in the style and trajectory of the improvisation. As an audience, we know we are involved in the creation of something powerfully unique and special.

Anastasio often acknowledges Phish's onstage music-making as part of a two-way, reflexive communication with the audience. In a 1993 interview, Anastasio observed that "the closer you can get to directly communicating with the other musicians, that thing that you're trying to say . . . I think the more powerful the experience is for somebody that comes to the concert."[27] Even more explicitly, Anastasio reflected on a jam from late 2019 during a 2020 interview by pondering how, in a particularly serene and quiet moment, "whoever just went to the bathroom had as much of an effect on this jam as any of the musicians."[28] He further noted how in that moment it seemed as though "the conscious thinking minds of everybody in this room, as individuals, had momentarily vanished," suggesting that individual identities of both band and audience had sublimated into a singular collective identity.

With Phish, the conversation between band and audience allows the music and the overall experience to permeate aspects of identity and meaning in phans' lives both at the show and beyond, constituting a deeper mode of communication between band and phans. This brings us back to the question of how Phish might co-perform Jewish identity alongside the Jewish subset of their phans. Certainly, the musical performance of "Avenu Malkenu" engages with Jewishness. But it is not merely the fact that Phish plays a song from the Jewish liturgy that resonates so strongly with Jewish identity in this moment, but specifically, it is that they play this particular melody.

The "Right" Tunes

Ethnomusicologist and rabbi Jeffrey Summit argues that musical choices during prayer services are central to the ways Jews construct their Jewish identity.[29] A congregation that chooses to sing Debbie Friedman's popular melody for the "Mi Shebeirach" prayer sets itself apart from one where the rabbi quickly chants the same words; the former is more likely to resonate with elements of Reform Judaism, such as greater reliance on English-language prayer and a more secular level of observance, and is more likely to embrace the use of instruments such as acoustic guitars in the prayer service. Despite music's ability to mark difference among Jews, Summit argues that melody choice can also foster connections between disparate Jewish communities, and that music is one area "where we find significant overlap among certain groups of Jews in America."[30]

With this in mind, it is worth examining bassist Mike Gordon's decision to bring "Avenu Malkenu" into the Phish repertoire in 1987, early in the band's career.

Gordon recalls that "it was pretty much my idea to start playing it as a band," and in a 1996 interview, he admitted that "it's an acknowledgment of my heritage."[31] Gordon notes how performing "Avenu Malkenu" has become a way to identify with and commune with Jewish audience members: "When we play ['Avenu Malkenu'], I can always look up and see the Jews in the audience smiling."[32] Significantly, a whopping 96 percent of Jewish phans said that the "Avenu Malkenu" melody is familiar to them from outside of listening to Phish, and so their smiles suggest that perhaps they, too, revel in acknowledging a shared musical heritage with Gordon.[33]

One of the reasons for this rate of recognition is the sheer popularity of the "Avenu Malkenu" melody that Phish performs. While the composer of this melody is unknown (the tune is typically attributed as "traditional" in most liturgical publications), ethnomusicologist Gordon Dale notes that this particular melody is "simply the default" in many synagogues.[34] He elaborates, "Those of us who were raised hearing it invest it with a great deal of personal meaning."[35] Rabbi Lawrence Hoffman notes that specifically the music of "Avenu Malkenu" has made the prayer "so central in [Jewish] consciousness."[36]

Not only is this melody widely used, but the prayer is sung during services that see higher attendance from secular American Jews. "Avenu Malkenu" is a central part of synagogue services on both Rosh Hashanah (the Jewish New Year) and Yom Kippur (the Day of Atonement), collectively known as the Jewish High Holidays.[37] These are often the holidays on which less observant American Jews, such as my own family, attend synagogue. Among Jewish phans in my survey, 65 percent said that while growing up they always attended High Holiday services, while only 16 percent reported that they rarely or never attended as children. Regardless of their level of observance, Jewish phans are likely to have attended High Holiday services at some point in their lives, and it is at those services that phans would have heard, and perhaps participated in, communal singing of "Avenu Malkenu."

As such, nearly 72 percent of Jewish survey respondents said that they were or would be "more excited than average" to hear "Avenu Malkenu" played at a Phish show. Jewish phans ranked the fact that they "recognize this song from outside the Phish world," likely from their Jewish upbringing and exposure in synagogue, as the main source of their excitement at hearing "Avenu Malkenu" live. In contrast, only 35 percent of non-Jewish phans indicated that they would be "more excited than average" to hear it, and recognition from outside the Phish world was the least important cause for their excitement ("it's musically interesting" and "it's rare" were the two highest-ranked sources of excitement for non-Jews).

Jewish phans also reported a heightened sense of communal belonging with other Jews when this song is performed live. Seventy-four percent of Jewish respondents indicated that they often or sometimes sing along with the Hebrew lyrics when Phish plays "Avenu Malkenu," a significant figure because, as Gordon Dale observes, "the experience of singing ['Avenu Malkenu'] surrounded by a congregation of voices blending together is a deeply moving event."[38] The immersive experience of singing "Avenu Malkenu" along with the band, whose amplified voices fill the concert space, as well as with fellow audience members transforms the Phish show into the congregation of voices blending together. Dale goes so far as to note that "the music of 'Avenu Malkenu' serves as an important connection to Jewish identity, to the Jewish community, and to the Jewish religion itself."[39] Indeed, 70 percent of Jewish phans agreed with the statement "I feel as though I am part of a larger Jewish Phish fan community," and I argue that Phish's performance of "Avenu Malkenu" is a key contributor to this communal sentiment. This moment is therefore apposite to Gordon Dale's observation that "the opportunity to melt into a collective through song can be a powerful reminder of the connection shared by Jews and the unity toward which we strive."[40]

In my research I asked Jewish phans to recall the moment they discovered that Phish performs "Avenu Malkenu." A number of phans noted how the band's performance of this prayer confirmed their sense of belonging within the Phish scene. Survey respondents shared comments such as "I felt included," "[Their performance of this song] drew me into Phish more than I had previously been," "I remember being deeply satisfied, deeply grateful, and feeling as though it confirms some aspect of my connection to Phish," and "It feels like a special thing to have grown up singing that song in temple and then to hear one of your favorite bands singing it." Certainly, many phans of all (or no) religious faiths find inclusion, familiarity, and connection, what Yeager theorizes as "affective authenticity," within the Phish scene. However, it is significant that this specific song instantiates that communal sense of belonging to the Jewish subset of fans within the context of the Phish show. These multiple layers of spiritualized belonging, both for Jews during this specific moment and for all phans throughout the entire show, are what lead to a double layering of identity construction for Jewish phans when Phish plays "Avenu Malkenu."

In an open response section of the survey, some Jewish phans noted a sense of communal identity among other Jewish phans when the band plays "Avenu Malkenu," with comments such as "I felt that they speak directly to our spiritual quest as wandering, Phish Jews." This particular phrasing is especially telling in that this respondent uses the term "Phish" to modify his identity as a "Jew," much in the same way one might say "American Jews" or "Orthodox Jews." It highlights how, for this fan, the twinning of phan identity and Jewish identity is not only possible but an essential part of his being—of his experience, and what it all means to him, in that moment—when the band plays "Avenu Malkenu." One respondent noted that when they heard the song live for the first time, they turned to an adjacent older fan and "asked him if he was Jewish. He looked surprised, said yes and then asked why i [*sic*] was asking. I told him, well, because you're singing along to 'Avenu Malkenu'!" For this younger fan, "Avenu Malkenu" served as a way to recognize and acknowledge fellow Jewish phans. In this moment, a Jewish fan singing the lyrics to the song is enacting a performance not just of and with the song but also of membership in the Jewish community. This public performance of Jewish identity thus marks fans qua Jews, in ways that make visible, and affirm, faith and/or cultural belonging.

These findings suggest that when Phish plays "Avenu Malkenu," many phans are given the opportunity to perform their Jewish identity in a way that is religiously or ethnically familiar while also fitting into their secular identity as Phish fans. As a diasporic community, Jews, and especially American Jews, seek to perform an identity that affirms an arbitrary or imagined authenticity to an idea of Jewishness intimately linked to our history as outsiders, one that we manifest in a varied and changing set of emplaced and embodied experiences. Each individual's performance of Jewish identity is bound up in what they personally believe to be authentically Jewish. For many Jewish Phish fans, a performance of "Avenu Malkenu" serves that affirmative purpose, allowing us to recognize and acknowledge other members of this diasporic community, and confirming the minority, dispersed status of Jews in the world. The song is what Rabbi Summit would call "the 'right' tune"; in other words, it is the familiar tune that most Jewish phans recognize from their Jewish home life, and as Summit argues, "The 'right' tune grounds one in history and becomes an assurance of authenticity."[41]

Part of this tune's claim toward authentic Jewish identity for American Jews is its use of the Freygish mode, a melody with specific intervals that signify Jewishness, especially for those of Eastern European descent.[42] Dale notes that this melodic scale is "the same mode that gives 'Hava Nagilah' its Jewishness," equating the melodic construction of "Avenu Malkenu" with a more predominant Jewish tune in American culture through its ubiquity at Jewish celebrations and even throughout popular culture.[43] Thus, not only is the "Avenu Malkenu" melody familiar to many Jewish phans, but it also "sounds Jewish." For phans who are not particularly observant or religious and do not understand the Hebrew words, "the tune *is* the prayer."[44] It is therefore especially noteworthy, then, that when Phish plays "Avenu Malkenu," it is the "right" tune for most of the Jewish phans in attendance.

Double Layering of Identity

Jewish phans' experience of Phish performing "Avenu Malkenu" can effectively be understood as a version of what Joseph Hermanowicz and Harriet Morgan call "collective identity affirmation," a process that occurs "when practices being cele-brated are both customary and already invested with a high level of sacredness."[45] Hermanowicz and Morgan refer to "ritualizing the routine" as a way of taking that which is customary and investing it with sacred meaning. The agency for affirm-ing this collective Jewish identity lies with the audience members themselves and not with the band. Phish is not trying to say, "We are part of your collective Jewish identity," but rather, their performance allows the space of the concert to become a site for what Yeager calls the "spatial articulation of affective authenticity," a place for the performance of collective identity for Jewish phans.[46]

Simultaneously, we might also say that Phish is "routinizing the ritual," that is, transubstantiating what is normally a ritual performance (a prayer in synagogue) into a nonreligious setting (the Phish show) while still retaining the main elements of that ritual performance, such as group singing of a common, Hebrew-language, Jewish-sounding melody. By playing a prayer that is associated with two of the most frequently observed religious holidays among American Jews, Phish allows for sacred meaning to permeate the secular custom of a rock concert. However, when discussing a Phish show in these terms, there is some slippage between con-cepts of sacred and secular, routine and ritual. For many phans, Jewish or not, the Phish show already borders on being a sacred ritual, born out of a shared, spiritu-alized musical experience.

Phans are already affirming their collective identity *as phans* within the space and time of a Phish show, and so when Phish plays "Avenu Malkenu," the perfor-mance adds a layer of Jewish collective identity affirmation. This performance of multiple identities is what Daniel and Jonathan Boyarin might argue is an essential feature of "diaspora culture and identity," namely, that it "allows for a complex con-tinuation of Jewish cultural creativity and identity at the same time that the same people participate fully in the common cultural life of their surroundings."[47] This is certainly not unique to Jewish phans, as other affinity groups (those based on sex-uality, for example, or sobriety) may experience that same sense of performing two separate yet simultaneous identities. What is distinctive is that both Jewish identity (indeed, Jewish identity that is activated by a liturgical prayer) and phan identity are performed within the spiritual realm.

As my ethnographic data suggest, Phish fans of all backgrounds have strong ten-dencies toward finding spiritual communal identity in the space of the Phish show. Among respondents, 68 percent agreed that music was a major source of spirituality in their lives. Individual phans also indicated that a Phish show is a highly spiritual experience, some even using the words "religious" to describe concert attendance. Jenn, an informant from Burlington, Vermont, notes that "Phish is like church," and opines that other than Phish fans, "born-again Christians are the only Americans who have this communal experience."[48] This sense is even perceptible to newcomers in the scene. Elissa Goldstein, a writer attending her first show at Madison Square Garden during the summer of 2017, humorously tweeted, "Ok, I'm starting to get it, this is a megachurch for secular software developers #Phish."[49]

Indeed, a Phish show is an excellent example of a situation where the routine is ritualized. Paraphrasing Mary Frances HopKins, Blau asserts that "a musical text is understood as far more than 'just' music; it is appreciated as an instance of *cultural memory*, of *participatory ritual*."[50] A Phish jam known as the "Tahoe Tweezer" (performed July 31, 2013) has become an infamous cultural signpost for phans, a moment to be forever recalled (regardless of whether we were there) in future discussions, a moment where band and audience achieved a liminal state of oneness removed from the structures of the non-Phish world via the ritual of co-performing the musical event.[51]

Phans even ritualize multiple nonmusical elements of the showgoing experience; a "pre-show rituals" thread on the fan forum of Phish.net highlights how some phans "try especially for the week before a show to not listen to any [Phish] at all" (this is a common ritual among many phans), while another has called out "Ticket check!" at a precise time before every show, forcing everyone in his party to visually confirm that they have their ticket.[52] A group of phans known as "rail riders" who try to see every show from the front row endure their own specific show-day rituals that, at various times, have included waiting in line to receive numbered wristbands, hearing those numbers called out randomly to determine walk-in order, and entering in an orderly fashion to their spots once allowed inside the venue. Musical moments have become ritualized over the years as well, and in every instance, these are started and perpetuated by phans, although the band will often encourage participation. For example, starting in 2003 fans began loudly singing the lyric "We love to take a bath" in the song "Bathtub Gin," a lyric that Anastasio eventually stopped singing to allow for the fans to shine in that moment.[53] Beginning in 1994, fans started clapping in unison during a part of the song "Stash" that previously had drum fills, and so Fishman stopped playing those fills himself.[54] The Phish show contains these communal rituals that occur at specific moments throughout the evening (not unlike the coordinated cheers of a soccer fan base), but also infinite personal rituals that individual fans enact in the days before, during, and after the show.

For Jewish attendees already affirming their collective identity as phans, the double layering of identification that occurs during performances of "Avenu Malkenu" can have the effect of both reinforcing their place within the scene and also highlighting something unique about a subset of phans that does not apply to all. When

Phish performed "Avenu Malkenu" on December 1, 2019, at Nassau Coliseum in Uniondale, New York, I realized that I happened to be surrounded almost entirely by Jewish friends. This was certainly not planned, and our shared Jewish background hadn't entered my mind at all until the song began. Yet as we listened to "Avenu Malkenu," we all danced and hugged and noted the beautiful synchronicity of the moment. We mimicked the gestural dancing of Hasidic Jews (think Tevye from *Fiddler on the Roof*), and we all recalled at set break other times in our Phish experiences when we'd heard that song. During a recent live webcast of a different archival show that also contained "Avenu Malkenu," the same group of friends started reminiscing on social media about that Nassau performance of the song, sharing GIFs of dancing Jews and using colloquial Yiddish to express our *nachas* (joyous pride) in that moment, one that we imbued with cultural memory and participatory ritual.

Tied to the sense of collective identity affirmation is a sense of Jewish belonging. Jewish phans may therefore find a double sense of belonging at a Phish show when the band plays "Avenu Malkenu," as they feel at home with other phans as well as with other Jews. One Jewish phan expressed this precise sentiment, noting that hearing the band play "Avenu Malkenu" "made me feel like this could be a band for me." Implicit in this statement is the idea that Phish's performances resonate with multiple elements of this fan's identity, both Jewish and non-Jewish, making them feel included as both a fan and a Jew in the Phish scene. There is no singular Jewish phan archetype; rather, there are only myriad individual expressions of Jewishness among the fan base. Hearing "Avenu Malkenu" live in concert, then, becomes a powerful moment that can cut across the multiple performances of individual Jewish identity into a collective performance of Jewish phan identity.

"I Tell Myself I'm Part of a Tribe"

One non-Jewish survey respondent noted that their Jewish friends "feel as though they have their own community inside of the community." The Jewish members of Phish are part of that community and help build it, too. Mike Gordon remembers that his attraction to the "Avenu Malkenu" melody stemmed from his childhood rabbi, Lawrence Kushner, who "just used it for everything."[55] By way of example, Gordon tells of how Rabbi Kushner would sing a *nigun*, or wordless song, using the "Avenu Malkenu" melody as part of the Havdalah service that ends the Sabbath. Like many secular American Jews, Gordon admits that he never fully accepted Judaism's belief system or rituals and even rebelled against them, but that Rabbi Kushner singing the "Avenu Malkenu" melody at sundown "was getting not just into my ears but into my soul. And so, when I'm bringing that song to the table [with Phish], in some ways . . .

I'm referencing back to an experience that was a deep soul experience for me, using that melody." Gordon then specifically elaborates on the communicative power of "Avenu Malkenu" and its ability to make a connection that goes beyond the immediate context of the concert space, likening it to "looking at the audience and taking in their energy. It's another way of doing that, and saying, okay, two band members are Jewish and there's this sort of experience in our beings that . . . well, we're going to let this connection live here. And this is part of what we are and we're gonna let it, for a moment, live and breathe here in this song."

These thoughts from Gordon seem to confirm what many Jewish phans had already understood through their own experience of performing their Jewish identity during Phish's renditions of "Avenu Malkenu." The band opens a space, within the concert, both physical and musical, for the connection to the "Jewish experience in our beings" to "live and breathe" for both the band members and the audience, whose energy the band is "taking in." When Gordon looks out from the stage and sees Jewish fans smiling and singing along to "Avenu Malkenu," he is affirming our collective Jewish identity and consciously allowing for the double layering of identity to occur, intermingling his (and our) experience as American Jews with his (and our) experience as members of the Phish community.

Furthermore, Gordon notes that while he rebelled against the dogma and rituals of Judaism, the melody of "Avenu Malkenu" served as a way for him to maintain his connection to his Jewish heritage and culture. For secular Jewish phans who have likewise turned away from Jewish observance, hearing "Avenu Malkenu" live can be understood as a performance of Jewish resistance: they are able to affirm their secular, cultural identity as Jews while still resisting conforming to Jewish religious practice and beliefs. Yeager argues that phans "seek out communitas as a resistance to the social and cultural structures of middle- and upper-middle-class cultural identity," that we go to Phish shows to escape from the establishment of middle-class American life and construct an identity that is somehow apart from the mainstream, while never fully rejecting the privileges of white middle-classness.[56] Understood in this way, Jewish phans may also be performing a double layering of resistance, both to generic American culture and to dogmatic religious Jewish belief systems.

"Avenu Malkenu" is a moment that has a lasting effect on Jewish phans because, as Blau asserts, "what Phish do onstage as performing musicians matters long after the actual performance event is over."[57] Perhaps this is because Jews, as a diasporic community, have suffered a long history of displacement, and Phish gives them a place to feel "at home": an overwhelming 93 percent of survey respondents of all backgrounds said they agreed with the statement "I feel 'at home' at a Phish concert," while 85 percent agreed with the statement "I feel 'among family' when I am at a Phish concert." As one survey respondent noted, there seems to be something about the Phish experience that lends itself to Jewish affinity: "I definitely think that there is a correlation between our upbringing as Jews (no matter what religious level you were raised and are now) and feeling that sense of belonging to a bigger community just like we do with Phish." For Jewish phans, that sense of home and family is affirmed doubly at a Phish show when the band performs "Avenu Malkenu." We feel at home at the Phish show being among other fans and in a situation that feels safe, familiar, and comfortable, but we also feel at home among other Jews, secure in our ability to perform our Jewish identity within an otherwise non-Jewish space. We feel as though we are part of a "phamily" as well as a mishpocha (Yiddish for "family" or "kin"), connected to other phans through our shared and individual ritualizations of the Phish show and our communal experience of a spiritual musical phenomenon. Furthermore, we are connected to other Jewish phans though our shared ability to perform our Jewish identity during "Avenu Malkenu" as we sing words and remember events from our Jewish lives outside of Phish. In double layering their performance of identity during "Avenu Malkenu," Jewish phans may experience a swelling sense of belonging to both groups—Phish fans and Jews—through this affective intensification of meaning.

NOTES

1. An earlier version of this chapter was presented at the Phish Studies Interdisciplinary Conference in Corvallis, Oregon, in May 2019. Many thanks to attendees and copanelists at the conference for their helpful comments and suggestions, as well as Jnan Blau and the editors of this volume for comments on drafts of this chapter.

2. Phish, "The Wedge," track 7 on *Rift* (Elektra, 1993); Phish, "Foam," track 5 on *Junta* (self-released, 1989, rereleased by Elektra, 1992); Phish, "Simple," track 3 on disc 2 of *A Live One* (Elektra, 1995).

3. Phish does not use a consistent transliteration of this Hebrew song title in their official live releases, which have used three different spellings, including the one used in this volume, "Avenu Malkenu." Trey Anastasio, "The Man Who Stepped into Yesterday," track 2 on *The Man Who Stepped into Yesterday* (senior thesis, Goddard College, 1987); Phish, "Avenu Malkenu" (live debut 1987).

4. For example, Dan Berkowitz, founder and former CEO of the music-related travel company CID Entertainment, admits "Avenu Malkenu" helped "bridge the gap" in convincing his parents to allow him to attend a show when he was in high school. "The Island of Misfit Toys," in Budnick, *Long May They Run.*

5. Phish has performed one other Hebrew song, Naomi Shemer's "Yerushalayim Shel Zahav," written in 1967 as a statement of Israeli nationalism. However, this song was only performed twelve times between 1993 and 1994 and is no longer part of Phish's repertoire.

6. Hermanowicz and Morgan, "Ritualizing the Routine."

7. Du Bois, "Strivings of the Negro People."

8. Throughout this chapter I use the colloquial "phan" (sometimes in addition to "Phish fan") both as a way to recognize the term's use as part of a community vernacular and as a way to distinguish the "phan" as part of a larger culture of Phish fandom that encompasses a variety of situated social and stylistic practices, norms, and collective history (much as "Trekkie" connotes far more cultural weight than "Star Trek fan"). A scholarly model for this distinction exists; see Blau, "More than 'Just' Music."

9. Yeager, "Understanding 'It,'" 160.

10. Phish, "Harry Hood," track 4 on disc 2 of *A Live One* (Elektra, 1995).

11. This rapturous state was captured on the band's official webcast of the Madison Square Garden concert on December 29, 2016, when the camera focused on a fan named Nicholas Peter Orr in the middle of a numinous experience at the climax of the "Harry Hood" jam. "MSG Hood Guy" soon went viral on the internet. In subsequent interviews, Orr noted that he was sober for these shows, and that his emotional reaction was entirely due to the music. Equally telling is the woman in sunglasses directly behind Orr, who stands motionless with her hands clasped in a prayer pose during the first shot, and then arms fully extended upward in the second shot.

12. Turner, *Ritual Process*, 96.

13. The survey mentioned here was administered by the author as part of ethnographic research undertaken during the fall of 2018, which involved an online survey as well as in-person informal interviews outside Phish shows in Albany, New York, and Hampton, Virginia. This data is available to anyone upon request. For the purposes of this chapter, when I refer to Jewish fans I include fans who either grew up in a Jewish household, had at least one Jewish parent, came to Judaism later in life by choice or marriage, or self-identify as

Jewish (these groupings are not mutually exclusive). Of the 665 respondents to my online survey, 149 (22.4 percent) affirmed that they currently self-identify as Jewish, regardless of religious observation or belief system. By comparison, the American Jewish Population Project for 2019 estimates that only 2.3 percent of the American population identifies as Jewish (Tighe et al. 2019).

14. All quotes from fans in this chapter are taken with permission from respondents to my 2018 online survey, unless otherwise noted.

15. Goffman, *Presentation of Self*.

16. Frith, *Performing Rites*, 204.

17. I explore this phenomenon in greater depth in "On Tweezermania and Not Being There."

18. Frith, *Performing Rites*, 204. For more on the links between the theater and the Phish scene, see Allaback, "Theater of Jambands."

19. Blau, "Phan on Phish."

20. Bakhtin's theory of the carnival and carnivalesque are expressed most fully in his *Rabelais and His World*.

21. According to a 2013 Pew Research Center report, 62 percent of American Jews say that "being Jewish is mainly a matter of ancestry and culture," attesting to the "long tradition" of secularism in Jewish life in America. See Pew Research Center, "Portrait of Jewish Americans."

22. Fleet, "Phish and Judaism."

23. Notable exceptions to this include the concert from April 18, 1992, in Palo Alto, California, which took place during Passover. During "Avenu Malkenu," Anastasio announced that Gordon would now take a "Happy Passover bass solo." During the concert on August 7, 1993, in Darien Center, New York, Fishman yelled out, "Dreidel, dreidel, dreidel!" just before Gordon's bass solo in "Poor Heart," and Trey then referred

to Mike by his Hebrew name. This show did not take place during Hanukkah, and the stories behind these utterances are unknown. Thanks to Twitter user @PhishTalmud for these references.

24. Blau, "More than 'Just' Music."

25. Blau, "Phan on Phish," 316.

26. Ibid.

27. Allan, "Interview with Trey Anastasio."

28. Budnick, "Trey Anastasio."

29. Summit, *Lord's Song.*

30. Ibid., 21.

31. Horowitz, "Mike Gordon"; Garnick, "Gefilte Phish."

32. Garnick, "Gefilte Phish."

33. This percentage is taken from the 2018 Phish fan ethnographic survey.

34. Dale, "Music of *Avinu Malkeinu*," 67.

35. Ibid., 68.

36. Hoffman, "History, Meaning, and Varieties," 13.

37. When these holidays fall on a Friday night or Saturday (Shabbat), "Avenu Malkenu" is not included in the service. In this case, some congregations use the tune for other prayers on Shabbat to make sure it is still sung and heard.

38. Dale, "Music of *Avinu Malkeinu*," 68.

39. Ibid., 70.

40. Ibid.

41. Summit, *Lord's Song*, 33.

42. In particular, these include a lowered (or flat) second and sixth scale degrees. This melodic character was frequently used throughout the nineteenth century in Western European concert music to signify exoticism and an orientalized "Easternness" often applied to groups such as Jews, Hungarian Romani, and Arab Middle Easterners. See Bellman, "Hungarian Gypsies," 83–86, and Locke, "Cutthroats and Casbah Dancers," 134.

43. Examples of "Hava Nagilah" appearing in American pop culture are Bob Dylan's early outtake "Talkin' Hava Negeila Blues" from 1962 (track 9 on disc 1 of *The Bootleg Series Volumes 1–3 [Rare & Unreleased] 1961–1991* [Columbia, 1991]), many Jewish wedding scenes in movies ranging from 1980's *Private Benjamin* to 2005's *Wedding Crashers* and beyond, and a 2014 *Saturday Night Live* sketch featuring the half-Jewish hip hop megastar Drake in which he sings the melody over the rapid fire electronic hi-hat associated with the trap subgenre of hip hop. The jam band moe., whose fan base often overlaps with Phish's, even occasionally performs "Hava Nagilah" in their concerts.

44. Summit, *Lord's Song*, 33.

45. Hermanowicz and Morgan, "Ritualizing the Routine," 200.

46. Yeager, "Understanding 'It,'" 160.

47. Boyarin and Boyarin, "Diaspora," 721.

48. "Jenn," in discussion with the author, Hampton, Virginia, October 21, 2018.

49. Tweet from user @goldsteinelissa, August 1, 2017, https://twitter.com/goldsteinelissa/status/892549571448107008.

50. Blau, "More than 'Just' Music."

51. Phish, "Tweezer," track 11 on *A Picture of Nectar* (Elektra, 1992).

52. GHOST8 and slack91 in "Pre-show rituals" (chat thread), Phish.net, December 22, 2018, https://forum.phish.net/forum/show/1378241982.

53. Phish, "Bathtub Gin," track 6 on *Lawn Boy* (Absolute A Go Go, 1990).

54. Phish, "Stash," track 5 on *A Picture of Nectar* (Elektra, 1992).

55. All quotes from Mike Gordon in this section are from "The Island of Misfit Toys" episode of Budnick's *Long May They Run* podcast.

56. Yeager, "Understanding 'It,'" 182.

57. Blau, "More than 'Just' Music."

REFERENCES

Allaback, Christina L. "Theater of Jambands: Performance of Resistance." PhD diss., University of Oregon, 2009.

Allan, Marc. "Interview with Trey Anastasio." Produced by Alan Berry. *The Tapes Archive*, August 28, 2019. Podcast. https://www.thetapesarchive .com/trey-anastasio.

Bahktin, Mikhail. *Rabelais and His World*. Translated by Hélène Iswolsky. Cambridge, MA: The MIT Press, 1968.

Bellman, Jonathan. "The Hungarian Gypsies and the Poetics of Exclusion." In *The Exotic in Western Music*, edited by Jonathan Bellman, 74–103. Boston: Northeastern University Press, 1998.

Blau, Jnan. "More than 'Just' Music: Four Performative Topoi, the Phish Phenomenon, and the Power of Music in/ and Performance." *TRANS–Transcultural Music Review* 13 (2009). https:// www.sibetrans.com/trans/article/44.

———. "A Phan on Phish: Live Improvised Music in Five Performative Commitments." *Cultural Studies ↔ Critical Methodologies* 10, no. 4 (2010): 307–19.

Boyarin, Daniel, and Jonathan Boyarin. "Diaspora: Generation and the Ground of Jewish Identity." *Critical Inquiry* 19, no. 4 (Summer 1993): 693–725.

Budnick, Dean, host. *Long May They Run*. Produced by C13Originals. Released September–November 2019. Podcast. https://shows.cadence13.com/long-may -they-run.

———. "Trey Anastasio on the Power of Live." *Relix*, June 29, 2020. https://relix .com/articles/detail/trey-anastasio-the -power-of-live.

Cohen, Jacob A. "On Tweezermania and Not Being There." *Smooth Atonal Sound* (blog), July 29, 2014. https://smootha tonalsound.wordpress.com/2014/07/29 /on-tweezermania-and-not-being -there.

Dale, Gordon. "The Music of *Avinu Malkeinu*." In *Naming God: "Avinu Malkeinu"—Our Father, Our King*, edited by Lawrence A. Hoffman, 67–70. Woodstock, VT: Jewish Lights, 2015.

Du Bois, W. E. B. "Strivings of the Negro People." *Atlantic Monthly*, August 1897, republished June 16, 2020. https://www .theatlantic.com/magazine/archive /1897/08/strivings-of-the-negro-people /305446.

Fleet, Josh. "Phish and Judaism: Going to Synagogue at Madison Square Garden." *HuffPost*, February 24, 2011. https:// www.huffpost.com/entry/the-phish -concert-as-a-je_b_826260.

Frith, Simon. *Performing Rites: On the Value of Popular Music*. Cambridge, MA: Harvard University Press, 1996.

Garnick, Darren. "Gefilte Phish." *Jerusalem Report*, December 26, 1996. https:// darrengarnick.wordpress.com/2009/05 /24/phishing-for-jewish-heritage.

Goffman, Erving. *The Presentation of Self in Everyday Life*. Garden City, NY: Doubleday, 1959.

Hermanowicz, Joseph C., and Harriet P. Morgan. "Ritualizing the Routine: Collective Identity Affirmation." *Sociological Forum* 14, no. 2 (1999): 197–214.

Hoffman, Lawrence A. "The History, Meaning, and Varieties of *Avinu Malkeinu*." In *Naming God: Avinu "Malkeinu"—Our Father, Our King*, edited by Lawrence A. Hoffman, 3–15. Woodstock, VT: Jewish Lights, 2015.

Horowitz, Jacob. "Mike Gordon Brings a New Flavor to Phish." *JVibe*, February 15, 2001. https://web.archive.org/web

/20010215003457/https://jvibe.com
/popculture/phish.shtml.

Locke, Ralph P. "Cutthroats and Casbah
Dancers, Muezzins and Timeless
Sands: Musical Images of the Middle
East." In *The Exotic in Western Music*,
edited by Jonathan Bellman, 104–36.
Boston: Northeastern University Press,
1998.

Pew Research Center. "A Portrait of Jewish
Americans: Findings from a Pew
Research Center Survey of U.S. Jews."
October 1, 2013. https://www.pewfo
rum.org/2013/10/01/jewish-american
-beliefs-attitudes-culture-survey.

Summit, Jeffrey A. *The Lord's Song in a
Strange Land: Music and Identity in
Contemporary Jewish Worship*. New
York: Oxford University Press, 2000.

Tighe, Elizabeth, Raquel Migidin de Kramer,
Daniel Parmer, Daniel Nussbaum,
Daniel Kallista, Xajavion Seabrum, and
Leonard Saxe. *American Jewish
Populations Project, Summary and
Highlights 2019*. Waltham, MA:
Brandeis University, Steinhardt Social
Research Institute, 2019. https://ajpp
.brandeis.edu/documents/2019/Jewish
PopulationDataBrief2019.pdf.

Turner, Victor. *The Ritual Process: Structure
and Anti-Structure*. Ithaca, NY: Cornell
University Press, 1977.

Yeager, Elizabeth A. "Understanding '*It*':
Affective Authenticity, Space, and the
Phish Scene." PhD diss., University of
Kansas, 2011.

3.

"Finest in the Nation"

THE FOOD OF PHISH AND THE JEWISH EXPERIENCE

Evan S. Benn

The taste of tahini—the ground sesame seed paste that's blended with chickpeas to make hummus, or with sugar to make halva—takes me to Jerusalem.[1] Tahini has an unmistakable, and unforgettable, contrast in flavors and textures. It's nutty and earthy, creamy and unctuous—like almond butter on steroids—but also a little bitter and tannic, like a hoppy India pale ale or a red wine with a bone-dry finish. Like good olive oil, tahini is a foundational component of everyday foods in the Middle East and throughout the world: hummus and halva, of course, as well as a million variations of savory dressings and sauces for crispy falafel, cucumber salads, charred eggplant, egg noodles, roasted cauliflower, and more.

It was the summer of 1995, I was just turning thirteen, and my parents, brother, aunt, uncle, and cousin traveled together to Israel for my bar mitzvah. The ceremony, a quick and intimate Reform service complete with a rent-a-rabbi who met us at our hotel the night before to go over my Torah portion, took place atop the ancient fortress Masada, a rocky plateau in southern Israel's Judean Desert that overlooks the Dead Sea. It was 114 degrees Fahrenheit that day, so it's forever known in my family as my bar schvitzvah.[2] The trip was remarkable and memorable for all the reasons one would expect; seeing the birthplace of so much of our world's shared religious history while having a unique Jewish experience elevated my bar mitzvah in Israel beyond a rite of passage. But that mid-'90s journey to Israel also unknowingly planted the seeds for two passions that would greatly influence both my personal and professional lives—food and Phish.

The journal that I dutifully kept during that trip contains excited mentions of food revelations interspersed with more religious and academic reports of experiences like praying at the Western Wall and seeing the gold-topped Dome of the Rock for the first time. There were falafel sandwiches with tangy pickled onions and eye-watering hot sauce. There was deep-red, fresh-squeezed pomegranate juice. There was rich, sweet chocolate babka, and there were oven-warmed bagels dusted with za'atar. There were olives and nuts and dried fruit and shawarma and shakshuka.

And there was tahini. At Jerusalem's bustling Machane Yehuda outdoor market there's a popular stand called the Halva Kingdom. There, you can buy dozens of kinds of halva, the dense and crumbly dessert confection made primarily with tahini and sugar and studded with nuts, fruit, or spices. Halva Kingdom also has a working tahini mill on display, so you can see—and, if you ask nicely, taste—impossibly fresh sesame paste dripping from stone grinding wheels down a bobsled chute into a collection barrel. That's where I first had true, pure tahini; its complex and distinct flavors and textures have stayed with me ever since. The creamy, oily texture, the intensely nutty and slightly tannic flavor—I'm instantly reminded of that flavor memory in the market every time I have a scoop of hummus, a bite of a sesame-seed bagel or sesame-crusted ahi tuna, or, of course, a sliver of halva.

That trip to Israel was also the first time I'd really listened to reggae music. I remember that I had packed my Green Day cassettes and Walkman for the overseas flight and the drives from stop to stop. But I stopped bringing the Walkman in our tour van once I heard the music our guide was grooving to. He played an Alpha Blondy tape almost exclusively when we drove, and I was hooked on the syncopated beat and the lyrics that sounded to me like a rhythmic chant. Alpha Blondy, an Ivorian musician whose songs often touch on political, social, and religious equality, integrates Hebrew and Arabic into his lyrics. The whole experience—jamming to an African reggae song about Jerusalem while I was in Israel—was really the first time I felt like music connected the whole world. I suddenly didn't feel like an awkward teen with a mouthful of braces. I didn't feel like an outsider, the only Jew in my class back at home. When I listened to that music—when I allowed myself to truly hear it—I felt the kind of swagger you only get when the sound is flowing through you and your head begins to nod along with the beat (a feeling I'd later experience hundreds and hundreds of times while listening to Phish). In hearing Alpha Blondy sing of Jerusalem's ability to unite Jews, Christians, and Muslims, and of the sun rising over Masada, I felt a shift in our trip, away from a personal rite of passage and toward a universal sense of interconnectedness. I felt like a larger force had brought me to this sacred place for a reason, and I felt like I belonged—to Israel, to Judaism, to the world. The music is what made it all click.

Up until that summer, I had been aware of Phish only as a band known more for their live shows than their studio albums or radio hits, for their long, improvisational songs, and for their dedicated fans who followed them from city to city, show to show, much like the Grateful Dead's fan base. My older brother, Merrick, was very much a loyal Deadhead by that summer—he let my dad and me accompany him to a Dead show on June 20, 1992, at RFK Stadium in Washington, DC, with the Steve Miller Band opening—so jam bands were in my blood. But I hadn't yet gotten into the music of Phish until soon after returning home from Israel that summer in 1995. Our tour guide on that trip had unknowingly prepped my soul to embrace Phish by playing reggae music that I loved, and a neighbor at home played Phish for me at the right place and the right time. I've been hooked ever since.

When I returned to Pennsylvania as a bar mitzvah, I rode to middle school that fall with a neighbor who listened to Phish in the car. He played the *Rift* studio album constantly, and I loved it all.[3] *A Live One*, Phish's first official release of songs recorded live at their shows, came out during the summer when I was in Israel, and it was the first Phish album that I bought.[4] Listening to Alpha Blondy was a gateway that freed me to experiment with music beyond that of Green Day (which I still love). And Phish was a natural next step in my musical progression: my brother introducing me to the Dead showed me that I had a predilection for improvisational music, and my neighbor putting Phish in my ears on those rides to school put me on the path to "phandom" (Phish fans are affectionately known as phans). The fact that two of Phish's four members are Jewish—bassist Mike Gordon and drummer Jon Fishman—also spoke to me during that moment in my life when, as a fresh bar mitzvah coming off a trip to Israel, I felt very connected to Judaism. It didn't take me long to get hooked on *A Live One*—its tracks feature an easily digestible mix of shorter, catchy tunes and a few longer jams, and the energy between the band and the live audience is undeniably infectious. I love all of that two-CD set, but I discovered the first of my lifetime's many ah-ha Phish moments while listening to the *A Live One* version of "Harry Hood."[5] The upbeat, rhythmic mini-jam toward the beginning of the song, before the dark and chaotic turn into the "Thank you, Mr. Miner" lyrics, always reminds me of the kind of reggae riff I fell in love with in Israel. I hear Alpha Blondy in that "Hood" riff; like tahini, it takes me back to Israel.

In addition to being the year I became a bar mitzvah, tasted tahini, and bought my first Phish CD, 1995 was also the year I first stepped into a professional newsroom and discovered my life's calling: journalism. I and my school newspaper staff were on a field trip to the *York Dispatch*. York, Pennsylvania, was—and, remarkably given the news industry's rapid and astounding consolidation in recent decades, still is—a two-newspaper town, with the white-collar and more conservative *York Daily Record* publishing in the morning and the more rough-and-tumble, left-leaning *Dispatch* coming out in the afternoon. The other kids on the trip that day were bored or otherwise checked out of the experience, but something about the atmosphere and the cacophony of deadline—the ringing phones, the clanking keyboards, the reporters shuffling to and from their editors' desks—made me want to experience more. I asked the *Dispatch*'s managing editor if I could come back and learn more about what journalists do. She obliged, and I started going there every day after school to shadow reporters, photographers, and editors. After several months of tagging along to house fires and press conferences and murder trials, the editor asked me to write something of my own: a story about a York woman who was appointed to a governor's commission for women. It was short and buried deep inside the Local section of the paper the next day, but seeing my byline in print sealed the deal. I studied journalism at Northwestern University and interned at places like the *Denver Post* and the *Miami Herald* before being hired full-time at the *Herald* out of college. I started writing about food for the *Herald* as a side gig to my breaking-news beat by contributing short reviews about takeout joints and eventually bigger profiles of chefs and stories about restaurants and home cooking. I haven't stopped since.

My interests in Phish and food began to build around the same time that Phish's mainstream visibility was making commercial gains. *A Live One* was the first Phish album to reach the Billboard Top 20 upon its release in 1995, and it was the first Phish album to hit platinum status of one million sales just two years later, in the fall of 1997. A few months prior, Phish marked another milestone at an intimate and sweet show at Burlington, Vermont's Flynn Theater. That night, March 18, 1997, Phish welcomed fellow Vermonters Ben Cohen and Jerry Greenfield to the stage to unveil Phish Food, a new Ben & Jerry's ice cream that the band had helped to develop.

Everyone in the audience got a scoop, and proceeds from that night's show were donated to the newly formed WaterWheel Foundation.[6] It was the first time Phish had licensed its name to a commercial product, and it was rare for the creamery's Jewish cofounders to collaborate with outsiders while developing a flavor—Ben & Jerry's website reveals that Ben wanted raspberry in the Phish Food blend but the band nixed it in favor of caramel. The partnership between these two Vermont icons—Ben & Jerry's was founded in the Green Mountain State in 1978, Phish in 1983—came about because of the similar values they shared, which prioritized community, the environment, and giving back. Not everything was about making money. "The band and their music and their fans and everything they stand for is right up our alley. It's a great association," Greenfield said.[7] The band decided to donate all royalties they receive from Phish Food, and Ben & Jerry's contributes a portion of sales from every scoop and pint of Phish Food sold to benefit Vermont's Lake Champlain watershed conservation efforts. "When the Ben & Jerry's ice cream flavor was coming along, it was kind of established, 'Well, we're going to give away the proceeds,'" drummer Fishman said.[8] The packaging for Phish Food—a kosher-certified base of chocolate ice cream with gooey marshmallow, caramel swirls, and chocolate fudge "fish"—features a cow wearing Fishman's ubiquitous donut dress. Phish phans reacted enthusiastically at the new flavor's arrival—it had been ten years since Ben & Jerry's gave Deadheads a flavor of their own with Cherry Garcia, a nod to Grateful Dead front man Jerry Garcia—and so did ice cream consumers as a whole. Almost twenty-five years after its debut, Phish Food remains among Ben & Jerry's best-selling flavors.[9] As a phan, I can't help but smile whenever I see Phish Food in our grocer's freezer. It's a symbol that our beloved Phish subculture is recognized in the most mainstream way, with placement in an American grocery store aisle, but in a cool way, collaborating with an ecofriendly partner that is using the ice cream's profits for good. I also can't help but smile when I eat it, because of the connection I feel to the band I love.

Phish and Ben & Jerry's continue to partner together on ice cream flavors and good causes. In 2018 Ben & Jerry's released It's Ice . . . Cream, a limited-edition caramel malt ice cream with almond toffee, fudge fish, and caramel swirls, its name inspired by the Phish song "It's Ice."[10] The flavor combination is rumored to have been in the running to be Phish Food back in the '90s, and Ben & Jerry's unearthed the recipe to commemorate the twenty-first anniversary of Phish Food and the company's collaboration with Phish and the WaterWheel Foundation. A portion of proceeds from It's Ice . . . Cream went to the foundation. And in 2017, during the band's thirteen-show Baker's Dozen run at Madison Square Garden, Ben & Jerry's cooked up a special-release flavor called Freezer Reprise—sweet cream ice cream with vanilla glaze, chocolate donut pieces, chocolate donut swirls, and fudge fish—that played off the Baker's Dozen's donut theme and Phish's song "Tweezer Reprise," a show-ending phan favorite.[11] Artist and longtime Phish collaborator Jim Pollock created special Freezer Reprise artwork for T-shirts that were sold during the Baker's Dozen run to benefit the WaterWheel Foundation.

To me, the long-standing relationship between Phish and Ben & Jerry's, and the concept of Phish Food in particular, exemplifies the Venn diagram intersection of Phish, Judaism, and food. The concepts of community, of coming together for the greater good, of deriving pleasure from our five senses as well as our mind, are what connect the Phish experience with Judaism and food. All of those concepts are present in every pint of this premium ice cream that was inspired by and created with Phish, that benefits a charity that helps local communities, that is a collaboration between a company founded by Jews and a band in which two of the four members are Jewish, that brings smiles to the faces of its fans and leaves them wanting just a little more.

As you may have guessed by now, I did not take on this project to uncover Talmudic references in the food-related lyrics of "Reba" or to seek out references of roasted eggs and shank bones in shows Phish has played during Passover.[12] I wanted to explore the intersection of Phish food (lowercase f) and Judaism in a way that was more personal, showing how my perspective as a Phish-loving Jew and food journalist squared with the experiences of other phans who may or may not be Jewish or food experts.

Of course, Phish Food (uppercase F) is not the only food that connects dots between the music of Phish and the Jewish experience. For most phans, if you ask them about a food memory that includes Phish, odds are they'll tell you a story about buying and eating something in a stadium parking lot either just before or after seeing a Phish show. The parking lot scene—you'll hear phans refer to it simply as "the lot" or "Shakedown Street," a carryover reference to a Dead song title that was used to describe a similar lot scene on Dead tours—is like a tailgate outside a sporting event crossed with a carnival midway.[13] You'll find off-the-books vendors selling everything from cold beer and water to homemade T-shirts and knit hats, from cannabis-infused Rice Krispies treats to grilled cheese sandwiches, vegetable burritos, French bread pizzas, and other lot favorites. And you'll find people playing music, burning incense, hanging out, killing time. It's a friendly scene, and while I don't find myself eating much food from the lot these days—I'm all for street food, but I've witnessed sanitation lapses on "Shakedown Street" that I wish I could unsee—you'd be hard-pressed to find a phan, including me, who hasn't ponied up for freshly fried falafel on warm pita in the lot before or after an epic show.

I wasn't thinking of food when I was riding the El to see Phish at the Allstate Arena outside Chicago on September 22, 2000. It was a few days after I moved to Evanston to start my freshman year at Northwestern, and I was going to the show with some other students I met through a pre-frosh message board. None of us had known one another for more than a few minutes, and up until this point I had only gone to concerts, Phish or otherwise, with close friends. Rumbling on a train through a new city to a twenty-thousand-person Phish show accompanied by a handful of strangers gave me a decent surge of anxiety, and I was more focused on that than what I might eat once we got there. Would these new people like me? Have I seen as many shows as they have? Will they think I'm enough of a phan? But when the train stopped and we made our way over to the lot, those anxious thoughts drifted as our group found some common ground beyond our shared love of Phish: We were all hungry, so we agreed our first stop should be food in the lot. I remember walking past a guy selling Sierra Nevada Pale Ale and Samuel Adams Boston Lager from a cooler (always one for three dollars, two for five dollars), and then, the next step, smelling the unmistakable scent of something frying in hot oil. My eyes looked up and saw a sign hawking six-dollar falafel pita sandwiches, and I knew I'd found my spot. A few others in our group also craved falafel and stayed with me to order and grub, while others split to keep searching Shakedown, and we planned to meet up in half an hour to go into the show together. When my falafel was ready, I handed over my cash, asked for extra hot sauce, and stepped between parked cars to unwrap that beauty from its foil blanket and dig in. Like all good falafel, this was drizzled with tehina, the smooth, tangy sauce made from pure tahini blended with lemon juice, garlic, and salt. And of course, that instantly zapped me back to Machane Yehuda in Jerusalem and flooded me with memories of being in Israel with my family and the comfort of feeling connected to them in this moment when I was still adjusting to new surroundings away from home.

As a staple lot option, falafel is forever tied to the Phish experience, and is most certainly a Phish food. Falafel's origins in the Middle East led to its current status as an Israeli culinary icon, where it is omnipresent in the diets of Israeli Jews and their relatives and descendants the world over, making falafel a Jewish food, too.[14] Speaking more broadly about this particular episode of my Phish experience, it points to the values of community and coming together that link Phish, Judaism, and food. The community of Phish is what brought me together with a group of strangers to experience a show. When I was feeling nervous and awkward about the situation, the shared experience of desiring, looking for, and eating food brought us together in a way that only food can. Finally, the nostalgia and sense of family and identity that I felt from tasting the familiar flavor of tahini on a falafel as a Jew, a reminder of my bar mitzvah experience in Israel, brought it all together. In that moment in the Phish lot with my falafel sandwich and new friends, I was where I was supposed to be.

The person who served us that falafel had a portable fryer set up on a folding table, and while deep-frying is somewhat rare to see in Phish lots, it's usually reserved for savory things like falafel and french fries, not sweets. So while you're not likely to encounter freshly fried donuts in a Phish lot, donuts are inextricably linked to the Phish experience. And this Phish food also happens to be a Jewish food. It's a

Jewish tradition to eat *sufganiyot*—round donuts filled with jelly and dusted with powdered sugar—during Hanukkah, one that puts donuts right up there with latkes as the most popular food that Jews eat on the holiday.[15] For decades, Phish drummer Jon Fishman has performed in a sleeveless muumuu, a navy blue dress with red "donut" circles all over it. Fishman explained on a 2019 episode of the *Long May They Run* podcast that his friends pulled it out of a Salvation Army freebie pile in the '80s.[16] He wore it on stage for a gig at Nectar's in Burlington on July 25, 1988. At a show the next night, Fishman explained, he showed up without the dress, and guitarist Trey Anastasio told him he had to wear the dress or else it would ruin the gig. "I then wore the dress for the next thirty-six years," Fishman said on the podcast.[17]

Beyond being a Phish food, donuts are a marker of Phish phans. One can purchase Fishman donut bathrobes, button-down shirts, and blazers from companies like Section 119, a wink-and-nod to the world that you're a phan, that you're in on the joke.[18] I joke with my wife about getting a Fishman donut-print flag to hang outside our home—I imagine that seeing it waving in the wind would bring me a similar sense of joy that spooning into a pint of Phish Food does. A red-circle emoji—a Fishman donut, not the regular, chocolate-glazed donut emoji—on a Twitter bio is a pretty good indicator you've found a phan. And it was phans who helped connect Phish with Philadelphia's Federal Donuts ahead of the band's epic thirteen-show Baker's Dozen residency at Madison Square Garden in July and August 2017.

Federal Donuts is the fried-chicken-and-donuts shop established by star chef Michael Solomonov in Philadelphia in 2011. Solomonov, an Israeli-born Jewish chef, rose to success along with his James Beard Award–winning Zahav restaurant, also in Philadelphia, which since 2008 has showcased Israeli and Jewish cooking in an upscale, ultra-hospitable setting.[19] With Federal Donuts, Solomonov and his partners, including Steve Cook (a Jewish former Wall Street financial guy turned culinary-school graduate) and Phish superphan Felicia D'Ambrosio, could be more playful than Zahav's fine-dining setting allows. Federal Donuts, whose kitchens until early 2022 were led by culinary director Matt Fein, also Jewish, had rolled out Phish-themed donuts from time to time—like the Fishman (blue vanilla raspberry with red glaze, inspired by Fishman's donut dress) and the Fluffhead (topped with marshmallow fluff and chocolate "pill" sprinkles, inspired by the song of the same name)—which made the rounds on social media and caught the attention of phans and foodies alike.[20] When Phish went looking for a donut baker to help out with an idea for its Baker's Dozen MSG residency, they wound up calling Federal Donuts after being tipped to the Philly restaurant by a chef in nearby New York. Fein took the band's ideas for donut flavors, came up with a Federal Donuts interpretation of each one, and things took off from there. "It's neat to get their take on what they

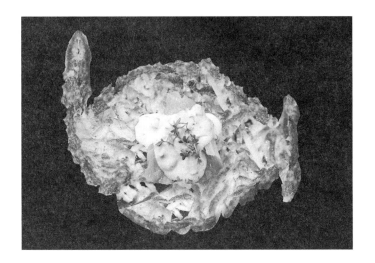

FIG. 3.1 Phish-shaped latke. Design by Ariane B. Davis.

wanted and then be able to put my name on it," Fein told the Associated Press.[21] Fein and crew baked the creations and trucked the donuts—every night of the thirteen-show run—from Philly to New York to hand out to the first few thousand fans through the doors at MSG each night (the exact number of free donuts prepped per show is unclear, but each night's available donuts were scooped up within minutes).

The Federal Donuts team had to keep each donut flavor a secret, because on the day of each show, usually about twelve hours before showtime, Phish would post on its social media channels a picture and description of that night's donut, which also doubled as the theme for that night's music. For example, on the morning of July 25, 2017, before night 4 of the Baker's Dozen shows, Phish tweeted a picture of Fein's creation of honey-dipped donuts with raspberry jam in the center, declaring that night's flavor as "Jam-Filled."[22] Those jam-filled donuts, which looked a lot like Hanukkah *sufganiyot*, foretold a show that featured long, jammed-out songs, like a thirty-minute rendition of "Lawn Boy," a song whose studio version lasts two and a half minutes.[23] The night before, with "Red Velvet" as the featured donut flavor, Phish worked a song from the Velvet Underground into its show and closed the second set with "Wading in the Velvet Sea."[24] Phish is beloved by phans for giving us little hidden treasures and inside jokes, like when the band dons a "musical costume" for their Halloween shows and plays another band's full album in its entirety, or back in the early '90s when Phish injected live shows with secret musical signals that only phans understood (for example, guitarist Anastasio would play a few notes of *The Simpsons* theme song, prompting the crowd to shout, in unison, "D'oh!" like Homer Simpson). Those clever antics help inspire a sense of community among Phish phans. Food also inspires a sense of community; it can bring people together.

By incorporating food—donuts, a traditional Jewish celebratory food, made by a Jewish chef working at a Jewish-owned restaurant company, as well as the identifying emblem of Phish's Jewish drummer—into the core of the Baker's Dozen concept, Phish extended the sense of "we're all in this together" beyond in-the-know phans and to a larger community. Between Fishman's dress and the Baker's Dozen shows, donuts will forever be linked to the legacy of Phish and its community.

Phish has always managed to foster a sense of community among its phans by making us feel special and seen in unique ways. Giving us awesome flavors of Ben & Jerry's ice cream and donating the proceeds, and playing thirteen shows in a row at an iconic New York venue in a donut-themed residency without repeating a single song are just two of many examples. Other prominent examples include hosting elaborate festivals complete with Ferris wheels and late-night jam sessions, as well as epic New Year's Eve shows, including one in the middle of the Florida Everglades as 1999 turned into 2000. And perhaps never did phans or anyone need to feel special and seen as much as we did in 2020, when the coronavirus pandemic brought so much fear and loss throughout the world. Soon after announcing in the spring of 2020 that they were postponing their summer concerts, Phish gave phans something wonderful: starting in March 2020, the band began streaming high-definition, archival video footage of one show a week for free online. And while the shows were free to stream, Phish also accepted donations during each installment through the WaterWheel Foundation to benefit different charitable organizations. They posted a companion recipe to go along with each show, so phans could cook and eat and watch the show—again Phish tapping into the power of food and music to foster a sense of togetherness and gathering even when we were apart and at home. The band aptly called the series Dinner and a Movie, after one of Phish's oldest songs of the same name.[25] For that first installment in March, the accompanying recipe was for a vegetarian chili from Sue and Trey Anastasio. The ingredient list and instructions were simple by design—this was at the beginning of the pandemic, and the Anastasios wanted people to be able to use what they already had at home without having to make a special trip to the grocery store. Some of the Dinner and a Movie recipes were more advanced, with professional chefs and others from the Phish universe offering their culinary pairings. For the nineteenth installment, on July 28, 2020, Phish broadcast its show from exactly three years earlier, July 28, 2017, from the "Chocolate" night of the Baker's Dozen run. The recipes that accompanied that night's Dinner and a Movie episode—a double-chocolate donut and a fried chicken sandwich—came from Federal Donuts and were probably out of reach for most home cooks (the donut recipe alone has nineteen ingredients and eighteen steps).

I appreciated not only the range of recipes and difficulty levels that accompanied the Dinner and a Movie shows, but also the thought that went into that element of the production. In the culinary world, food pairings are often limited to beverages like beer and wine—what drink pairs best with what you're eating. Before Dinner and a Movie, I hadn't given much thought to pairing food with music, and I love the way that Phish did that in their typically smart and humorous way: a three-set show goes with a three-course meal, a scorcher of a summer show from Alpine Valley goes with blistered shishito peppers, the "Chocolate" show from Baker's Dozen goes with a chocolate donut. It was perfectly Phish, and perfectly communal: a quick search of #phishdinnerandamovie any night of the series pulled up dozens of pics from phans who were all cooking the same recipes and jamming to the same music.

I tuned in to every Dinner and a Movie that I could, including the 2020 New Year's Eve installment, the twenty-ninth installment, which featured Phish's first NYE show from Madison Square Garden, December 31, 1995, exactly twenty-five years earlier. Phish paired that episode with recipes to build your own charcuterie and cheese boards—the cheese-board recipe is a riff on a chess board, because at their shows in 1995, including NYE, Phish would play chess against the audience, each side making one communal move per show. Many Phish phans I know started to look forward to Dinner and a Movie nights with a similar anticipation to that we have when seeing Phish live, with the bonus in 2020 of being a much-needed escape in an otherwise dreary year. Early in my Phish phandom, I would rack up as many shows as I could afford to get to and pay for. As I've gotten older, with a family and career and mortgage and all their inherent responsibilities, seeing Phish live has become less of an every-time-they're-within-five-hundred-miles-of-here sure thing and more of an occasional treat. Which is why I and, I suspect, other phans with similar life circumstances embraced the Dinner and a Movie concept so enthusiastically and loved the experience of watching (and cooking and eating) together while in the comfort and privacy of our own homes. Nothing replicates the energy and experience of a live concert, but being able to curl up on the couch, bathroom and kitchen breaks a pause button away, on a Tuesday night when the kid is asleep to watch my favorite band on the planet, knowing that thousands of other like-minded phans are doing the same thing? Yeah, sign me up every time.

Although I watched every Dinner and a Movie installment that I could, I only cooked along with the suggested recipes once, for episode 22, which took place on August 25, 2020, and featured a Phish show from nine years earlier, August 15, 2011, at the UIC Pavilion in Chicago. Something about the recipes, provided by longtime Phish HQ employee Betty Frost, spoke to me, with their emphasis on peak-season vegetables for dishes like cucumber gazpacho and sweet corn risotto. The one I wanted to try most, however, was her flourless chocolate brownies made with tahini, and it did not let me down. The recipe is straightforward and gives a double dose of tahini, calling for some in the batter and more swirled on top for a beautiful black-and-tan contrast between the cocoa and the tahini. I loved working through the dishes as the sets progressed, saving the brownies for a delightful, five-song encore. I wondered if other phans were doing the same thing, but I didn't have to look up the #phishdinnerandamovie hashtag on Twitter to confirm it—I know my people, I know this community, and I felt connected to every other phan who was eyeing a plate of still-warm brownies just like I was. Phish closed that show with "Harry Hood," and as I sat there, tahini brownie in hand, I closed my eyes, I pictured myself in Israel, I heard the reggae inflections of Alpha Blondy, and I smiled. I am home.

NOTES

1. The author acknowledges and thanks his wife, Teri, for seeing the joy that Phish brings him and allowing him to pursue creative endeavors like music, food, and journalism; his parents, Joyce and Niles, and family for the trip to Israel; his former neighbor Brian Smith for playing Phish on those rides to school; and members of the Journophish community for this opportunity and for daily smiles.

2. *Schvitz* is the Yiddish word for sweat.

3. Phish, *Rift* (Elektra, 1993).

4. Phish, *A Live One* (Elektra, 1995).

5. Phish, "Harry Hood," track 4, disc 2, on *A Live One* (Elektra, 1995). Each track on the album was recorded at a different live Phish show in 1994. The album's "Harry Hood" was from October 23, 1994, at the University of Florida in Gainesville.

6. Established in 1997, the WaterWheel Foundation is Phish's charitable arm that gives to nonprofit groups in local communities where the band tours as well as to Vermont-based nonprofits. The foundation primarily seeks to benefit organizations that provide social services, focus on environmental causes, or improve access to food and clean water.

7. Fishman and Greenfield, "Water-Wheel | Ben & Jerry's."

8. Ibid.

9. According to Ben & Jerry's, Phish Food was the company's sixth most popular flavor in 2019, the most recent year that data were available. Cherry Garcia was the second.

10. Phish, "It's Ice," track 12 on *Rift* (Elektra, 1993).

11. Phish, "Tweezer Reprise," track 16 on *A Picture of Nectar* (Elektra, 1992).

12. Phish, "Reba," track 2 on *Lawn Boy* (Absolute A Go Go, 1990).

13. Grateful Dead, "Shakedown Street," track 3, on *Shakedown Street* (Arista, 1978).

14. Raviv, *Falafel Nation*.

15. From a Talmudic description meaning "spongy dough," adapted to the Hebrew word *sufganiyot*.

16. Budnick, *Long May They Run*.

17. Ibid.

18. Section 119, established in 2017, is an upscale men's clothing brand with apparel that features the red-donut-on-blue-background motif of Fishman's dress, as well as designs with the Grateful Dead's iconic dancing bears. It got its name from

Section 119 at Madison Square Garden, which the company's founders said is the best section in that venue because of its "Page-side" view of Phish keyboardist Page McConnell and because of its proximity to Fuku, the fast-food offshoot of star chef David Chang's Momofuku empire whose spicy fried chicken sandwiches were heralded by phans during the Baker's Dozen run at Madison Square Garden in 2017.

19. Presented by the James Beard Foundation, the Beard Awards are considered the Oscars of the food world. Solomonov has won them for Best Chef: Mid-Atlantic in 2011 and Outstanding Chef in 2018; his *Zahav* cookbook won three Beard Awards, including Cookbook of the Year, in 2016; and Zahav won the Beard Award for Outstanding Restaurant—the best in the United States—in 2019. The author of this chapter served as a volunteer member of the Beard Foundation's Restaurant and Chef Awards committee from 2017 until 2021.

20. Phish, "Fluffhead," track 1, disc 2, on *Junta* (Elektra, 1992).

21. Cornfield, "For Philadelphia Phish Fan." Cornfield, the AP writer who penned the above-cited piece about Federal Donuts' involvement in the Baker's Dozen, along with the author of this chapter, are among the roughly one hundred members of Journophish, a group of journalists who have a shared love for the music of Phish.

22. The tweet read, "*TONIGHT'S FLAVOR IS JAM FILLED (mini honey dipped donuts with raspberry jam in center). #phish #bakers dozen*" (@phish, July 27, 2017, https://twitter.com/phish/status/889835445911257088).

23. Phish, "Lawn Boy," track 4 on *Lawn Boy* (Absolute A Go Go, 1990).

24. Phish, "Wading in the Velvet Sea," track 12 on *The Story of the Ghost* (Elektra, 1998).

25. Phish, "Dinner and a Movie," track 6, disc 1, on *Junta* (Elektra, 1992).

REFERENCES

Budnick, Dean, host. *Long May They Run*. Produced by C13Originals. Released September–November 2019. Podcast. https://shows.cadence13.com/long-may-they-run.

Cornfield, Josh. "For Philadelphia Phish Fan, It's Time to Make the Doughnuts." *Associated Press*, July 27, 2017. https://apnews.com/article/cd6247156d1c4eb5b1ddc6f4f2e6ef98.

Fishman, Jon, and Jerry Greenfield. "Water-Wheel | Ben & Jerry's." YouTube video, December 10, 2014, 2:01. https://youtu.be/FvJaUOdBkDc.

Raviv, Yael. *Falafel Nation: Cuisine and the Making of National Identity in Israel*. Lincoln: University of Nebraska Press, 2015.

4.

Exploring Jewishness and Queerness on Phish's Dance Floor

Isaac Kandall Slone

> Because I'm a Jew, Sergeant. I *am* different.
> —PHILIP ROTH, "DEFENDER OF THE FAITH"

Before seeing my first Phish show, I struggled to enjoy dancing. I could not get my body to move like others could, or in ways that felt physically liberating. I took dance classes in middle school for physical education credits. Though I was relieved that they offered a way out of organized sports, I still struggled to perform the choreography. I sensed that others enjoyed dancing and found it liberating. I wanted to experience that physical liberation myself, and I was able to finally have that experience while seeing Phish.

When I look around an amphitheater during a Phish show, I see hundreds of smiling faces and bodies in motion as fans let go of their cares and move in uninhibited ways. Limbs fly freely, without choreography or coordination, in direct reaction to the music. The band's jams encourage particularly lively ambulation. As the band composes on the spot, riffing off one another to produce moments of rhythmic groove, dissonance, and climactic rock and roll energy, the audience responds by synchronously embracing each moment, moving their bodies in any way the music takes them. I feel drawn to this kind of dance, as it helps me feel immersed in Phish's music and free in my own body. The dancing I experience at Phish does not emphasize a dancer's singular capacities but rather the collective surrender to the show's flow.[1]

On August 16, 2009, I attended my twelfth Phish concert of the summer, at the Saratoga Performing Arts Center in Saratoga Springs, New York. I was fourteen years old. Throughout the summer tour, my eyes opened to the band's extensive and diverse songbook, their rich improvisational style, and the ethos of creativity and kindness that follows them. While I swayed and moved my feet to Phish's music at the previous shows I'd seen, I felt a particular sense of unity and connection dancing among the crowd that evening, participating in joyful and uninhibited movement from the moment the band played their first notes until they took their final bows. I left my seat, which was located close to the stage, in favor of dancing through the aisles and on the lawn—a sacrifice that would have felt foolish at any other concert, where sightlines would overrule the chance to interact with the audience. As I danced in the aisles of SPAC, I felt a newfound sense of joy and belonging.

The music resonated deeply with me, as did my embodied experience. I felt enlivened as I shared "in the groove" with an amphitheater full of others gathered in celebration.[2] The experience was thrilling as I came to feel heightened sensations throughout my body. As I moved with abandon, I connected with parts of my identity that I had not imagined such movement could tap into. While dancing at this particular Phish concert, I sensed an ephemeral connection to my Jewish identity. Though I do not believe that Phish shows are essentially Jewish spaces, jam-band music and specifically the music of Phish has a particular influence on some of its Jewish fans, in part because of the style of dance the music evokes and invites. The unscripted and expressive qualities of jam-band music and the dancing that it invokes help me move without care and simultaneously pushes me to explore the queerness of my Jewish body.

My uses of the terms "queer" and "queerness" refer to experiences of feeling and identifying as outside the mainstream, particularly in performing masculinity. Queer individuals look to countercultural spaces, such as Phish concerts, for acceptance and for the freedom to explore aspects of themselves in ways that otherwise might feel dangerous or inaccessible given the pressures of societal norms. In his research on queer world-making and the affirmation of minoritarian lives, José Esteban Muñoz suggests that one can extract great meaning from the ephemeral elements of lived experience—the "traces, glimmers, residues, and specks of things."[3] Ephemeral evidence is essential to queer world-making, as there are varying degrees of social vulnerability that come with explicit displays of difference. Ephemeral moments occur in innumerable ways at Phish shows. These moments may take the form of an encounter with a smiling stranger, a memory caused by a particular music riff, or an embodied experience provoked through dance. Like Muñoz, I look to ephemeral experiences at Phish and analyze those ephemeral qualities of Phish concerts that create the space for me to dance in ways that conquer my feelings of inadequacy and offer points of connection.

The Phish concert space often feels free of societal expectations and accompanying judgments. This distinguishes the Phish show experience as one that exists outside the cultural framework of my daily life and allows for the band and fans to have an expressive and unmediated exchange. Once the lights go down at a Phish show and the band begins playing, I feel free to move my body, unrestricted by preoccupations or feelings of self-consciousness. In fact, from the moment I depart for a Phish show, my engagement with the world shifts. As I ready myself for the concert, I separate from the confines of my day-to-day existence. Victor Turner's research on the liminal provides a theoretical framework through which to analyze how this phenomenon manifests at Phish shows. Turner identifies the liminal state as one in which fixed structures and conditions no longer apply, wherein individuals or groups separate from their set social structures and cultural conditions. An individual or group enters this state, then aggregates back into a stable and fixed form with structures and norms.[4] Like many Phish followers, I take time away from my daily life and travel great distances to see Phish concerts. I often shed formal clothing for a T-shirt and cargo shorts, in which I can move more comfortably. Although casual, I can feel assured that the attire will mirror what other audience members are wearing. While my chosen garb marks a departure from my daily clothing, some Phish fans see a Phish concert as an opportunity to wear everything from colorful tie-dyes to creative costumes.

At the start of a show, I silence my phone. In contrast to most other rock concerts taking place on a similar scale (in arenas or amphitheaters), very few people photograph or video Phish concerts on their phones. Beyond the distraction, phones are links to the world outside of the concert space. Silencing my phone at a Phish concert creates a further separation between myself and the obligations, images, and potential communications that exist outside the show. It allows for a singular focus, which is in and of itself liminal in our culture.

Phish's long compositions and complex improvisations require attention from their audience, thus the common opinion among Phish fans that one has to see the band live to fully understand them. To be in step with Phish, leaning into the heightened sensory experience and ephemeral moments their concert space creates can mean being out of step with normative concert practices in ways that can feel liberating—dancing in ways that would look odd when set to other kinds of music, moving through aisles, and giving full attention to the music and environment.

When I attended the SPAC show referenced above, Phish played their rarely performed but highly sought-after song "Harpua."[5] The song includes improvised narration from guitarist Trey Anastasio about the song's protagonist, a young boy named Jimmy, and his dog Harpua. In this particular narration, Anastasio described Jimmy as suffering from "perennial blues that has overcome his body [and] his spirit." Anastasio continued, describing Jimmy's spirit guide, who assumes the form of a "funny little man wearing a dress." At this moment, Phish drummer Jon Fishman, who is of Jewish descent, left his drum kit and took center stage to sing a rendition of Katy Perry's pop song "I Kissed a Girl."[6] He was wearing his signature blue and red donut dress. The singing was off-key and the instrumentation was jumbled, subverting the song's pop style and subject matter. It did not resemble anything close to Perry's original recording. Following "I Kissed a Girl," Fishman approached the front of the stage, threw up his hands victoriously, and greeted the audience. He then ran and jumped across the stage as the rest of the band performed a cover of Argent's "Hold Your Head Up."[7] "That didn't work on so many levels," Anastasio exclaimed after the stunt. Reflecting on the moment, I recognize that the performance did actually work. Before seeing Phish, I felt like Jimmy in Anastasio's story—overcome by the blues. Furthermore, my spirit guide assumed the form of a "funny little" Jewish man wearing a dress, unabashedly playing up his strangeness and the queerness of his masculinity, moving across the stage chaotically, and finding an ecstatic audience all the while.

Phish takes musical risks that leave them vulnerable to the potential for failure. These moments often occur during the band's improvisational jams, although other instances occur during shows: the performance of a new, unreleased song or the inclusion of a gag or stunt such as the aforementioned Katy Perry cover. Phish's openness to vulnerability resonates with me as an audience member. They are brave and authentic, and reject mainstream expectations that a band play their hit songs in ways that resemble their recordings. With these risks comes the immense reward of a jam, song, or stunt going well. In these instances, the band and audience both share in the newfound creative space. Fans often memorialize these moments as part of Phish's lore and often discuss them following the show.

I interpret the band's aesthetic choice of valuing risk-taking over consistent flawlessness as queer because it succeeds in being off script and not conforming to traditional systems of valuation as defined by a heteronormative, capitalist society.[8] This in and of itself is queer, as are Phish's lengthy songs and usage of odd time signatures. Their artistic choices define Phish as anything but mainstream. Muñoz intriguingly interrogates queer artists' relationship to what he calls "straight time": "Within straight time the queer can only fail; thus, an aesthetic of failure can be productively occupied by the queer artist for the purpose of delineating the bias that underlies straight time's measure."[9] Phish's long shows and improvisations delineate the bias of straight time's measure while inviting the audience to participate in an escape from straight time. In this space of escape, I can embrace queerness in a bodily way: through dance. That experience of queerness is tied to my male Jewish body.

According to Daniel Boyarin, premodern and modern European culture feminized the male Jewish body, emphasizing characteristics, traits, and behaviors that read as nonmale.[10] The characteristics bestowed on the Jewish male body typically indicated a lack of something: a lack of strength, height, athletic ability, dominance, and even masculine pride. This assessment of male Jewish bodies as deficient still resonates today. Boyarin notes a "widespread sensibility that being Jewish in our culture renders a boy effeminate. . . . To be sure, this meant being marginal and it has left me with a persistent sense of being on the outside of something, with my nose pressed to the glass looking in."[11] Boyarin's experience of being on the outside has felt true for me as a flamboyant short man with thinning hair in my early twenties. Boyarin suggests that "the 'normal' male in our social formation, and especially the adolescent, is engaged in a constant project of demonstrating to himself that he is not queer, that he does not desire other men."[12] But at Phish concerts, men embrace, hugging and dancing among other men. Though maleness is dominant at Phish, the masculinity performed at Phish differs from what popular society prizes as manly. It's maleness that embraces creativity and fluidity, in which a man has nothing to prove. It is also a rejection of heteronormative masculinity that can be harmful to many men (including Jewish ones) and to women and nonbinary individuals through the idealization of manhood that it creates.

As I dance at Phish, I am free to embrace my effeminized male Jewish body and all that it offers through dance. Dancing serves as a reclamation of my body as worthy and a means of eradicating my fears concerning being judged as queer. The sense of freedom that I feel at Phish shows echoes my experience in synagogue. So does the dancing. To me, Phish's audience members always look as if they are engaged in prayer as they sway and bow. I, too, dance to Phish's music in a way that mimics the act of *shuckling*, a Yiddish word meaning "to shake," that refers to the way observant Jews sway when deep in prayer, a bodily method meant to foster total physical, mental, and spiritual immersion. The soul is like a flame, moving and flickering in prayer as one's body moves back and forth.[13] Both in synagogues and at Phish shows, this kind of movement enables the audience to achieve total spiritual immersion.

Zachary Braiterman notes that the synagogue was a historically safe space for Jewish males to participate in movement. According to Braiterman, "In cultic space, the body does without the expression of personality. . . . Dance is a cultic act in Judaism. . . . Whereas dance shatters the walls of the church as it proceeds outside the church and into the village, in Judaism, dance occurs inside the synagogue."[14] As an observant Jew who *shuckles* at synagogue as well as at Phish, I find in both settings a familiar and welcome feeling of giving my full body over to the experience. While dancing or *shuckling* at a Phish concert, my physical stature is not under observation or at threat of being judged. The concert space is more public than a synagogue but still allows me to engage in this sacred and powerful movement that is divinely sanctioned in the temple of Phish.

Though this type of movement is liberating for me, it is steeped in a complex history. In nineteenth-century Europe, the Jew was closely bound to the idea of the diseased hysteric.[15] At the time, hysteria was seen as a diagnosable and treatable illness, most commonly seen in females. Feminized males such as Jews were also diagnosed as hysterics.[16] In fact, much popular and scientific literature of nineteenth- and early twentieth-century Germany argues that hysteria is what sets Jewish men apart from other men.[17] Such ideas highlight the antisemitism and implicit misogyny that underwrote representations of Jewishness at the time. Today, hysteria is no longer a diagnosis but rather is used in its descriptive form *hysterical* to describe a display of uncontrolled emotions. This kind of hysteria can be observed in many forms at Phish concerts. In its most physically observable way, one could determine many behaviors of Phish fans to be hysterical, including their unwavering dedication to the band, their predilection toward drug use, and the behavior of fans on the dance floor, especially during the band's musical peaks.

Indeed, Phish's musical peaks encourage me (and so many others) to give myself up to ephemeral moments of performed hysteria. I experience these peaks with my whole body, often basking in them with eyes closed and arms outstretched—or in an ecstatic frenzy, rocking back and forth and jumping up and down. In these moments, I may look observably hysterical to uninformed outsiders. Yet I feel liberated and joyful in the moment, unbound from the worry of what my movements may convey. Dancing ecstatically—and perhaps hysterically—at Phish shows helps me embrace and reclaim the power of my male Jewish body, a body that has been othered and feminized by Western culture. So too, in moving my body, along with so many others, in ways that decidedly do not conform to general American societal

FIG. 4.1 "I Always Wanted It This Way," Madison Square Garden, New York, July 22, 2017. Photo: Andrea Z. Nusinov.

expectations, I reclaim aspects of my identity that have been othered and find a space in which my otherness is celebrated.

Though I focus on the male Jewish body, dance can offer embodied experiences of freedom for all Phish fans. However, gender identity certainly informs fans' abilities to "surrender to the flow." The gender dynamic of the Phish community skews heavily male. The maleness of the space becomes particularly apparent to me as I dance among the crowd during shows. Within the space of a Phish concert, I move my body and consequently feel simultaneously liberated and vulnerable. And yet that opportunity is not available to all fans. Sexism, racism, and other forms of discrimination cannot be ignored or made light of simply because Phish concerts are safe and spiritual places for some. Not all concertgoers are focused on creating a safe and spiritual place. Indeed, some fans engage in abusive and prejudiced behavior at shows. Phish fans are responding to this reality by reflecting and investigating how to make the Phish community more inclusive. For example, a support group called GrooveSafe has recently formed in response to unwanted touching and sexual assaults at concerts, while Phans for Racial Equity strives to make Phish a more welcoming and equitable concert space for fans of all races and ethnicities. Along with these community efforts, the emerging academic field of Phish studies has the opportunity to unpack these dimensions of identity as they pertain to Phish and their community.

Phish creates a unique aesthetic in their music, one that forgoes perfectionism to embrace what comes naturally in the moment of performance. And they ask their fans to participate in the improvisational moment. Dancing at Phish concerts among other Jewish and non-Jewish bodies has for me proven to be a necessary means of self-emancipation from the need to adhere to traditional social norms.[18] As I exit the liminal space of a Phish show and aggregate back into a more fixed state, I take with me the experience of bodily freedom. Outside the Phish concert space, I feel empowered by the sense of belonging I feel at concerts. In fact, my experiences of dance at Phish concerts inspired me as a high schooler to participate in my school's annual dance. I found I was able to access the embodied sense of joy I felt at Phish in other contexts. Despite my inability to land choreographed dance moves, my Jewish body needs and wants to dance and move beyond its insufficiencies and past what was historically deemed, both by culture and science, as capable of a Jewish body. In the space of a Phish concert, I experience bodily freedom among Jews and non-Jews alike, reveling in that which makes us similar: the chance to be nurtured through dance.

NOTES

1. My use of "surrender to the flow" explicitly references Phish's song "The Lizards," which comes from Phish guitarist Trey Anastasio's concept album and senior thesis, *The Man Who Stepped into Yesterday*. Phish fans often use this phrase as an expression of a shared philosophy, the essence of which is to give over to the experience—in this case, of the concert. Trey Anastasio, "The Lizards," track 3 on *The Man Who Stepped into Yesterday* (senior thesis, Goddard College, 1987).

2. Phish, "Weekapaug Groove," track 7 on *Slip, Stitch, and Pass* (Elektra, 1997). Phish's "Weekapaug Groove" includes the lyrics "Trying to make a woman that you move / And I'm sharing in a Weekapaug groove." Though the band has said that the lyrics are meaningless, fans often use this phrase to describe the collective experience of a Phish concert. Phish.net, "Weekapaug Groove History," https://phish.net/song /weekapaug-groove/history.

3. Muñoz, "Ephemera as Evidence," 10.

4. Turner, "Liminality and Communitas," 95.

5. Phish, "Harpua," track 18 on *8/16/2009 Saratoga Performing Arts Center, Saratoga Springs, NY* (LivePhish.com, 2009).

6. Katy Perry, "I Kissed a Girl," track 2 on *One for the Boys* (Capitol, 2008).

7. Argent, "Hold Your Head Up," track 1 on *All Together Now* (Epic, 1972).

8. Muñoz, *Cruising Utopia*, 174.

9. Ibid., 173–74.
10. Boyarin, *Unheroic Conduct*, xiii, 5.
11. Ibid., 4–5.
12. Ibid., 15.
13. Donati, "Moving Prayer," 20.

14. Braiterman, "Modern Mitz-vah-Space-Aesthetic," 262–63.
15. Gilman, *Jew's Body*, 63.
16. Ibid.
17. Pellegrini, "Jewishness as Gender."
18. Boyarin, *Unheroic Conduct*, 4.

REFERENCES

Boyarin, Daniel. *Unheroic Conduct: The Rise of Heterosexuality and the Invention of the Jewish Man*. Berkeley: University of California Press, 1997.

Braiterman, Zachary. "A Modern Mitz-vah-Space-Aesthetic: The Philosophy of Franz Rosenzweig." In *The Art of Being Jewish in Modern Times*, edited by Barbara Kirshenblatt-Gimblett and Jonathan Karp, 257–69. Philadelphia: University of Pennsylvania Press, 2008.

Donati, Julie S. "Moving Prayer." *St. Anthony Messenger* 114, no. 2 (2006): 18–22.

Gilman, Sander. *The Jew's Body*. New York: Routledge, 1991.

Muñoz, José Esteban. *Cruising Utopia: The Then and There of Queer Futurity*. New York: New York University Press, 2009.

———. "Ephemera as Evidence: Introductory Notes to Queer Acts." *Women and Performance: A Journal of Feminist Theory* 8, no. 2 (1996): 5–16.

Pellegrini, Ann. "Jewishness as Gender." *Shofar: An Interdisciplinary Journal of Jewish Studies* 14, no. 1 (1995): 138–41.

Turner, Victor. "Liminality and Communitas." In *The Ritual Process: Structure and Anti-Structure*, 94–113. Chicago: Aldine, 1969.

5.

I've Been Wading in the Whitest Sea

REFLECTIONS ON RACE, JUDAISM, AND PHISH

Caroline Rothstein

In 2017, in the wake of the Movement for Black Lives and the national conversation around White supremacy and systemic oppression, Phish fan and racial justice activist Adam Lioz wrote a seminal article called "Phish Scene So White: Let's Talk," urging fellow fans to consider race and White privilege within the Phish community.[1] Lioz called out the pervasive Whiteness in the Phish scene and invited fans to recognize and discuss the role White privilege and systemic racism play in creating an exclusive and racially biased music scene.[2]

In the article, Lioz reflected on his own Whiteness, interviewed fans of color, and posed questions about how White privilege might operate in the scene. He challenged fans to help transform the Phish community into "a force for racial equity."[3] Lioz argued that the Phish scene is built on a foundation of White privilege and broke down the unguarded and extensive use of drugs at festivals and shows. How at Phish shows, police and security officers often watch and waver on the sidelines as thousands of mostly White people openly consume drugs.

Despite equal drug usage across racial identities in the United States, Black Americans are six times more likely than White Americans to be incarcerated for drug-related charges.[4] Similarly, nearly 80 percent of people federally incarcerated for drug-related charges are Black or Latinx.[5] So Lioz rightfully pointed out how the Phish scene was and is built on a foundation of White privilege. If a festival heavily attended by people of color exhibited the same unabashed usage of drugs, there's no way cops would respond with seemingly little concern.

The article received mixed reviews from the fan community. According to Lioz, while plenty of fans and readers were excited by and on board with what he wrote, the vast majority of responses and backlash he received veered on vitriolic, further exposing the way White privilege, White supremacy culture, and systemic racism permeate societal norms and ideologies in the United States, especially in predominantly White spaces like at Phish.[6] As a result, Phish fans and sociologists David L. Brunsma, Joong Won Kim, and Nathaniel G. Chapman produced a paper breaking down just how racialized the online responses, specifically, were to Lioz's piece.[7]

As a fan of twenty-plus years, I often say that Phish is the "Whitest" thing I do. Once in a while, frustrated and overwhelmed by the Whiteness of the scene, I'll Google "Phish and Whiteness," just to see if anyone's publicly talking about it, and Lioz's article is always the top search result. So his piece validates one of my long-standing critiques of the scene: it's overwhelmingly White and it's also overwhelming male, neither of which tends to create the liberatory and inclusive spaces I seek.

As a White Jewish woman committed to racial equity and inclusivity in its myriad forms, it's always complicated for me when I attend Phish shows, despite my deep devotion to the band's music, my lust for dancing en masse, and my fervent commitment to my many friends and this community that I've been a part of for much of my life. I imagine that challenge might only amplify the further a fan is from White and male.[8] As Lioz notes, "Whiteness tends to build upon itself—once a scene or culture is overwhelmingly White it becomes very difficult for it also to be welcoming for people who don't fit neatly into the mold."[9] While this reality can easily apply to other social identities like socioeconomic class, gender, sexuality, and others, it holds up a mirror as to why the Phish scene is so White. This reality also offers an examination as to why so many White Jews—like me—have easily blended into the fold, relatively unscathed.

I saw my first Phish show on July 8, 2000, at Alpine Valley in East Troy, Wisconsin. I was seventeen. I went with two freshmen from my competitive, mostly White and affluent public high school in the northern suburbs of Chicago. One guy I knew from theater; the other was his friend. While I had my license and a car, my parents wouldn't let me drive, claiming the hour-and-a-half trip up I-94 from

Wilmette, Illinois, to East Troy, Wisconsin, was too far. Instead, my parents had a family friend—Vladimir, who owned a limousine company—drive us in a fancy black sedan. I was mortified.

As we neared the venue on that sunny Saturday afternoon in July, stuck in traffic, I got out of the car to walk alongside the cornfields that kissed the midwestern highway. As far as the plains stretched, White hippie kids in patchwork clothing ambulated with their fingers in the air, looking for tickets to get inside. Even before entering the show, I felt arrived, home. I felt like I had found my people. I wanted more. I never wanted to leave.

I'd spent most of my life fetishizing and worshipping 1960s American counterculture. Attending my first Phish show felt like the closest I had ever gotten to that counterculture, and I wanted in. I was wealthy and White, also Jewish and female. I did theater, sang, wrote poetry, and danced. I was popular and had friends across social groups and moved throughout my high school like a butterfly or a chameleon, depending on the day. I was a tinge "Jewish American Princess"—the antisemitic term "JAP" was rampant in the 1990s, even among Jews before we realized how classist and self-loathing it was—but at heart, I was a lefty radical anticapitalist antiestablishment artist with bulimia and depression who felt othered and alone in so many ways. But at that first show in Alpine Valley, I finally found a container that might be able to hold my many nuanced identities and selves. Though I still loathed getting there in a shiny luxury sedan.

We had seats in the pavilion next to some dude who bought me a beer. The show was explosive. Everyone seemed like they were in on some inside joke or secret world—chanting at the end of certain lines, moments they knew to shout and yell specific things. It was like everyone there belonged. The music was decadent, guttural, determined, melodic, whimsical, and vulnerable, all while simultaneously building toward some monumental and otherworldly anticipatory rock and roll revolution and risk. I'd been listening to Phish for several years by now, repeating their *A Live One* album over and over on my bedroom stereo and Discman.[10] But seeing Phish live was something else entirely. It was transcendent and transformative.

At some point during the first set, I felt an awakening burst as the soundwaves hit not only my ears but now my skin. I pushed my way out of my seat and erupted into the aisle to dance. Something broke. For the first time in my life, my body took over my brain. It was incredible. Liberating. The countercultural experience for which I'd long dreamed. I'd been totally sold—the anticipation, the arrival, the lot, the crowd, the music, the entire scene.[11] I was in. I became a devotee.

But what did it mean that after seventeen years of feeling all too often othered I found sanctity wading in a velvet sea of Whiteness?[12]

I am a fourth-generation American. My great-great-grandparents left Lithuania to flee anti-Jewish oppression in the late 1800s. My ancestors benefited from assimilation and White privilege here in the United States as White Ashkenazi Jews, just as I have. And yet despite the various privileges and many ways from which my family and I have long profited and prospered in the United States, our experiences of antisemitism endure.

My maternal grandmother shares childhood memories of encountering signs posted at Chicago beaches that read "No Dogs, No Jews." She often recalls an incident that took place in the 1990s when her friends were enjoying lunch and a man who had been dining at the next table said to them, upon leaving, "They should have kept the ovens burning longer." Six years before I was born, there was a proposed—and ultimately blocked—Nazi march in Skokie, Illinois, the town next to where I grew up. Skokie was, and is still, known for having a large Jewish population that included hundreds of Holocaust survivors at the time.[13] Other neighboring towns, especially Kenilworth, were notorious for housing discrimination preventing Jews from owning property there.

The local public high school I attended matriculated a handful of suburban Chicago towns, including some with significant Jewish populations. As a student, I befriended people who grew up in actively antisemitic towns. Some of my non-Jewish friends fed micro-aggressions off their tongues like PEZ dispensers. I viscerally remember what it felt like to be othered, even though plenty of my friends in junior high and high school were also Jews. But when White Christian friends were mean to me, or I got bullied for being chubby and overweight as a kid and teen, I always assumed it was because I was a Jew. Just as it had for my maternal grandmother, the impact of these incidents became internalized and engrained.

My experience growing up in the Chicago suburbs was not filled with instances of overt antisemitism. I was never beaten in the street or at school, like my father had been in the 1960s. I never found a swastika plastered on my door, like plenty of other Jews had. But the constant chance of being othered and targeted as a Jew always lurked in every part of my life. It still does.

Throughout my career as a public writer, poet, and performer, I've experienced significant online harassment, especially as a woman and as a Jew, ranging from emails to social media comments and messages. In particular, comments on my YouTube poetry videos have long been a cesspool for antisemitism, with comments like "LOL, where are you horns, ROTHSTEIN?"; "nice one kike, im gonna shoot you in your forehead when i have the time for it [*sic*]"; and "It is time to deport all of the nose goblins from the West. To Israel you go!"

There was nothing thematically compelling or directly related to my being a Jew that baited the harassment. It was as simple as a bunch of White supremacists and neo-Nazis finding an outspoken artist and harassing her because she happened to be a Jew. I ultimately disabled comments on all of my YouTube videos because the harassment got so bad.

It's impossible to ignore the overt antisemitism that is prevalent in the United States today. Examples are abundant: the events in Charlottesville in 2017, where White supremacists marching in the streets chanted "Jews will not replace us"; or the Tree of Life synagogue shooting in Pittsburgh in 2018 that killed eleven Jews while they worshipped; or the desecration of Jewish tombstones in Michigan amid the 2020 presidential election; or the White supremacist insurrection at the United States Capitol mere days into 2021, where one person wore a "Camp Auschwitz" sweatshirt amid a field of neo-Nazi paraphernalia and hate symbols.[14] Each incident was perpetrated by someone seeking to intentionally, unabashedly uphold White supremacy in America by targeting Jews as a religious, ethnic, and cultural group that does not belong. These events illustrate a more widespread phenomenon of Jews being targets of hate crimes in the United States. In 2017, the FBI reported the largest increase in hate crimes committed in the United States since 9/11, with 900 of the 1,564 religion-based incidents—a staggering 58 percent—targeting Jews.[15] That same year, the Anti-Defamation League found antisemitic hate crime incidents rose by 57 percent, the largest single-year increase on record.[16] Despite this alarming data, Alexander Gutfraind argues that "today's Jewish America has probably the safest existence of any Jewish community in history. In this generation, a Jew is much more likely to suffer a car accident than a hate crime."[17]

That is, of course, if the Jew is White.

During a panel on race and racism in the Phish community at the first academic conference on Phish, Joong Won Kim highlighted the question "Is this your first show?" which fans often ask people they perceive to be new to the scene. "This idea of 'Is this your first show?' is a discourse that reveals a perception about who is valued as the best fan," says Kim.[18] This reality echoes the experiences of Jews of Color who recall being asked if they are Jewish while in synagogues and at Jewish events. It also confirms that race remains a steadfast marker of belonging at Phish shows. Kim explains, "The closer you are to White and male, the more likely you are to be perceived to be a knowledgeable fan." Social interactions at Phish shows are thus inherently racialized, yet that racialization is "rendered invisible for people who are not people of color."[19] That includes White Jews.

So while my Whiteness grants me privilege and protects me from systemic racism, my Jewishness still makes me a target for discrimination, hate, and abuse. And while I feel unencumbered by that threat at Phish, will that potentially ephemeral illusion of safety ultimately save me from being a very real and prospective target for antisemitism and White supremacy?

Phish is a way I connect with myself and the people I love. It is one of the many communities that holds me and keeps me whole. Part of that is the undeniable fact that being a Phish fan has a complicated relationship with identity, whether it's gender, body ability, socioeconomic status and class, or Whiteness and race. But if it is my Whiteness that allows me to travel around the country relatively unencumbered to follow my favorite band on tour, where does my Jewishness fit into and complexify this dynamic?

According to anthropologist Karen Brodkin, "The eagerness [for Jews] to be white is not hard to understand, since whiteness is a state of privilege and belonging. The Jewishness created by postwar Jewish intellectuals laid Jewish claim to these privileges and to belonging to the mainstream."[20] My Jewish ancestors assimilated into Whiteness both to survive and to access privilege. But regardless of why my ancestors—and any other White and White-passing Jews—assimilated into Whiteness, I am aware that by assimilating, I am inherently adopting the racist ideologies on which the United States was founded and built. As Brodkin writes, "With slavery, blackness became stigmatized as servile and worse, and whiteness became a privileged condition made visible by its never-ending efforts to distinguish itself from blackness."[21] White Jewish assimilation thus perpetuates systemic racism because assimilation is inherently built on anti-Blackness, and it also risks silencing Jews of Color by painting a narrative trope that overlooks the multiracial, multiethnic, and multicultural reality that is and has been the Jewish diaspora throughout time.

So Whiteness comes at a cost, both for people of color and for White people as well. Scholars and activists have long noted that participation in Whiteness—and assimilation, especially for White American Jews—is tantamount to the erasure of culture, ethnic ancestry, and history. Eric L. Goldstein, for example, describes this tension: "Exhilarated, on the one hand, with the possibility of achieving success and acceptance of a kind unimaginable even twenty years ago, some are also afraid that the Jews may cease to exist as a distinct group."[22] Of course, that collective assimilation has by no means been uniform, as an estimated 12 to 15 percent of the American Jewish population identifies as Jews of Color.[23]

Furthermore, in a renowned 1967 essay about Whiteness and American Jewry, James Baldwin writes, "In the American context, the most ironical thing about Negro anti-Semitism is that the Negro is really condemning the Jew for having become an American white man—for having become, in effect, a Christian. The Jew profits from his status in America, and he must expect Negroes to distrust him for it."[24] While Baldwin doesn't explicitly take into account Black Jews or non-Black Jews of Color, he does suggest that by accepting Whiteness, Jews simultaneously adopt particular elements of Christian culture that are prevalent in mainstream White American society. Because Phish became my ultimate haven for both assimilation and culture, my fandom necessitates that—like Baldwin suggests—I've assimilated as a Jew into Whiteness while adopting certain Christian hegemonic norms.

And still I struggle to reconcile my Whiteness and Jewishness within a contemporary American landscape that targets Jews and privileges White people, with my love of Phish, a band that exists fully within this same framework. Even though the band is known for being quirky and unconventional by rejecting the expectations of that same contemporary American culture, they're able to do so because of their own privilege as four cisgender middle-class White men. One of the many reasons I go to Phish shows is to disengage from my life and the world at large. Loving Phish is my surrender. But one could then argue that at Phish shows, I'm also disengaging from my Jewishness. The privilege I have to take a break from the world in a sea of Whiteness as a White Jew is the ultimate act of assimilation. It is the ultimate leveraging of my privilege.

As I wrestled with these concerns around my own White Jewish assimilation, as well as the racial homogeneity of the Phish scene, I reached out to speak with Marc Dollinger. Dollinger, whose research touches on Jewish participation in the counterculture and the historical relationships between Black and Jewish people in America, explained that in the 1950s, Jews were among the most upwardly mobile of European ethnic groups with regard to socioeconomics and class.[25] This upward mobility and assimilation into Whiteness "was done without self-reflection in many cases, even consciousness," Dollinger told me.[26] "The classic example I use is when Jews moved to the suburbs in the '50s because the antisemitic housing covenants eased. But the anti-Black covenants didn't. So the achieving of the American dream—home ownership in the suburbs—translated into complicity in a racist system." He helped me to understand that for me, and many other White Jews like me, seeing Phish may be "what the quest for inclusion looks like." Phish is my version of the White suburbs in the 1950s. It is what embracing Whiteness looks like.

I had a visceral reaction to his words in that specific moment and it all clicked into place: I feel comfortable at Phish concerts because, even though antisemitism genuinely looms in the world and potentially even at Phish, the experience affirms my Whiteness as a Jew.

Despite my love for the band, it feels imperative to grapple with and confront the Whiteness and privilege inherent to the Phish scene and think about the ways that White privilege—along with other kinds of privilege—is ingrained within it. That is why Lioz's call to action is critical in naming that our scene exists within the larger framework of American society and its history, even though so many fans want desperately to believe that we are part of an entirely altruistic, loving space that exists on its own.

"[White] Jews are liminal," Dollinger shared. "In one sense, we've gained the privilege of Whiteness. We get to hang around and . . . go to Phish concerts. And it's . . . great because we enjoy the privilege that's been conferred on us. And we know we will never be fully embraced by White America, because as Jews, we will always have antisemitism." Dollinger believes that this feeling of never being fully included is specific to White Jews. When he says this, my belly unlocks. I breathe more deeply into my lower torso and core, as if he's given me permission to fully feel the nuanced complexity with which I've always grappled throughout my life. The word "liminal," in particular, makes tangible the ethereal experience I live and breathe every day of my life in America as a White Jew, Phish fan or not, because liminality is an integral part of my identity as a Jew. Liminality has come to epitomize my desire to be in countercultural spaces.

As a White American Jew whose Jewish identity has been subject to erasure through my complacent assimilation into Whiteness, I've lost part of my connection to my ancestral heritage. Even though I care deeply about Judaism and practice daily, I am fully integrated into mainstream White American society. As Brunsma, Kim, and Chapman note in their paper breaking down the racialized online backlash to Lioz's essay, "White spaces have a strong assimilating effect, reinforced by white actors, creating an invitation for cultural membership of whiteness, rather than cultural pluralism."[27] I am no longer countercultural by virtue of markings betrothed to my Jewish identity, as my ancestors might have been. Instead, I flock to Phish to fulfill my countercultural fix.

While countercultural movements have existed throughout history, today we tend to commodify and romanticize our thinking around the 1960s, both in the United States and worldwide. The 1960s counterculture was—and remains—expansive, intersected, and vast: the Civil Rights Movement; the Chicano Movement; the American Indian Movement; antiwar and antiimperialist sentiments of the Asian-American Movement; the Puerto Rican–led Nuyorican Movement; the Free Speech Movement; antiwar; feminism; queer liberation; avant-garde art; alternative fashion; sexual liberation; psychedelics and other drugs.

And yet.

In pop culture, the common depiction of 1960s—and current—American counterculture is of a White hippie on acid listening to the Grateful Dead or flailing their arms at Woodstock. This image beckons, asking us yet again to center history and culture around Whiteness. I grew up both fetishizing and nostalgically wishing I had been part of the 1960s counterculture, while also having an image in my head of what it would look like if I were to adopt that behavior myself.

Dollinger contends that 1960s counterculture manifested in two distinct ways: one he calls the "Berkeley" Movement, illustrated by student protests at the University of California, Berkeley, and rooted in the Free Speech Movement and anti–Vietnam War ideals, and an underlying determination to stay engaged politically in order to actively change the system.[28] The other he calls the "Haight" Movement in reference to the Haight-Ashbury district in San Francisco, which became known for exemplifying the "Turn on, tune in, drop out" psychedelic, drug-induced, music-loving, long-haired cultural pushback on societal American norms.[29]

I've always felt like an intersection of both countercultural movements: a "Berkeley" activist (armed with an elite education and committed to the ideals of social justice and communal liberation) and a "Haight" hippie (White and socioeconomically secure enough to follow Phish with little consequential risk). By embodying both of these countercultural elements, I enable and perpetuate their histories of upholding and maintaining privilege. Dollinger confirms this, noting that "the ability to go to San Francisco and drop out requires you to be in a particular whiteness." Similarly, my ability to regularly go on Phish tour since I was seventeen has required a particular kind of privilege.

Phish tour, as a countercultural phenomenon, therefore reinforces the idea of Whiteness as normative and thereby participates in the larger systems of oppression and racism that are undoubtedly part of America's fabric and history. Even fans like myself who personify both the Berkeley and the Haight elements of the counterculture—who are committed to liberal, progressive, and antiracist values—participate in this. It took well into college and early adulthood for me to begin unpacking and understanding how so much of my performance of liberalism still centers around my Whiteness. I will probably spend the rest of my life continuing to interrogate this and holding myself accountable for the balance between my intentions and my impact, because no matter what I do to help dismantle oppression, I remain White.

Despite the hippie vibes of peace and love that draw so many to follow Phish, I've been on Phish tour and heard racial slurs. I've watched people bother a fan with a yarmulke after a show. The overt racism in the Phish scene is real, to say nothing of the blatant misogyny, ableism, classism, transphobia, and queerphobia that exists both on tour and in online fan forums and social media.[30] One prominent example took place during a 2018 Phish show at the Gorge Amphitheatre in George, Washington, when fans of color were physically assaulted in what appears to have been a series of racially motivated attacks.

As a response to incidents like this, as well as the long-term challenges the Phish community faces around other forms of structural inequality, some fans have created organizations specifically dedicated to building an antiracist and tolerant fan community. For example, Phans for Racial Equity formed as a result of the positive and proactive responses Lioz received for his article about the Phish scene's lack of racial inclusivity. By centering their work around the voices of fans of color, PHRE's mission is to help make the Phish scene more inclusive, while simultaneously mobilizing the community at large to help create systemic change around racial equity.[31] Another example of a fan group working toward social justice is Mike Side / Dyke Side, which is creating "a way for dykes and their allies to easily network within the Phish community—online, at shows, and beyond."[32] Similarly the fan group Brian-Robert is "a gathering place for LGBTQI Phans and their Phriends in the Phish community."[33] A group called GrooveSafe seeks to create "a movement within the musical community to bring awareness about unwanted touching and sexual assault at concerts."[34] There is also Access Me, a collective of Phish fans with disabilities along with allies who together focus on "dismantling ableism and promoting accessibility."[35] The Phish community is not safe for everyone. These groups help make it safer.

This activist fan community is the kind of countercultural experience I was seeking. Phish—both the band and the community—predominantly organizes around Whiteness and maleness despite the band's quest to revolutionize sound, and we fans took what we knew from the non-Phish world and created social currency rooted in Whiteness, maleness, able-bodiedness, Christian hegemony, and wealth. Perhaps for me, as a White Jew in the Phish community, there is space to help subvert that, to call my musical idols and our beloved community out—or rather in—on its structural inequalities.

So why am I so devoted to this band? Why do I follow four White dudes in the Whitest sea? I am devoted to the way I feel at a Phish show. Connected to my body. Connected to the people around me. Connected to the music. To people I love. I feel liberated. Free. But at who's expense? Am I really liberated and free when I'm in the midst of a mostly White audience in an already racist country and world inundated by systemic inequity and oppression?

We may be "wading in the velvet sea," as the Phish song states, but our experiences are not all the same.[36] Velvet—in all its complex histories and frequent associations with royalty and hierarchy—is, more than anything, so delicate, so silky, so thick because of its closely woven threads. So too, our liberation is bound up in one another. Not any of us are free until all of us are free.

The seas, the oceans—they cover the majority of Earth's surface. They are vast, expansive, and filled with mystery and so much and so many profound inhabitants and habitats and life. I'd like to think that—as Lioz calls us to do—we can simultaneously share in the groove as we celebrate Phish's music and one another, while also confronting systemic racism and dismantling White supremacy. The velvet sea of Phish fans is not a monolith. Never has been. Never will be. And that's worth a long and glorious jam.

NOTES

1. Lioz, "Phish Scene So White."

2. I have intentionally chosen to uppercase White and Whiteness throughout this chapter. There is much debate and discussion both in the journalism world, which is part of my own professional background as a writer, as well as in academia, around whether "White" should be uppercased in regard to race. I am leaning on the notion that, as my friend and colleague Adam Falkner would say, "capitalizing White is a move toward removing the comfort of racial invisibility. Folks capitalize it (myself included, now) to reject the notion that Whiteness is absent as a racial identity."

3. Lioz, "Phish Scene So White."

4. Pearl, "Ending the War on Drugs."

5. Ibid.

6. Lioz, Aly-Brady, and Budiansky, "White Phragility."

7. Brunsma, Kim, and Chapman, "Culture of White Space."

8. Kim, Chapman, and Brunsma, "Is This Your First Show?"

9. Lioz, "Phish Scene So White."

10. Phish, *A Live One* (Elektra, 1995).

11. Phish fans gather in the venue parking lot, or "the lot," before and after shows to socialize and to sell and purchase food, clothing, and other consumer goods.

12. Reference to Phish's "Wading in the Velvet Sea," track 10 on *Story of the Ghost* (Elektra, 1998).

13. For more, see Goldberger, "Skokie Case."

14. The Charlottesville, Virginia, march and rally took place on August 11 and 12, 2017. The Tree of Life mass shooting took place on October 27, 2018, in Pittsburgh, Pennsylvania. The Capitol insurrection took place on January 6, 2021, in Washington, DC. Armus, "'Trump' and 'MAGA.'"

15. Farivar, "FBI Reports Largest Spike."

16. Anti-Defamation League, "2017 Audit of Anti-Semitic Incidents."

17. Gutfraind, "Is Anti-Semitism?"

18. Kim, Chapman, and Brunsma. "Is This Your First Show?"

19. Ibid.

20. Brodkin, *How Jews Became White Folks*, 182.

21. Ibid., 70.

22. Goldstein, *Price of Whiteness*, 211.

23. Kelman et al., "Counting Inconsistencies."

24. Baldwin, "Negroes Are Anti-Semitic," 26.

25. See Brodkin, *How Jews Became White Folks*.

26. Marc Dollinger, in discussion with the author, November 5, 2020.

27. Brunsma, Kim, and Chapman, "Culture of White Space," 19.

28. Marc Dollinger, in discussion with the author, November 5, 2020.

29. "Turn on, tune in, drop out" was a popular counterculture-era phrase attributed to Timothy Leary beginning in the mid- to late 1960s.

30. Livingston and Livingston, "This Is Your Song Too."

31. Adam Lioz, in discussion with the author, January 8, 2021; Phans for Racial Equity, "About PHRE," https://phansforra cialequity.wordpress.com.

32. Mike Side / Dyke Side, "About This Group," Facebook, https://www.facebook .com/groups/148090072436676.

33. BrianRobert, "About This Group," Facebook, https://www.facebook.com /groups/75481393776.

34. GrooveSafe, "Our Story," https:// groovesafe.org.

35. Access Me, "Birds of a Feather Affinity Groups," Phans for Racial Equity, https:// www.facebook.com/groups/32740490459 63292.

36. Phish, "Wading in the Velvet Sea."

REFERENCES

Anti-Defamation League. "2017 Audit of Anti-Semitic Incidents." February 25, 2018. https://www.adl.org/resources /reports/2017-audit-of-anti-semitic -incidents.

Armus, Teo. "'Trump' and 'MAGA' Spray-Painted on Gravestones in Michigan Jewish Cemetery." *Washington Post*, November 3, 2020. https://www.wash ingtonpost.com/nation/2020/11/03 /michigan-jewish-cemetery-trump -maga.

Baldwin, James. "Negroes Are Anti-Semitic Because They're Anti-White." *New York Times Magazine*, April 9, 1967.

Brodkin, Karen. *How Jews Became White Folks and What That Says About Race in America*. New Brunswick, NJ: Rutgers University Press, 1998.

Brunsma, David L., Joong Won Kim, and Nathaniel G. Chapman. "The Culture of White Space, the Racialized Production of Meaning, and the Jamband Scene." *Sociological Inquiry* 90, no. 1 (2020): 7–29.

Farivar, Masood. "FBI Reports Largest Spike in Hate Crimes Since 9/11." *Voice of America*, November 13, 2018. https://

www.voanews.com/a/fbi-hate-crimes -report/4656468.html.

Goldberger, David. "The Skokie Case: How I Came to Represent the Free Speech Rights of Nazis." *ACLU*, March 2, 2020. https://www.aclu.org/issues/free -speech/rights-protesters/skokie-case -how-i-came-represent-free-speech -rights-nazis.

Goldstein, Eric L. *The Price of Whiteness: Jews, Race, and American Identity*. Princeton, NJ: Princeton University Press, 2007.

Gutfraind, Alexander. "Is Anti-Semitism Really at Unprecedented Levels in the U.S.? Not According to Data." *The Forward*, July 29, 2019. https://forward .com/opinion/428463/is-anti-semitism -really-at-unprecedented-levels-in-the -us-not-according-to.

Kelman, Ari Y., Aaron Hahn Tapper, Izabel Fonseca, and Aliya Saperstein. "Counting Inconsistencies: An Analysis of American Jewish Popula-tion Studies, with a Focus on Jews of Color." May 2019. https://jewsofcolor fieldbuilding.org/wp-content/uploads

/2019/05/Counting-Inconsistencies
-052119.pdf.

Kim, Joong Won, Nathaniel G. Chapman, and David L Brunsma. "Is This Your First Show? White Racism and Subcultural Capital in the Phish Community." Paper presented at the Phish Studies Conference, Oregon State University, Corvallis, May 17, 2019. https://media.oregonstate.edu /playlist/dedicated/0_xrymaobl/0 _fcsxdolu.

Lioz, Adam. "Phish Scene So White: Let's Talk." *HeadCount*, September 2017. https://www.headcount.org/music-and -activism/phish-scene-white-lets-talk.

Lioz, Adam, Kate Aly-Brady, Daniel Budiansky, and Rupa Mitra. "White Phragility: Race-Talk and Backlash in the Phish Scene." Paper presented at the Phish Studies Conference , Oregon State University, Corvallis, May 17, 2019. https://media.oregonstate.edu /playlist/dedicated/0_xrymaobl/0 _fcsxdolu.

Livingston, Laura J., and Paul Livingston. "This Is Your Song Too: Race and Exclusivity in the Phish Community." Paper presented at the Phish Studies Conference, Oregon State University, Corvallis, May 17, 2019. https://media .oregonstate.edu/playlist/dedicated/0 _xrymaobl/0_fcsxdolu.

Pearl, Betsy. "Ending the War on Drugs: By the Numbers." *Center for American Progress*, June 27, 2018. https://www .americanprogress.org/issues/criminal -justice/reports/2018/06/27/452819 /ending-war-drugs-numbers.

6.

"Feeling Weightless in the Sea"

PHISH AND OVERCOMING CANCER

Benjamin David

When I was diagnosed with cancer, I turned in various directions for help. I sought out esteemed medical professionals. I spoke with others who had battled life-threatening illness. I took refuge in prayer and community. I reflected at length. I read, diving into fiction as I attempted to escape the painful reality of my circumstances. I tried to rest. I spent time with loved ones when I was able. Still, somehow, I felt bereft. I felt empty. I was missing out on so much and missing so many.

During those trying months, maybe more than anything, music offered me hope. It took me to a place that no medicine, no book, no religious text fully could. It was the music of Phish specifically that lifted my spirits when I needed it most. Experiencing an aggressive form of chemotherapy had me bound to a drip for days at a time. I was confined within hospital walls. I felt not unlike the Torah's infamous *tzaraat*: isolated and pained.[1] The *tzaraat* was made to feel alone, different, and dangerous. I felt all of it, too.

With cancer, not only does the body suffer, but the mind must come to terms—or not—with the unforgiving predicament. Consciousness would come and go. Nurses appeared and vanished. Even if the days and nights rejected consistency, I tried to regularly listen to my music. I perked up when my earbuds brought back the Phish verses I had heard so often. I longed to be free, feeling "the feeling I forgot," as the song "Free" captured so perfectly for me.[2] I wondered what it would really mean to come back to a self I could scarcely remember, a music-loving community I adored, and the songs that had galvanized me since my youth.

From my hospital bed, if I tried, I could almost picture an eventual return to a concert venue to see the band in person. I could almost feel the joy of walking in and finding my seat. I could experience the shift from a world of stress and anxiety and obligation to a world of sound and color and artistry. I could almost see the sights, the lights and colors arrayed across an animated crowd. I could again take in the spectrum of personalities in attendance at every show. If I closed my eyes and held still, I could hear the sounds and feel the joy emanating deep within me once more.

Music is at the heart of the Jewish experience and central in the Torah, the age-old scroll of commandments and stories on which Jewish life is based. Moses led the Jewish community in song as the Israelites celebrated their freedom from Egyptian slavery by singing "The Song of the Sea."[3] Miriam famously takes a timbral in her hand as they revel in their sudden liberation.[4] Later biblical literature also presents music as fundamental to the human experience. King David, the poet and warrior, played his lyre amid distress and jubilation.[5] In these examples, music is an expression of arching emotion, of human outcries that could never be captured fully by spoken language.

Music is indeed aligned with transcendent emotion and also with exultation throughout biblical literature and Jewish foundational texts such as the Mishnah and Talmud.[6] Early Israelites recognized the limitations of speech as a means of communicating feeling and as a vehicle for declarations of belief in a divine and benevolent power. As such, Psalm 150 urges the community to praise God "with lute" and "resounding cymbals."[7] There are numerous such instances of miraculous moments in Jewish history that are set to song, from the soaring melodies associated with the Book of Esther, which Jews sing at the holiday of Purim as they mark salvation from a would-be tyrant, to the rabbis' recounting of deliverance of the Jewish community at the Festival of Lights, when the Temple was spared ultimate destruction, to the resounding melodies of Hallel, the series of Psalms incorporated into festival worship throughout the year. Music both helps convey the events detailed in these hallowed moments in Jewish time while reinforcing the importance of those moments themselves.

Jews turn to music not only as a means of jubilation, however. Music has long helped Jews and Judaism climb from the depths of despair. Jews worldwide have long mourned the two fallen Temples in Jerusalem with the soul-churning expressions of the biblical book of Lamentations. Yizkor, the service reserved for individual and communal remembrance, is replete with melancholy renditions of Psalms 23 and 121. The dour tones embedded in observance of Yom HaZikaron, a day marking Israel's fallen soldiers, and Yom HaShoah, a day memorializing the six million Jewish lives lost amid the Holocaust, grant a semblance of meaning to unspeakable tragedy.[8] At funerals the haunting hymn of "El Maleh Rahamim" gives full voice to the mourner's longing for the departed.[9]

Music does more than give voice to joy and pain; music mends the soul. How many have returned from Shabbat services feeling better, lighter, more whole, because the familiar melodies of prayer and song placed a palpable salve on an aching heart?

As Moses sang for his sister's health in Numbers chapter 12, Jews sing prayers of healing at the bedside of loved ones while praying for their recovery.[10] Whether adopting an age-old melody or the popular Debbie Friedman arrangement, the very notes of prayers for healing bring comfort to the hurting and their caretakers.[11] A community sings in the name of healing during daily worship, amid Torah services, and often quietly from the pews in the midst of personal prayer. As a rabbi, whether at the podium or in hospitals or nursing homes, I have watched with wonder as music offered hope to the aggrieved and calm to racing minds. I have also experienced the unequivocally transformative power of music personally, as well as the power of a shared musical experience to foster elation and togetherness vis-à-vis lyrics that inspire, melodies that embolden, and enchanting improvisation that can only lift one's spirits.

I first attended Phish shows in the summer of 1998. Some of the band's songs have stayed with me almost despite myself as I moved through the phases of my life, becoming a husband, a dad, and a rabbi. I love the raw sense of contentment found in solitude in "Brian and Robert."[12] The outlier status conveyed in "No Men in No Man's Land" always resonates as well, especially the notion that one can proudly "Stand on a rock / Suspended in air" and thus revel in being different and even apart from a kind of mainstream mode of being.[13] The idea of finding "a place to hide" somehow captured for me the idea that, amid a chaotic existence, all beings must stake out a place where they can fully be themselves.[14] Yet it was "Free" that spoke to me as I faced cancer.

Written by Trey Anastasio and Tom Marshall, "Free" details the trying relationship of a couple and their anticipation of freedom from each other. A broader longing for freedom, itself echoed in "Hatikvah," the national anthem of the State of Israel, is profoundly Jewish, a longing expressed by ancient Israelites and throughout history, from those Jews who lived in Europe in the 1940s to those in the Soviet Union of the 1980s to those across the globe whose lives have been rattled by antisemitism in recent years.[15] The lyrics from "Free," which state "in a minute I'll be free," harness that relentless hopefulness Jews have clutched at throughout multiple chapters of hardship.[16] For someone enduring cancer or another life-threatening illness, such hopefulness is itself a form of medicine. It reminds us that there will be another "minute" and perhaps another day, another year, still.

Jews and Judaism join in shared fascination with freedom achieved through divine providence, incorporating gratitude for that freedom into nearly every ritualized experience. For the Jewish people, the very idea of freedom is part of the daily vernacular. Liberation from Egyptian bondage is the foundational story told and retold every Passover. More than that, it is a motif Jews come back to time and again in prayer and in conversation, a perpetual reminder that "you were slaves in the Land of Egypt."[17]

As a cancer patient, I struggled with questions around freedom and liberation. I was certainly not "bouncing gently 'round the room," as "Free" notes.[18] Instead I was tethered to my pole, imprisoned in a cramped space, and under the unmoving eye of a host of doctors at the Hospital of the University of Pennsylvania. Even while unable to leave, in my mind I could forever "see the path ahead of me" to which the narrator of the song refers.[19] It was this vision of freedom and a would-be triumphant return to my life that so often kept me going as the hours passed slowly on the oncology wing.

Prior to my diagnosis, I'd gone to Phish festivals. I had seen the band at Madison Square Garden in New York City dozens of times, watched them play the Mann Music Center in Philadelphia each summer, and had caught the band in Hershey, Pennsylvania, and Hampton, Virginia. I was there when Jay-Z joined them in Brooklyn and when B. B. King showed up at the Meadowlands.[20] I had been so present and now I was not. More than that, my lengthy fandom had been rewarded in that I had been an eyewitness to these numerous defining moments for Phish. Such shows were legendary and would be talked about for years. I was there, living it with my own eyes and ears. I had been taking it in firsthand and now, suddenly, I was entirely distant from such spaces and opportunities. I longed for the community and the culture and aspired to be again "bouncing gently 'round the room" with my friends, living those aspirational ideals of "Free."[21]

Phish became an antidote for me, pulling me, ever slowly, despite the many medications and accompanying side effects, from sickness back to health. It was not only the hallowed melodies but the thought of rejoining the community that brought me hope. I could picture myself returning to see Phish once more. I could imagine myself "floating," as the song suggests, rather than stuck in a hospital room.[22] As Steve Magness and Brad Stulberg note, trees do not reach deep into the ground for sustenance but often outward, attaching their roots to those of trees around them, thereby ensuring that they help one another remain upright and sturdy amid life's storms.[23] It is in this togetherness, whether in a synagogue sanctuary or amid thousands of upbeat fans, that both Jews and fans of Phish feel whole and wholly fulfilled. Community reminds us in both spaces that we are alone neither in our times of distress nor in our moments of triumph.

As I neared the end of my treatment, the Baker's Dozen was announced, a thirteen-night series of donut-themed Phish concerts at Madison Square Garden.[24] This would no doubt become another in the growing list of iconic moments created by the band. I attended the seventh show, cinnamon night, with my brother-in-law. The band treated us to an exquisite concert, fittingly highlighted by an encore performance of Neil Young's "Cinnamon Girl."[25] I went to night 8 with my brother. The theme that night was "Jimmies." The inevitable playing of "Runaway Jim" in the first set was followed by an iconic rendering of Jimi Hendrix's "The Wind Cries Mary" at show's end, both a tribute to the jimmies promised in the show's billing.[26]

On both of these memorable nights, as I entered the venue, I was released from my isolation and enveloped at last in the smells and sights of a sea of gathered beings united in musical experience. Just being there furthered my healing. While the band didn't play "Free," each tune affirmed for me that I was finally present again. With a full heart and endless appreciation, I felt the music fully and the joy of the crowd in my heart. The music emanating from the stage reached a place deep within me. With scars still fresh and hair that hadn't fully returned, I had been granted entrance back into the community not by a Levitical priest but by a band that had allowed for a symbolic validation of my well-being. It was the music, and the community, like a religious experience, that affirmed that I was indeed alive, still.

Gazing around the venue, I felt part of something, no longer the biblical *tzaraat*, alone and cast out. The healing power of Phish had helped me to overcome my trial, just as music has done for Jews for millennia. Moreover, the promise of live music provided me with hope. Coming back to Phish shows, getting "back on the train," thus became for me and so many others a dream realized.[27]

NOTES

1. Chapter 13 of Leviticus introduces the concept of the skin disease, *tzaraat*. A biblical priest would examine the affected area to determine whether an afflicted individual was impure. If designated as impure, an individual was placed in isolation for a period of seven days (Lev. 13:2–5, 13:45–46).

2. Phish, "Free," track 1 on *Billy Breathes* (Elektra, 1996).

3. Exod. 15.

4. Exod. 15:20.

5. As in 2 Sam. 6:1–23.

6. These rabbinic works of the second through sixth centuries provide extensive commentary on the Torah, oft-cited fables, and guidance on the inner workings of early Jewish life.

7. Ps. 150:4–5.

8. Yom HaZikaron, or Israeli Remembrance Day, is a day of remembrance for soldiers who fell in defense of the State of Israel. Yom HaShoah, which translates as the Day of Tragedy, is a day of mourning and prayer. In Israel, a siren sounds on the morning of Yom HaShoah, bringing the entire nation to a halt for one minute.

9. A traditional Hebrew-language funeral benediction dating back to 1096 through 1271 in eastern Europe and first recited for those who perished at the hands of the Crusaders.

10. Num. 12:13.

11. Debbie Friedman, born 1951, remains a beloved Jewish singer and songwriter, even after her passing in 2011. Her setting of "Mi Shebeirach" is sung regularly at Reform and Conservative synagogues on Shabbat.

12. Phish, "Brian and Robert," track 9 on *The Story of the Ghost* (Elektra, 1998).

13. Phish, "No Men in No Man's Land," track 9 on *Big Boat* (JEMP, 2016).

14. Ibid.

15. "Hatikvah" ("The Hope") was written by Naftali Herz Ingber in 1878 in then-Austrian Poland. Composer Shmuel Cohen provided the musical arrangement in 1887. It was adopted as the national anthem when statehood was officially declared in May 1948.

16. Phish, "Free."

17. Deut. 15:15.

18. Phish, "Free."

19. Ibid.

20. On June 18, 2004, at KeySpan Park, Brooklyn, New York, and on February 24, 2003, at Continental Airlines Arena, East Rutherford, New Jersey.

21. Phish, "Free."

22. Ibid.

23. Stulberg and Magness, *Passion Paradox*.

24. The Baker's Dozen shows took place from July 21 through August 6, 2017.

25. Neil Young with Crazy Horse, "Cinnamon Girl," track 1 on *Everybody Knows This Is Nowhere* (Reprise, 1969).

26. Phish, "Runaway Jim," track 4 on *Live Phish 06* (Elektra, 2001); Jimi Hendrix, "The Wind Cries Mary," track 7 on *Are You Experienced* (Track, 1967).

27. Phish, "Back on the Train," track 4 on *Farmhouse* (Elektra, 2000).

REFERENCES

Ginsberg, H. L., Harry Orlinsky, and E. A. Speiser, eds. *Hebrew-English Tanakh.* New York: Jewish Publication Society, 1985.

Plaut, Gunther, ed. *The Torah: A Modern Commentary, Revised Edition.* New York: CCAR Press, 2005.

Stulberg, Brad, and Steve Magness. *The Passion Paradox: A Guide to Going All In, Finding Success, and Discovering the Benefits of an Unbalanced Life.* New York: Rodale Books, 2019.

SET 2

GOD ON TOUR

Judaism and the Live Phish Experience

7.

Beyond "Avenu Malkenu"

FAN RESPONSES TO SACRED MUSIC IN PHISH'S MUSICAL CANON

Ariella Werden-Greenfield

I attended my first Phish show on December 30, 1995. The boisterous crowd entering New York's Madison Square Garden thrilled me—a naive and yet self-assured thirteen-year-old from the suburbs. Once the lights dimmed and the band began to play, I knew that I had found something special. And that was before Phish played "Avenu Malkenu." Upon hearing the prayer, I felt a poignant sense of belonging that was both familiar and yet radically new. I was filled with emotion and excitement as I listened to a melodious supplication that I had chanted many times before fill an unexpected venue. In the concert hall turned sanctuary, the prayer elicited feelings of elation and a sense of connection. I felt united with a sea of music lovers, all moving rhythmically to a holy petition of the Jewish people. And I felt profoundly linked to my Jewish heritage. Some Phish fans chase "Avenu Malkenu" for years. I heard the band's rendition at my first show.

"Avenu Malkenu," or "Our Father, Our King," is a traditional Jewish prayer most associated with Rosh Hashanah, the Jewish new year, and Yom Kippur, a day of reckoning that caps a period of reflection beginning with Rosh Hashanah.[1] Hearing

Phish play the petition, which expresses submission to God and pleads for divine forgiveness, carries deep meaning for many Jewish fans. For a moment, a Phish show becomes a site of sacred prayer and tradition. A concert venue transforms into a space wherein one can celebrate Jewish identity in a way that is explicitly Jewish and unique to the cosmos of Phish.

My recollection of hearing "Avenu Malkenu" is not exceptional; numerous Jewish fans detail impactful encounters of hearing Phish play the sacred tune. In these particular live Phish moments, Jewish people feel affirmed as Jews in the Phish community. Experiences of elation and connection during a Phish show are not isolated to Jews, nor are they only conjured by hearing the prayer. However, that Jewish fans interpret this elation and connection—sometimes transcendental transformation—in a profoundly Jewish way en masse is distinct. Jewish cultural identity and religiosity are kindled and celebrated during Phish's renditions of "Jewish" songs, as fans bestow a layer of Jewish meaning on the live Phish experience.

Is the affinity of Jewish Phish lovers for "Avenu Malkenu" unique? My investigation of Phish-focused online chat forums and Facebook groups proves that the widespread celebration of and performance of Jewish identity during Phish concerts, and during "Avenu Malkenu" specifically, is indeed remarkable and that the band's integration of Jewish songs into their catalog encourages Jewish fandom. For American Jews searching, whether consciously or unconsciously, for mediums through which to connect Jewishly, Phish shows serve as stages for the performance of Jewish identity in part because Phish's choice to play Jewish songs creates that space. Though Phish also plays songs with Christian origins, Christian fans respond to Phish's renditions of those tracks with concerns related to faith and comportment. Jewish and Christian fans, as assumedly the two most well-represented religious traditions among the Phish fan population, relate to religiously significant tracks in differing ways, and those responses offer a unique insight into fan religiosity and the role of religion in the live Phish experience.[2]

Jewish songwriters are behind some of the most cherished music of the last century, including Christmas favorites.[3] Yet, through most of the twentieth century, traditional Jewish music made few inroads into the American pop culture arena.[4] Though popular artists of the past few decades are increasingly engaging the "Jewish" catalog, including Anderson .Paak, who samples the Israeli national anthem "Hatikvah" in his 2016 hit "Come Down," Jewishness is still not a frequent element of American popular music.[5] Conversely, it is not uncommon to hear a rock and roll band cover a gospel song or spiritual. Christian messages and Christian songs are constant features of American pop music. In a cultural landscape structured around a Christian, white majority as cultural arbiter, these religious tunes have become American favorites, while the music of minority religious and ethnic groups has historically been relegated to the fringes of the music industry.

In the mid-1990s, Jewishness began presenting more prevalently in popular music and in music-centered subcultures.[6] In famed punk band NOFX's 1994 "The Brews," the band boasts of sporting "anti-swastika tattoos" and identifies as Orthodox, going so far as to deem themselves Hasidic.[7] Though edgy, their humorous and celebratory approach to Jewish identity echoes that of Adam Sandler's "The Chanukah Song," which debuted on *Saturday Night Live*'s "Weekend Update" sketch on December 3, 1994. The parody became an instant hit. In it, Sandler admits that he wrote the song for melancholy Jewish children who don't hear many Chanukah songs during the holiday season.[8] He goes on to list Jewish celebrities as he highlights Jewish success and stardom. Rabbi Irwin Kula shares, "What's amazing about that song—what makes it important—is that Jews are being outed, and it's no big deal. It's funny and it's normal. This is a remarkable moment in Jewish history and American history. There is no way that song could have been played 40 years ago."[9]

Popular rapper and comedian Lil Dicky depends on the same fusion of humor and Jewishness. In 2013's "Jewish Flow," he repeats in the chorus "Dicky spit that Jewish flow, Lil Dicky spit that Jewish flow / Sicker than the holocaust, that motherfuckin' Jewish flow / That Third Reich raw, concentration camp cold / Now we rollin' in that motherfuckin' dough, that's that Jewish flow."[10] In the video for the track, he triumphs in a rap battle against Adolf Hitler. In Dicky's "Jewish Flow," NOFX's "The Brews," and Sandler's "Chanukah Song," Jews survive and thrive, whether it be by achieving celebrity status or by "rollin'" in "dough."[11] By crafting and then playing distinctly Jewish songs, these popular artists claim space for themselves as American musicians and as Jews, thereby carving out room for Jewishness in pop culture. Their humorous approach helps the general public adjust to their proud outings of minority identity.

Phish's objective in playing their funk-heavy version of "Avenu Malkenu" may not be to create space for American Jewishness in the larger cultural landscape. Nonetheless, their choice to include Jewish songs in their catalog is impactful for American Jews, even as Phish's catalog includes other sacred music.[12] Jack Zaientz reflects on Phish's addition of Jewish and Hebrew songs to their repertoire: "When I was growing up in the 80s, I was constantly awash with pop music full of Christian imagery and themes. I dealt with it, but always wondered why a popular music so full of Jewish musicians never seemed to slip in some Jewish material. It seems like it's finally happening. About time."[13] Enthusiasts find in the band's engagement with Jewish culture via music a way to confirm their identity, as Jews and as participants in American pop culture.

Jewishness is audible and visible at Phish concerts, both on and off the stage. One finds amusing T-shirts sold in parking lots outside of venues printed with adages including "Whatever you do, take care of your Jews" (a nod to the "Cavern" lyric "Whatever you do, take care of your shoes") and "Fish side, knish side" (a reference to the area in arenas nearest Jon Fishman's drum kit where Jewish fans—who assumedly enjoy knishes—congregate during shows).[14] Fans wear kippahs, or skull caps, printed with a blue and red donut design made famous by Fishman's patterned muumuu worn at every show (one such product is brilliantly dubbed the "OhKeePah" in a nod to the band's "The Oh Kee Pa Ceremony").[15] And of course, "Suzy Greenberg" is Jewish.[16]

In 1998, Rabbi Shmuel Skaist started Gefilte Phish, an outreach organization aimed toward engaging unaffiliated Jews. He began setting up a Shabbat Tent for worship and community at Phish festivals, including Camp Oswego, Coventry, and Festival 8 (see fig. 8.1).[17] Jewish outreach happens at one-night affairs as well. Leib Meadvin encourages Jewish concertgoers to lay tefillin in venue parking lots before showtime, thus allowing them to fulfil an essential mitzvah, or "precept" (see fig. 12.1).[18] And Rachel Loonin Steinerman distributes packages of candles and matches before and during Phish shows, complete with a traditional Jewish blessing for candle lighting on the Sabbath so that recipients can complete the mitzvah of lighting Shabbat candles. She distributes these "Love and Light on Friday Night" packages to inspire Jewish women to celebrate their heritage.

During a set break, you might find a gathering of observant fans who meet to pray in a minyan, chant, and dance in celebration of faith and community (see fig. 11.1).[19] They likely used the "PHIShalom" Facebook page to find details about the get-together. Marc Silberstein recalls, "These set breaks were some of my favorite moments of the run, especially with what had just happened in Jersey City. Such a beautiful moment of pride."[20] Here, Silberstein references the band's four-night residency at Madison Square Garden from December 28 through December 31, 2019, and how his Jewish experiences during that run helped him process the tragic and deadly December 10 antisemitic attack at a kosher market in Jersey City, New Jersey.

Jewish things are happening at Phish shows. These assertions of identity are expressions of love for Phish, as Jewishness exists for many as an integral part of the Phish experience. In an article for the *Times of Israel*, Tracy Frydberg writes, "The band couldn't be more Jewish if they called themselves 'gefiltephish.'"[21] While it is problematic to call Phish a Jewish band, for a spectrum of Jewish fans, from affiliated and observant to secular, Phish serves as a site of religious and/or cultural connection. The inclusion of Jewish songs facilitates this.

Many Phish fans who identify as Jewish connect to their cultural identity, ancestry, and/ or religious upbringing during Phish shows. Furthermore, they are talking about it online, frequently posting about Jewishness and Phish in chat forums and on social media. After concerts conclude, enthusiasts recount Jewish experiences at concerts, staying engaged as Jews and as Phish lovers through forums including Facebook groups like "Gefilte Phish" and chat threads, one notable example of which is titled "Phish has even helped Jews feel and become more Jewish."[22] Jewish Phish fans associate with, interrogate, and celebrate the intersections between Phish and Jewish identity.[23] A review of active online forums offers a glimpse of how identities are expressed and confirmed both during and after the live concert experience.

FIG. 7.1 Saying Kaddish after the show, Gorge Amphitheatre, George, Washington, August 28, 2021. Photo: Bob Fishel.

According to bassist Mike Gordon, he introduced "Avenu Malkenu" and "Yerushalayim Shel Zahav" to the band to "revisit something Jewish."[24] The introduction of this content was not lost on fans. "Yerushalayim Shel Zahav," or "Jerusalem of Gold," was written in 1967 by Naomi Shemer. Despite its minimal religious messaging, Phish enthusiasts perceive this unofficial Israeli anthem, which praises the holy city of Jerusalem, as traditionally Jewish because its lyrics are in Hebrew, but also because many learned the song in Jewish spaces, including synagogues and summer camps. Phish includes the song as a secret concluding track on their 1994 album, *Hoist*; the lyric "Halo l'chol shiraich ani kinor," or "In all your songs I am a violin," is printed in Hebrew inside the CD's liner notes.[25] Phish played "Yerushalayim Shel Zahav" twelve times between July 16, 1993, and December 31, 1994. Before its debut at Philadelphia's Mann Center for the Performing Arts, "the band worked hard to get it right to impress Gordon's grandmother and other Jewish relatives who were in the audience."[26] Gordon confirmed that their rendition was "good enough to move people."[27]

Jewish fans posting in chat forums routinely comment on the band's choice to play "Yerushalayim Shel Zahav." They also address the klezmer teased into the popular tune "Scent of a Mule."[28] However, posts and comments related to the band's rendition of "Avenu Malkenu" significantly outweigh those instances. Phish debuted

"Avenu Malkenu" at Nectar's in Burlington, Vermont, on May 11, 1987; it is most often woven into the middle of "The Man Who Stepped into Yesterday."[29] Writing in a chat thread on Phish.net, enthusiast The_Steiner writes, "I remember clearly the first time i got IT. . . . when TMWSIY began, i started getting goosebumps, because that of course meant Avenu Malkenu, a tune that i have known since before i knew words. as the first chords came in i was shell-shocked that this huge band, playing for so many people, was playing a song from my culture, my religion, my childhood. tears, man."[30]

Guitarist Trey Anastasio played an acoustic version of the prayer during his solo performance at Sixth & I in Washington, DC, on February 14, 2018 (plate 2). And while most Jews posting online excitedly comment on his choice to cover it, others share deep concern that he mispronounced several words, especially since the venue, now a community space used for cultural programming and synagogue services, was once a synagogue. Nonetheless, the members of Phish consistently articulate their respect for the prayer, which, according to Anastasio, was written by "Pete Rose and God."[31] Mike Gordon reflects, "'Avinu Malcanu' has that sort of deep, lurking, familiar melody and I think [Jewish fans] feel something. It's part of my heritage and I feel a real warmth because of their reaction."[32] Their reaction is significant, and Gordon rightly recognizes that Phish's renditions mean something to many Jewish fans. Gordon continues: "To some, it seems blasphemous to take a holy prayer and play it in concert. I don't sing it as a joke. It's an acknowledgment of my heritage. . . . When we play it, I can always look up and see the Jews in the audience smiling."[33]

And the Jews are smiling. What defines those Jews in the audience as Jewish varies. For some, belief in God is paramount. Yet American Jewishness is not necessarily predicated on religious identity. For many contemporary American Jews, their Jewishness is rooted in a sense of cultural belonging. The 2013 Pew Research Center Survey report claims that 62 percent of American Jews see ancestry and/or culture as their main connection to Jewishness.[34] Only 15 percent reported religion to be the primary element of their Jewishness; 22 percent of American Jews felt no attachment to religion, with 32 percent of Jews born after 1980 falling into that category. In sum, the Pew survey shows a distancing from synagogues and other Jewish institutions that prioritize a Jewishness predicated on religious affiliation and temple membership. As younger generations seek out authentic iterations of Jewishness, they look to personally fulfilling cultural spaces in which to encounter Jewishness and to express it.

Rupert Till suggests that dedicated fan cultures, which he calls "popular music based new religious movements," answer the needs of younger generations who are searching for something left unfulfilled by organized religion.[35] Till argues that these new religious movements "have replaced many of the functions traditionally served in traditional cultures by religions, as those traditional religious cultures become increasingly irrelevant, refusing to discard outdated traditions."[36] While some Christian and Jewish Phish enthusiasts recount leaving religious backgrounds as they became involved in Phish culture, the majority of Jewish fans posting online report that their sense of themselves as Jewish is enhanced by their engagement with the band and the surrounding scene.[37]

Popular music culture, then, can function as a site of identity making that depends on and simultaneously reinvigorates those "traditional religious cultures" that Till deems irrelevant. Phish tour answers unaffiliated Jews' want for such a revitalized meeting ground, but it also offers much to religious Jews who might be active in synagogue communities—or even lead them. Rabbi Yehoshua "Shu" Eliovson, founder of PHIShalom and JamShalom, for example, looks to band members as spiritual teachers. Rabbi Shu shares, "Trey is my rebbe. I love all of the guys. Every one of them has a meaningful place in my heart and I've gotten great Torah from them over the years. Trey is my rebbe though. As far back as I can remember, there are times when Trey is in a jam and I truly know the next bar before he gets there because I am learning a Torah with him that is so deeply connected to my own soul that it is like being in love."[38]

For the spectrum of Jews represented at shows, Phish concerts are venues in which to connect with an inclusive community, one that integrates self-identified Jews of all kinds into a music-loving family. No formal institution determines membership. During Phish concerts, individuals authentically convey their religious and cultural Jewish identity without required institutional mediation. In the "Gefilte Phish" Facebook group Rebecca M. Ross remarks, "Whenever Phish plays Avenu Malkenu I feel absolved of any residual guilt from no longer attending shul on Rosh Hashanah and Yom Kippur."[39] Ross's sense of freedom from perceived communal expectations is echoed in the reflections of other Jewish fans. Other listeners share recollections of hearing the song and being moved to participate in (or joke about enacting) popular practices associated with American Jewish life and institutional involvement, including philanthropic giving and support of Israel.[40] Mandy Berman quips, "I send Phish a check for $18 every time they play it."[41] Russell S. Glowatz responds to Mandy, "Whenever they play it I have a tree planted in Israel."[42] As people encounter a profound audible expression of Jewishness at Phish shows, they negotiate their own belonging, to the Phish community and to a Jewish peoplehood. Hearing Phish play "Avenu Malkenu" amplifies and encourages distinctly Jewish behavior among fans. What that Jewish behavior looks like varies from humor-filled posts in Facebook groups that recall Jewish Phish experiences, to participation in prayer services during set breaks, to a mere acknowledgment of the potently Jewish energy enveloping the crowd. Perhaps that acknowledgment leads to a smile.

In a Phantasy Tour chat thread, The_Steiner recounts that sense of togetherness that hearing the prayer cultivates among concertgoers: "Some guy was dancing next to me, singing along out loud, and i asked him if he was jewish too. he gave me a funny look and said 'yeah, but how did you know?' i said, 'because you know all the words to Avenu Malkenu!!' and he laughed. . . . that was when i knew IT was real, and that i'd be listening to this band for the rest of my life."[43] "Avenu Malkenu" can also offer concertgoers an opportunity to commune with God. PT_Barnum comments, "i keep a yamuka on me just for when they play it . . . then im jewish."[44] Traditionally, Jewish men wear a yarmulke or kippah on their head as a way of showing respect to God. By placing one on his head during Phish's rendition of "Avenu Malkenu," PT_Barnum signals that God has entered the arena.

Les Skolnik reminisces on Facebook about Phish playing "Avenu Malkenu" at the Magnaball festival: "I turned to my friends and said, well, summer's over. Phish just rang in the High Holy Days!"[45] As Phish played the prayer, they ushered in the Jewish new year for Skolnik, and the festival grounds became a temple filled with the sounds of Rosh Hashanah. For him and so many others including Kevin Samuel Haber, "Phish is Synagogue."[46] Hearing Phish play "Avenu Malkenu" can serve as a substitute for attendance in conventional Jewish sanctuaries, or it can add a bit of a twist to hearing the prayer in synagogue. In either case, as user Gwexler shares on Phantasy Tour, "Phish makes temple fun!"[47]

Liz Zimmerman asks, "Anyone else see phans getting thrown in the chair bar mitzvah style during the Alpine 'Avenu'?"[48] She witnessed an extremely physical, bodily activity associated with Jewish *simchas*, or moments of joy, while listening to Phish play the prayer. At Phish concerts, individuals can articulate their relationship to Judaism and Jewish culture through movement, jest, and meditation as they listen to sacred tunes mediated by a revered band. Dance, especially Jewishly inspired dance, becomes a corporeal declaration of religiosity and a mode for reaching higher consciousness.

Mike Gordon shares, "I've always compared my movements on stage to *davening* [praying]. . . . To me, music has always served as that type of religious release."[49] The experience of hearing, dancing to, and playing powerful religious music no doubt amplifies the release that Gordon speaks of. Playing—or dancing—to these Jewish "bust outs" leaves Jewish listeners with a sense of themselves as profoundly connected, in a Jewish way, to the music, the band, coreligionists, and sometimes God.

But Phish also plays Christian classics. The band first played "Swing Low, Sweet Chariot" on October 15, 1986.[50] Since they debuted it, Phish has played the African

American spiritual thirteen times; the band last played it on November 16, 1994. "Amazing Grace," a Christian hymn written by Reverend John Newton in 1772, has appeared on set lists 111 times since its debut in 1993, most recently on October 3, 1998.[51] These traditional songs are beloved both in and beyond Christian worship communities. And yet, Christian Phish lovers do not detail impactful episodes of listening to Phish play them live, in part because it is not unusual for rock and roll artists to cover Christian songs and because Christianity is a presumed backdrop for the American cultural arena. Ostensibly, the frequency with which Christians encounter Christian messaging in pop culture defuses the impact of hearing Phish play songs like "Amazing Grace."

Rock and roll music owes much to the southern gospel tradition. As Randall J. Stephens notes, "In the American South, a region that consistently ranked as the most conventionally religious section of the country, musical influences crossed back and forth over the thresholds of church doors," and the "culture of southern Pentecostalism helped give birth to the new genre of rock 'n' roll."[52] The creative liberties taken by early rock and roll artists did not please most churchgoers, as their engagement with church music and their music more generally was considered abhorrent, earning the genre the tantalizing title "the Devil's music." The ensuing debate over whether Christians can listen to rock and roll shapes much Christian commentary on Phish, at least what few conversations are taking place online. In accounts like that of Phish.net user Gausssplit, Christian Phish enthusiasts share concerns about the band's approach to Christian songs or recount tests of faith during their rehearsal. Gausssplit writes, "Here's one of my first experiences, phish show couple hits of L and little fungus, crazy show and then break into AMAZING GRACE and because of my upbringing I thought God was punishing me for over indulging."[53]

An interrogation of Christian Phish fans, who are presumably the most well-represented religious group on Phish tour, proves that they do not generally celebrate the band's iterations of Christian classics, nor do they frequently integrate Phish into their articulation of Christian identity. Conversely, Jews celebrate Phish's choice to include Jewish songs in their repertoire, writing frequently about being deeply moved by hearing those songs played live. Because Christians are a cultural and religious majority, both in America and at Phish concerts, Christian identity becomes assumed and is therefore invisibilized. The historical infusion of Christianity into American pop culture means that Christian fans may not need to search to find communities and cultural institutions to connect with in Christian ways. Christian rock serves this purpose for many seeking a musical vehicle for religious expression and an acceptable and righteous means of enjoying popular music.[54] For some, listening to secular rock and roll bands that cover Christian classic raises too many concerns related to faith.

Phish's rendition of "Daniel Saw the Stone," "Don't You Want to Go?," and "Paul and Silas" occasionally cause such distress.[55] The band played "Daniel Saw the Stone" for the twenty-third time on August 1, 2017. Though faithful to the original tune when playing this spiritual, Phish changes the lyrics of the chorus from "Jesus was the stone" and "I found the stone" to repeat "Daniel saw the stone."[56] This omission bothers Christian Forums user PS139, who writes, "I also don't like how they leave out the lines about Jesus in 'Daniel Saw the Stone.' Also they sometimes add a word in there that I do not appreciate (you might know what I mean) and I skip thru that part on my CD."[57]

PS139 also communicates concern about lyricist Tom Marshall, questioning whether Marshall is promoting an anti-Christian objective: "The songs (Bug) and Lifeboy definitely do convey this feeling, and for that reason I refuse to listen to them. I dont need that."[58] It is easy to understand why the lyrics to "Bug"—"There've been times when I wonder / And times when I don't / Concepts I'll ponder / And concepts I won't ever see / God isn't one of these / Former or latter / Which did you think I meant? / It doesn't matter to me"—could prove problematic to the faithful.[59] Similarly, the lyrics to "Lifeboy"—"But God never listens to what I say / God never listens to what I say / So very, so very hard / And you don't get a refund / If you overpray"— pose deep questions about the band's perspective on God and faith.[60] Though these songs might trouble religious Phish followers of other faiths, these lyrical questions are not a focus of public Jewish fan discourse.[61]

While many Christian enthusiasts involved in online dialogue about Phish and religion describe challenges associated with their fandom, others consider how they can integrate Phish into their worship committees. u/kernsomatic asks on a Phish-focused Reddit page for suggested Phish songs to add to his church band roster.[62] And Christian fans find religious meaning at Phish shows. Blogger Jen shares her "worshipping God at the Phish show moment": "During the Phish show, as the band was playing and the people around me were swaying to the sounds of the music, I looked up at the stage framed by the city we now call home and at the stars twinkling in the sky—and strongly felt the presence of God. As my body moved and my gaze fixed upward, I began to pray."[63] Drew shares a similar experience, recounting: "Christian guy and the alive one hood made me see heaven itself."[64]

Such accounts are slim, however. Most people posting in Phish-related chats who were raised as Christians mention their upbringing before describing their distancing from the church, highlighting Phish's role in their departure story. For example, FoolontheHill shares, "I went from being an evangelical Christian in high school listening to Christian rock to listening to Phish. The feelings of elation and joy I got from the praising the holy ghost I got from Phish's ethereal Ghost. . . . I was taught that (Lucifer) used his skills in rock-n-roll to deceive listeners into becoming hedonistic non-believers. Obviously, this made me very curious about rock music and when I left home I searched for what drugs and rock-n-roll were all about."[65] While such accounts are prevalent, it is not easy to find examples of Christian religiosity at Phish concerts, nor is it easy to connect with other Christian enthusiasts. Desertrat complains, "It looks like im the only Christian Phish Phan."[66] Christian fans do not often share stories of Christian belonging or faith enhanced or evoked by the live Phish experience. Further, Desertrat's comment implies that Christian listeners do not frequently seek each other out in Phish-centric spaces.

Self-identified Christian fans are writing little about Christian experiences of Phish, seemingly because they are not perceiving their relationship to Phish as elemental to their Christian identity. Most self-professed Christian enthusiasts instead write about the challenges of being enthusiastic about Phish. What online dialogue exists pits Phish and Christianity against each other. Many doubt that an individual can enjoy seeing Phish live while avoiding temptation and depravity assumed as inherent to the scene.

Some active posters describe the band as an enticement—one that tempts the unrighteous—and one that they have, in a sense, overcome. Original Phish guitarist Jeff Holdsworth shared these concerns. In a 1996 interview, Phish keyboardist Page McConnell recounts, "I joined the band in 85 . . . and they started with two guitar players. What happened to the second guitar player? He found God! He became a born again christian and he thinks that we play the devil's music."[67] Numerous chat contributors echo Holdsworth's unease, sharing their own stories of departure from the band and tour life. Bee7le shares how he found the church and left Phish tour behind: "My wife and I began to get our life straight as the light of Christ began to shine. . . . We began to realize the lifestyle these followers were living was not what we wanted. Phish was no longer for us. . . . My ears are now set to follow a much greater Sound."[68] PS139 responds to Bee7le, "A bunch of my friends are crazy about Jesus *and* crazy about Phish. The two are not mutually exclusive."[69] Yet, though that may be the case, many Christian fans struggle to find a way to balance their faith and their love for the band.

Some who once loved the band return to Phish concerts with hopes to missionize. Once an active enthusiast, Theoneway recounts enduring a Phish show after finding Christ in order to save "lost" fans: "I had planned an aggressive witnessing program that night, but I was so overwhelmed by it all. . . . It was sobering to be forcefully reminded of how out of it and lost these people are and how much

I wanted to tell all of them about Jesus. I did a lot of silent pleading to God for Him to send more laborers to the harvest. . . . They are truly like sheep without a shepherd."[70] While Theoneway worries about the spiritual life of others at Phish shows, the majority of people sharing online convey concern about their own temptation and salvation; drug use is generally the crux of that worry.

Drug consumption is a notorious aspect of Phish culture, as it frequently is in cultures structured around rock and roll bands.[71] The prevalence of drug and alcohol use at Phish concerts is troublesome for Christian fans struggling to remain righteous. Not all fans partake, and yet the question of consumption frequently appears in online dialogue. Rasheed shares his concerns: "I personally love them. Have seen them over 50 times, but always feel weird b/c most of their scene at shows has every drug you can imagine. . . . Granted, I have been weakened once or twice and taken some LSD and I must say it was a truly amazing experience, but I feel guilty about it in hindsight. They are the most talented band in the world currently, without question, and I cannot . . . there is so much temptation at those shows. Anyone else love the band Phish but have problems with the scene/lifestyle and it conflicting?"[72] KM Richards responds to Rasheed, "Find some good Christian bands to listen to and get involved with helping one of them make it in the biz. . . . Hangin out with dope fiends is just going to drag you down."[73] Others direct Rasheed to the Phellowship, a group of Phish devotees who choose to remain drug and alcohol free.

Most Christian fans posting online question whether one can love the band while remaining a good Christian. The live Phish experience seems to hinder this possibility, largely because of the prevalence of drugs in Phish culture. Jewish enthusiasts seldom worry publicly about this potential impediment. More common are accounts of drug-fueled transformative journeys tied both to hearing classic Jewish songs at shows and to other elements of live Phish.

Traditional Jewish thought cautions about the dangers associated with transcendental experiences, both those induced by drug use and those facilitated by other means, including musical journeys. Rabbi Darby Leigh explains, "The danger is that the spiritual (or physical) high of the Phish concert will become the goal of the attendees, rather than a tool to help them live more righteously . . . following the concert/transcendent experience."[74] Yet she acknowledges that there can be power in such episodes "if a Phish concert helps one to "recharge" their spiritual batteries, and therefore . . . live more righteously, performing more acts of kindness, and mitzvot."[75] Hillel Zerzen's transcendental experiences at Phish concerts did just that, leading him to embrace an Orthodox life. Zerzen, once an active member of the Shabbat Tent crew, "doesn't downplay the fact that magic mushrooms and LSD were an integral part of the process. 'It made me realize there was something beyond me,' he says, 'something larger than myself.'"[76]

Rabbi Shlomo Carlebach, who indelibly reshaped the Jewish musical and devotional landscape in the 1960s, admitted to psychedelic pioneer Timothy Leary that while he generally abstained from recreational drug use, he did try LSD once: "It was gewalt, but it did not compare to learning Talmud."[77] Rabbi Zalman Schachter-Shalomi, who founded the Jewish Renewal movement and dropped LSD with Leary, called MDMA "just as sweet as Shabbos," sharing of the experience, "I felt the great delight of loving the universe and being loved by the universe."[78] These significant Jewish thinkers represent a minority rabbinical perspective. Nonetheless, this outlook, however fringe, creates space for Jewish indulgence. It too enables drug-inspired transcendental experiences to become Jewish ones. Rabbi Zalman Schachter-Shalomi once noted, "When God saw that people, instead of turning to God, were turning to the medicine cabinet, God made himself available in the medicine cabinet."[79]

While it is challenging to locate online conversations about Christianity and Phish, the sheer number of sites, online groups, and chat threads related to Jewishness and Phish is staggering. The association Jews feel to Phish's Jewishly linked songs and to the band itself is distinct, as is the prevalence of Jewish culture and religious practice on Phish tour. In fact, religion and fandom can sometimes seem indistinguishable on tour. Andreas Hägar reflects on the relationship between popular music and faith: "These two spheres of contemporary culture exist in a complex relation: at times mutually repellent and at times closely intertwined to the extent that it is impossible to know where one ends and the other begins."[80] Phish offers an alternative space for Jewish expression and connection for many for whom established Jewish spaces (i.e., synagogues and community centers) are not meaningful. Furthermore, Phish serves as a venue through which Jews can carve out space for themselves in the pop culture arena.

Phish's renditions of Jewish classics arouse a sense of belonging and connection in affiliated and unaffiliated Jews who love the band. These fans find a unique home at Phish shows, and that sense of community remains intact after the encore concludes, in part because they actively engage in dialogue about their love of Phish and Jewishness. As devotees hear their favorite band sing a sacred Hebrew chant in a radically new venue as part of a hallowed musical experience, they might find community, celebrate their Jewishness, or commune with God. Jewish experiences at live Phish shows are not isolated to renditions of "Avenu Malkenu," nor are religious or spiritual experiences limited to Jewish ones. The nature of these occurrences is self-determined, as is their impetus. In "Sand" the band sings "I would choose my own religion / And worship my own spirit / But if he ever preached to me / I wouldn't want to hear it."[81] Perhaps Jewish Phish fans relate in such a deep way to the band and the culture surrounding it because the band enables them to define how they live Jewishly. They get to at once dance to their own tune and be enveloped in the prayer of their people.

NOTES

1. The liturgy is also recited on fast days, with the exception of the ninth of Av. Notably, many American Jews only attend synagogue on Rosh Hashanah and Yom Kippur.

2. I address Jewish and Christian fans in this chapter both because Phish plays Jewish and Christian songs and because Jewish and Christian fans are visible and outspoken. There is a glaring lack of source material regarding fans affiliated with other faiths. However, Islamophobic commentary sometimes appears in Phish-related chats. This topic requires further inquiry.

3. See Benarde, *Stars of David*.

4. Even while Jews have made up a significant number of popular American musicians, the Jewish identity of these artists was and is often downplayed in order to increase their marketability to a national audience. Artists including Bob Dylan (born Robert Allen Zimmerman) and Joey Ramone (born Jeffrey Ross Hyman) changed their names in pursuit of this goal. See ibid.

5. "Hatikvah" is the Israeli national anthem. Anderson .Paak, "Come Down," track 13 on *Malibu* (ArtClub International, Empire Distribution, OBE, and Steel Wool, 2016).

6. Croland, *Oy Oy Oy Gevalt!*, xxiv.

7. NOFX, "The Brews," track 8 on *Punk in Drublic* (Epitaph, 1994).

8. Adam Sandler, "The Chanukah Song," track 6 on *What the Hell Happened to Me?* (Warner Bros., 1996).

9. Farhi, "Do Sandler's Goofy Lyrics?"

10. Lil Dicky, "Jewish Flow."

11. Drake threw himself a "re-bar mitzvah" at age thirty-one, and Mac Miller had a Star of David tattoo. Yet, Jewishness plays little roll in their music.

12. In addition to the Christian classics mentioned in this chapter, Phish plays reggae songs that hold great meaning for Rastafari.

13. Zero, "Phish and Avinu Malkenu."

14. Phish, "Cavern," track 3 on *Picture of Nectar* (Elektra, 1992). A favorite Ashkenazi delicacy, a knish is a doughy pocket most often filled with a spiced potato mixture.

15. Phish, "The Oh Kee Pa Ceremony," track 5 on *Lawn Boy* (Absolute A Go Go, 1990).

16. According to fan lore. "Suzy Greenberg" is a Phish original played at 23.09 percent of concerts. Phish, "Suzy Greenberg" (live debut 1987).

17. Camp Oswego took place at the Oswego County Airport in Volney, New York, on July 17–18, 1999. Coventry took place August 13–15, 2004, at the Newport State Airport in Coventry, Vermont. Festival 8 took place October 30–November 1, 2009, at the Empire Polo Fields in Indio, California.

18. Deut. 6:8.

19. A minyan is a prayer group traditionally comprising at least ten men. Female fans posting in the "Gefilte Phish" page on Facebook (https://www.facebook.com/groups/2218655508163396) raise questions about the lack of female involvement in the

minyan. Some express a desire for an egalitarian minyan. These gatherings take place on the 100s level during Phish shows at Madison Square Garden.

20. Marc Silberstein, in "Gefilte Phish" (Facebook group), February 12, 2020, https://www.facebook.com/groups/22186555 08163396/permalink/3155414627820808.

21. Interestingly, it is not uncommon to hear someone in the Phish community refer to the Grateful Dead as the "Christian" jam band, in part because the Dead's list of Christian classics is extensive. Frydberg, "25 Years of Phishy 'Avinu Malkenu.'"

22. Hutsy, in "Phish Has Even Helped Jews Feel and Become More Jewish" (chat thread), Phish.net, June 7, 2019, http://forum .phish.net/forum/show/1378424407#page=1.

23. I focused on Phish.net, Phantasy Tour, and Facebook groups including "Phish Tour 2014" and "Gefilte Phish."

24. Benarde, *Stars of David*, 341.

25. Phish, "Yerushalayim Shel Zahav," track 12 on *Hoist* (Elektra, 1994).

26. Benarde, *Stars of David*, 341.

27. Gilmour, *Gospel According to Bob Dylan*, 138.

28. Phish, "Scent of a Mule," track 9 on *Hoist* (Elektra, 1994).

29. "The Man Who Stepped into Yester-day" is often abbreviated as "TMWSIY." Trey Anastasio, "The Man Who Stepped into Yesterday," track 2 on *The Man Who Stepped into Yesterday* (senior thesis, Goddard College, 1987).

30. The_Steiner, in "Phish and Religion" (chat thread), Phish.net, August 31, 2016, http://forum.phish.net/forum/show/137688 7127.

31. "Avenu Malkenu," Phish.net, https:// phish.net/song/avenu-malkenu/history.

32. Benarde, *Stars of David*, 341.

33. Garnick, "Gefilte Phish."

34. Pew Research Center, "Portrait of Jewish Americans."

35. Till, *Pop Cult*, 169.

36. Ibid.

37. These statements are not mutually exclusive.

38. Rabbi Yehoshua "Shu" Eliovson, in discussion with the author, May 11, 2021.

39. Rebecca M. Ross, in "Gefilte Phish" (Facebook group), December 1, 2019, https:// www.facebook.com/groups/22186555 08163396/permalink/2992452877450318.

40. See Corwin Berman, *American Jewish Philanthropic Complex.*

41. Mandy Berman, in "Gefilte Phish" (Facebook group), December 1, 2019, https:// www.facebook.com/groups/22186555 08163396/permalink/2992452877450318.

42. Russel Glowatz, in "Gefilte Phish" (Facebook group), December 1, 2019, https:// www.facebook.com/groups/22186555 08163396/permalink/2992452877450318.

43. The_Steiner, in "Phish and Religion" (chat thread), Phish.net, August 31, 2016, http://forum.phish.net/forum/show /1376887127.

44. PT_Barnum, in "Avenu Malkenu and Non-Jewish Fans" (chat thread), Phantasy Tour, July 15, 2019, https://www.phantasytour .com/bands/phish/threads/4544008.

45. Les Skolnik, in "Gefilte Phish" (Facebook group), December 1, 2019, https:// www.facebook.com/groups/22186555 08163396/permalink/2992452877450318.

46. Kevin Samuel Haber, in "Gefilte Phish" (Facebook group), December 2, 2019, https://www.facebook.com/groups/22186555 08163396/permalink/2992452877450318.

47. Gwexler, in "Avenu Malkenu Appreci-ation" (chat thread), Phantasy Tour, March 21, 2006, https://www.phantasytour.com /bands/phish/threads/965660/avenu -malkenu-appreciation#page/1.

48. Zimmerman refers to the July 14, 2019, show at the Alpine Valley Music Center in East Troy, Wisconsin, where the band played "Avenu Malkenu." Liz Zimmerman, in

Gefilte Phish (Facebook group), Facebook, December 1, 2019, https://www.facebook.com/groups/2218655508163396/permalink/2992452877450318.

49. Zero, "Phish and Avinu Malkenu."

50. Rock and roll musicians including Elvis, Eric Clapton, and the Grateful Dead have also covered the track.

51. The accompanying tune was written in 1835 by William Walker.

52. Stephens, *Devil's Music*, 27–28.

53. Gausssplit refers to his experience of ingesting LSD and magic mushrooms. Gausssplit, in "Phish and Religion" (chat thread), Phish.net, August 31, 2016, http://forum.phish.net/forum/show/1376887127#page=2.

54. This is a majority opinion, yet dissenting opinions exist.

55. Phish also played "Oh, Holy Night" on August 2, 2017, during their notable Baker's Dozen residency at New York's Madison Square Garden.

56. "Daniel Saw the Stone," Phish.net, https://www.phish.net/song/daniel-saw-the-stone/history.

57. PS139, in "The Phish Thread" (chat thread), Christian Forums, July 6, 2004, https://www.christianforums.com/threads/the-phish-thread.687259/page-6.

58. Ibid.

59. Phish, "Bug," track 3 on *Farmhouse* (Elektra, 2000).

60. Phish, "Lifeboy," track 6 on *Hoist* (Elektra, 1994).

61. See Pessin, *Jewish God Question*.

62. u/kernsomatic, in "Phish at Church" (chat thread), Reddit, October 4, 2019, https://www.reddit.com/r/phish/comments/ddbd2q/phish_at_church.

63. Jen, "Praise, Phish and Bob Weir: An Exceptional Trio," *Truly Yours, Jen* (blog), November 9, 2018, https://trulyyoursjen.com/2018/11/praise-phish-and-bob-weir-an-exceptional-trio.

64. *A Live One* is an album of live recordings released through Elektra Records on June 27, 1995. It includes the song "Harry Hood" (track 11), as referenced by this user. Drewthedevilstickinglawnboy, in "Phish and Religion" (chat thread), Phish.net, September 2, 2016, http://forum.phish.net/forum/show/1376887127#page=3.

65. FoolontheHill, in "Phish and Religion" (chat thread), Phish.net, September 1, 2016, http://forum.phish.net/forum/show/1376887127#page=2.

66. Desertrat, in "Phish and Religion" (chat thread), Phish.net, September 3, 2016, http://forum.phish.net/forum/show/1376887127#page=3.

67. McConnell, "Phish, le petit poisson."

68. Bee7le, in "The Phish Thread" (chat forum), Christian Forums, July 9, 2004, https://www.christianforums.com/threads/the-phish-thread.687259/page-8#post-8462986.

69. PS139, in "The Phish Thread" (chat forum), Christian Forums, June 27, 2004, https://www.christianforums.com/threads/the-phish-thread.687259/page-8#post-8462986.

70. Theoneway, in "The Phish Thread" (chat forum), Christian Forums, June 27, 2004, https://www.christianforums.com/threads/the-phish-thread.687259/page-6.

71. See Till, *Pop Cult*.

72. Rasheed, "How do you guys feel about the band Phish?" (chat thread), Christian Forums, May 19, 2010, https://www.christianforums.com/threads/how-do-you-guys-feel-about-the-band-phish.7468065.

73. KM Richards, "How do you guys feel about the band Phish?" (chat thread), Christian Forums, July 19, 2010, https://www.christianforums.com/threads/how-do-you-guys-feel-about-the-band-phish.7468065.

74. Benji, "Pop Jewish: Jewish Phish Food for the Soul," *Benji UnSpun: Connecting People Places and Things* (blog), July 15, 2012,

https://allmyprojects.wordpress.com/2012
/07/15/pop-jewish-jewish-phish-food-for
-the-soul.

75. Ibid.

76. Vikhman, "Phishers of Men."

77. The Yiddish *Gewalt*, translated as
"health," relates to a strong or violent force.
Carlebach uses the term to indicate the
power of psychedelic experience. Ferry,
"Love, Prayer, LSD."

78. Wilensky, "Can Psychedelics Heal?"

79. Jenkins, "Electronic Dance Music's
Love Affair."

80. Häger, *Religion and Popular Music*, 8.

81. Phish, "Sand," track 11 on *Farmhouse*
(Elektra, 2000).

REFERENCES

Benarde, Scott R. *Stars of David: Rock 'n'
Roll's Jewish Stories*. Lebanon, NH:
Brandeis University Press, 2003.

Corwin Berman, Lila. *The American Jewish
Philanthropic Complex: The History of a
Multibillion-Dollar Industry*. Princeton,
NJ: Princeton University Press, 2020.

Croland, Michael. *Oy Oy Oy Gevalt! Jews
and Punk*. Santa Barbara, CA: Praeger,
2016.

Farhi, Paul. "Do Sandler's Goofy Lyrics Fuel
Jewish Pride or Anti-Semitism?" *Los
Angeles Times*, December 3, 2002.
https://www.latimes.com/archives/la
-xpm-2002-dec-03-et-farhi3-story
.html.

Ferry, Josh. "Love, Prayer, LSD and Nina
Simone: Get to Know Soul Doctor's
Rock Star Rabbi Shlomo Carlebach."
Broadway.com, July 31, 2013. https://
www.broadway.com/buzz/170898/love
-prayer-lsd-and-nina-simone-get-to
-know-soul-doctors-rock-star-rabbi
-shlomo-carlebach.

Frydberg, Tracy. "25 Years of Phishy 'Avinu
Malkenu.'" *Times of Israel*, July 15, 2012.
https://www.timesofisrael.com/25
-years-of-phishy-avinu-malkenu.

Garnick, Darren. "Gefilte Phish." *Jerusalem
Report*, December 26, 1996. https://
darrengarnick.wordpress.com/2009/05
/24/phishing-for-jewish-heritage.

Gilmour, Michael. *The Gospel According to
Bob Dylan: The Old, Old Story for
Modern Times*. Louisville: Westminster
John Knox Press, 2011.

Häger, Andreas. *Religion and Popular Music:
Artists, Fans, and Cultures*. New York:
Bloomsbury Academic, 2018.

Jenkins, P. Nash. "Electronic Dance Music's
Love Affair with Ecstasy: A History."
The Atlantic, September 20, 2013.
https://www.theatlantic.com/health
/archive/2013/09/electronic-dance
-music-s-love-affair-with-ecstasy-a
-history/279815.

Lil Dicky. "Jewish Flow." YouTube video,
August 14, 2013, 5:37. https://www
.youtube.com/watch?v=BFVtamh
2dNU.

McConnell, Page. "Phish, le petit poisson
qui se transforme peu à peu en
dinosaure, à découvrir d'urgence . . ."
Djouls.com, July 12, 1996. http://www
.djouls.com/phish/interview.html.

Pessin, Andrew. *The Jewish God Question:
What Jewish Thinkers Have Said About
God, the Book, the People, and the
Land*. New York: Rowman & Littlefield,
2018.

Pew Research Center. "A Portrait of Jewish
Americans: Findings from a Pew
Research Center Survey of U.S. Jews."
October 1, 2013. https://www.pewfo
rum.org/2013/10/01/jewish-american
-beliefs-attitudes-culture-survey.

Stephens, Randall J. *The Devil's Music: How
Christians Inspired, Condemned, and*

Embraced Rock 'n' Roll. Cambridge, MA: Harvard University Press, 2018.

Till, Rupert. *Pop Cult: Religion and Popular Music*. New York: Continuum International, 2010.

Vikhman, Felix. "Phishers of Men." *Salon*, August 21, 1999. https://www.salon.com/1999/08/21/gefiltefish.

Wilensky, David A. M. "Can Psychedelics Heal the Jewish People? This Rabbi Is Exploring That Question." *Jewish News of Northern California*, August 20, 2019. https://www.jweekly.com/2019/08/20/can-psychedelics-heal-the-jewish-people-this-rabbi-is-exploring-that-question.

Zero, Jack. "Phish and Avinu Malkenu." *Teruah Jewish Music*, June 18, 2007. http://teruah-jewishmusic.blogspot.com/2007/06/phish-and-avinu-malkenu.html.

8.

"All Times and Seasons Are the Reasons"

HOW PHISH BROUGHT AMERICA TO SHUL

Mike Greenhaus

On the morning of December 2, 2019, "Avenu Malkenu" was trending. A night earlier, Phish had performed the tune—cased, as always, in the middle of Trey Anastasio's meditative instrumental "The Man Who Stepped into Yesterday"—during their first set at Uniondale, New York's Nassau Veterans Memorial Coliseum, and clips of the song quickly went viral on social media.

It's no secret to Phish fans that the Vermont quartet had already performed the musical prayer dozens of times dating back to the late 1980s; they'd even busted it out for the first time since 2015 earlier in the year on June 14 at East Troy, Wisconsin's Alpine Valley during an asterisk-adorned, rarity-filled show. But there was something about the time and place of that Nassau performance—on Long Island, at the end of the annual autumnal homecoming that is Thanksgiving—that helped this "Avenu Malkenu" go viral months after the Jewish High Holidays when many Jewish fans may have heard the prayer in a synagogue setting.[1]

For all intents and purposes, Phish is a secular band. While a few of their originals, like "Lifeboy" and "Dogs Stole Things," touch on God directly and several others contain veiled references (the titular number in "46 Days" can be seen as a reflection of the length of the Lent period), their music, by and large, steers clear of biblical references and the proper Psalms.[2] And only two of the band's four members—bassist Mike Gordon and drummer Jon Fishman—grew up in the Jewish faith. Yet their concerts have also long felt, for some fans, to have an innately Jewish feel and identity that stands apart from any other arena act of their size.

From rabbis conducting services in the parking lot of concerts to former bunkmates from Jewish camps using summer tours as their unofficial reunions, concertgoers and even band members have long treated the Phish experience as a place to openly express their connection with Judaism, sometimes by engaging in profoundly religious acts. So how did a secular band who has avoided talking directly about religious and biblical themes become one around which Jews of all backgrounds can congregate, both culturally and religiously?

The answer is varied, or to ape a line from "McGrupp and the Watchful Hosemasters," a cherished part of Trey Anastasio's "Gamehendge" saga, it's because "all times and seasons are the reasons."[3]

Of course, as the saying goes, one of the biggest reasons that Phish's music possesses a strong Jewish identity has to do with location, location, location. All four members of Phish lived in states with significant Jewish populations (New York, New Jersey, or Massachusetts) for at least a portion of childhood, and the band spent their formative years barnstorming clubs and colleges around the Northeast—a region of the country that has the greatest density of Jews anywhere in the United States.[4] Outside of Vermont, some of the first places Phish gained a foothold were in these collegiate areas with significant Jewish populations in New York and New England. At the dawn of the internet, college students would share tapes with their friends at other schools and pass the music down to their younger siblings, spreading their music down the family tree.

A lot of it has to do with the simple fact that Phish came of age playing prep schools, colleges, and small clubs in the Northeast, all of which have helped Phish bring a sense of Judaism to festival-sized stages around the world. It also has to do with the band's cerebral sense of musical discovery, which like Judaism itself places a deep emphasis on questioning and exploration, and that the band's music has traditionally swayed closer to Broadway and klezmer than traditional American roots music, drawing influence from the work of Jewish composer Leonard Bernstein.[5]

By the time their classic lineup solidified in the mid-1980s, Phish had already opened their sound to include a range of influences—from jazz and bluegrass to the classically minded fugues Anastasio was studying at Goddard College. Like their jam-rock forebears the Grateful Dead, the Allman Brothers, Little Feat, and Santana, the members of Phish used those traditional forms both to develop a shared language based on a synthesis of their influences and as platforms for open-ended improvisation.

On the 2019 "The Island of Misfit Toys" episode of the *Long May They Run* podcast, Gordon described their ability to genre-jump at such a dizzying speed at their early "tour of the world" gigs.[6] And indeed, as Phish matured as a band and developed their own style, they've been able to home in on a more nuanced approach that hints at the styles they've studied without replicating them note for note—like balancing a Fabergé egg.

It's only natural then that, as they were defining their sound, Gordon—who attended Jewish day school—brought in elements of his Jewish upbringing, just as he pushed to add some bluegrass tunes to the repertoire and cover his childhood heroes Max Creek. When he first suggested that the band learn "Avenu Malkenu," Gordon noted that the song's melody is malleable and thus would allow them to create their own variations when playing it in concert. His own experiences working with a forward-thinking rabbi when he was younger, on one level, may also have been an early entry into the jam-band mentality of not being tied to a song's classic structure.[7]

Phish's songbook includes one other Hebrew number, "Yerushalayim Shel Zahav," which the band played twelve times from 1993 through 1994. Though the song is no longer in rotation, they *did* record the popular Israeli tune for their 1994 album *Hoist*, which was released on the major label Elektra. The number appears at the end of "Demand," emerging as part of a reckoning sequence that falls after a bit of "Split Open and Melt" and car-crash noise effects—the driver, whom many listeners presume to be Jewish, crashes, there is a moment of silence, and he ascends to heaven or a place of spiritual bliss. (The band also wrote a few lines from the song in Hebrew in the liner notes, which has long been like finding the *afikoman* for Jewish fans.)[8]

In both cases, Phish usually runs through those Hebrew songs alongside other catalog material without making any particular reference to the tunes' religious or cultural origins. For fans, hearing the band riff on Hebrew liturgy felt just as natural as hearing them tease *The Simpsons* theme or riff on a popular radio song. Yet, much like the secret language the group introduced in 1992 to connect with audience members traveling from show to show, as they started to play bigger and more mainstream venues, those selections have long served as unifying rallying calls for Jews in the audience. Likewise, the klezmer-like breakdown and dance that Gordon inserted into his bluegrass song "Scent of a Mule" has long been a wink to the weddings, b'nai mitzvah, services, and other festivities where many Jews in attendance at a show may have first heard live music in any sort of formal setting.

In many ways, Gordon has done more than most rock stars to bring Jewish music and Jewish-influenced sounds to the popular rock lexicon. Perhaps his efforts are inspired by growing up in an overtly Jewish household where his father Robert Gordon, the former CEO and president of the popular Store 24 convenience store chain, did his part to help Jews overseas. "I actually had a strong Jewish upbringing," Gordon recalls.[9] "My dad was actually a leader in the Jewish community at the time of the Soviet Jewry movement, helping Jews who were denied exit visas to get out of Russia. He was a national leader of that. I feel like, in some ways, I'm doing something for Judaism, too."

Like much of the Phish world in general, the band's roots can be traced, in part, back to the 1960s countercultural movement. Proportionally speaking, many stars of the classic-rock movement were raised in the Jewish faith. While the hippie movement of the 1960s drew in freethinkers from all backgrounds and faiths, there were a disproportionate number of Jews involved, ranging from social activists like Abbie Hoffman and the Yippies like Jerry Rubin to writers like Allen Ginsberg to musicians like folk singer Phil Ochs and Simon and Garfunkel, who turned those voices into a musical revolution. Their voices represented a generation of Jews who were searching for a sense of community while feeling like outsiders in the conservative, Levittown-esque suburban diaspora that largely characterized the Jewish post–World War II era. Some were looking for a spiritual sanctuary they felt was missing in the traditional synagogue setting at the time.[10] (Many Jewish Americans who were involved in the civil rights and counterculture movements would later apply those progressive ideals to their own religious and cultural backgrounds as they grew older and became more involved in synagogue life.)[11]

Steely Dan singer/keyboardist Donald Fagen spoke with *Rolling Stone* about this very search for authenticity while also reflecting on the similarities between his and Paul Simon's upbringing. He said, "There's a certain kind of New York Jew. Almost a stereotype, really, to whom music and baseball are very important. I think it has to do with the parents. The parents are either immigrants or first-generation Americans who felt like outsiders, and assimilation was the key thought—they gravitated to black music and baseball looking for an alternative culture. My parents forced me to get a crew cut; they wanted me to be an astronaut."[12] In fact, as many of these immigrants or first-generation American Jews trained to Americanize, their children rebelled by searching for music and career paths that did not fit the mainstream. That rebellious spirit is heavily entwined in the poetry of Bob Dylan and Canadian singer-songwriter Leonard Cohen—both of whom are Jewish. Despite their Jewish identities, Dylan and Cohen often mined the New Testament and the Christian-rooted American songbook for inspiration—nodding to Psalms and biblical stories as they embraced, even agnostically, elements of Christian-rooted rock and roll and popular folk music. As they continued to grow as songwriters and spiritual searchers, both luminaries also touched on other religious disciplines: Dylan explored evangelical Christianity and the Chabad movement at different moments in the 1970s and 1980s, and Cohen spent five years in a Zen Buddhist monastery. And the practice of searching for spirituality while reflecting the mainstream continued, shaping the ideology of the Grateful Dead and their peers.

Rob Weiner, editor of *Perspectives on the Grateful Dead*, notes, "The Grateful Dead is a good example of people searching for the other, whatever that means, in terms of spirituality—trying to find something that goes beyond their own identity, beyond themselves. It's an important way to help them live their lives in a moral and reasonable way."[13] Simply put, the Dead, and by extension the larger jam-band universe that includes Phish, became a place for all types of freethinkers to follow their own "golden road."

So too, the Dead's symbiotic relationship with their fans—feeding off one another's energy—and ability to present themselves as "real people" on a stage instead of intangible rock-star characters, also left a mark on Phish, influencing how they interacted with their audience as their own concert ecosystem developed. "Deadheads felt like outcasts in America, yet we were outcasts who built a very strong and vital and joyful community," observes Steve Silberman, a writer who earned gold records for coproducing the *So Many Roads (1965–1995)* box set and penning liner notes for rereleases of *Workingman's Dead* and *Europe '72*.[14] He continues, "There's a *wink-wink* understanding that we're always in the same tribe. It's a feeling of being both outcast and deeply inside. Shows were very much like a secular Sabbath. [The Grateful Dead] were open to discovering [the sacred] every night, in the next set or the next song or the next transition. The possibility of the sacred being revealed was always there, but it was also never certain."[15]

Within that community surrounding the Dead, fans have long found a sense of spirituality. While the New York–bred percussionist Mickey Hart was the only Jewish member of the Grateful Dead—the band often played the Northeast around the High Holidays so that he could spend time with his family—that freethinking mentality and search for the sacred was heavily associated with the band throughout their career. And the search continued into the Phish scene, which, at least at the outset, looked to the Dead's grassroots approach and touring model as a blueprint.

While the Dead are just one of Phish's musical influences—they draw just as much from Frank Zappa, Talking Heads, and the Meters—the band looks to the Bay Area legends' intangible sacred element that has consistently ignited their community. No matter what one's cultural background, Phish's music, especially as they

FIG. 8.1 Reading Torah in the Shabbat tent. Photo: Eli Falk and Adam Broder.

segue into a deep jam, has always lent itself to mindful thinking and spiritual quest. Both textually and lyrically, Phish's music has historically left room for interpretation. Early on, their music favored story songs and seemingly nonsensical lyrics perfectly timed phonetically with their harmonic gymnastics. Later on, their material started to sway from the head to the heart, with bouncy but cerebral tunes like "The Mango Song" and "Reba" giving way to the tender "Billy Breathes," which was written for Anastasio's young daughter in the 1990s, and "Miss You," which deals with the passing of the guitarist's sister in 2009.[16] But even though those stories were often rooted in real-time experiences, they were also vague enough to leave ample room for listeners to insert their own experiences and perspectives and have true religious and cultural experiences.

Thus, it is no wonder that Jews of all stripes have continued to use Phish's concerts as their own shuls over the years, both formally and informally.[17] For over twenty years, musician and rabbi Shmuel Skaist has hosted the Shabbat Tent at Phish events and festivals as well as multiband gatherings like Coachella and Lockn' (fig. 8.1).[18] At times, minyans have even congregated to mark the Sabbath, both inside and outside venues.[19] As Phish welcomed in 2010 at the American Airlines Arena in Miami,

Florida, then Hasidic singer and longtime fan Matisyahu could be seen reciting a few words of prayer at set break in the arena concourse.

Phish fans have compiled their own Phish-themed Haggadah.[20] And for several years, New York's Brooklyn Bowl has organized a Phish-centric Purim show with Because Jewish and Shalom Ya'll Jams. The band is aware of the many ways that Jewish Phish fans connect Jewishly to their music. Furthermore, rumor has it that the band decided to revive "Avenu Malkenu" for the first time in three years at their Magnaball festival after seeing a Star of David flag waving from a campsite.[21] And, as a wink to both Hanukkah and fellow improv heroes Yo La Tengo's concurrent run at the Bowery Ballroom, Phish's management used the group's "Eight Candles" as their walkout music over the PA at Madison Square Garden on December 28, 2019.[22] Even the famous hotdog Phish used to fly around the Boston Garden in 1994—and again through Big Cypress in 1999 and Madison Square Garden in 2010—is kosher (see fig. 0.1). (The prop is now on permanent display in the lobby of the Rock and Roll Hall of Fame in Cleveland, Ohio.) "We actually had a rabbi come kosherify it, so my grandmother was happy," Gordon confirmed in a 1995 interview with Toni Brown.[23]

For some fans, Phish's overt and more subtle Jewish references are simply nods to their religious and cultural roots; for others they are moments to engage in prayer and reflection. And for some, it's simply a reminder that there are other Jews like them, living their parallel experiences in other parts of the world, who like Phish, too.

Intertwined with their clear reverence for the roots and rituals associated with the Jewish music in their catalog is a decidedly outsider—at least by US standards—style of music at some of the most esteemed theaters and arenas in the country. And, like Phish's music in general, that mix of broader pop-culture references and insular discussion is how four friends from Vermont managed to become one of the top-grossing bands of all time while remaining both underground and personal.

There seemed no more fitting moment for Phish to bust out "Avenu Malkenu" than on that early December evening in 2019, at the end of Thanksgiving weekend, at an arena that sits just outside New York City. Some fans posted video clips of the song before the set was even over as a sign of their Jewish pride or because they were already feeling connected to their roots after spending a few days with family at the start of the holiday season. Some posted it simply because they were excited to hear the song live for the first time. But no matter the reason Phish decided to segue into that tune, one thing that would decidedly please Gordon's family was clear: the Vermont quartet managed to get thousands of music fans to sing sacred Hebrew lyrics at a major sports arena amid an otherwise secular show.

NOTES

1. Including Rosh Hashanah, the Jewish new year, and Yom Kippur, a day of repentance and fasting.

2. Phish, "Lifeboy," track 6 on *Hoist* (Elektra, 1994); Phish, "Dogs Stole Things" (live debut 1997); Phish, "46 Days," track 8 on *Round Room* (Elektra, 2002).

3. Phish, "McGrupp and the Watchful Hosemasters" (live debut 1985).

4. It is worth noting that Phish connected with their longtime manager John Paluska when they played at his social club, The Zoo, in Amherst, Massachusetts.

5. Boilen, "'What Song Changed Your Life?'"

6. Budnick, *Long May They Run*.

7. Ibid.

8. An *afikoman* is a piece of matzah that, during the ritual Passover meal, is hidden. The meal cannot conclude until the *afikomen* is recovered and consumed as dessert.

9. Brown, "No Fear of Flying."

10. Gloster, "How the Summer of Love Changed."

11. Bush, "Judaism as a Counterculture."

12. Dawidoff, "Paul Simon's Restless Journey."

13. Goodwin, "Soapbox."

14. Ibid.; Grateful Dead, *So Many Roads (1965–1995)* (Arista, 1999); Grateful Dead, *Workingman's Dead* (Warner Bros., 2003); Grateful Dead, *Europe '72: The Complete Recordings* (Rhino, 2011).

15. Ibid.

16. Phish, "The Mango Song," track 12 on *A Picture of Nectar* (Elektra, 1992); Phish, "Reba," track 2 on *Lawn Boy* (Absolute A Go Go, 1990); Phish, "Billy Breathes," track 10 on *Billy Breathes* (Elektra, 1996); Phish, "Miss You," track 10 on *Big Boat* (JEMP, 2016).

17. *Shul* is a Yiddish-derived name for a synagogue or Jewish place of worship.

18. The Shabbat Tent website (http://shabbattent.org) explains, "Shabbat Tent is an oasis of chill based on Shabbat hospitality, mindfulness, and nourishment for the body and soul. A space to connect spiritually and communally with other Jews at festivals. A welcoming tent open to everyone regardless of religion or nationality. A realization of the spirit and practice of Abraham and Sarah, founders of the Jewish People."

19. Minyans are prayer quorums required for certain prayer services.

20. A Haggadah is the text used to guide the Seder meal on the first two nights of Passover.

21. Held from August 21 to 23, 2015, in Watkins Glen, New York, Magnaball marked the tenth time Phish staged a multiday camping festival since 1996.

22. Yo La Tengo, "Eight Candles," track 3 on *Hanukkah+* (Verve Forecast, 2019).

23. Brown, "Phish."

REFERENCES

Boilen, Bob. "'What Song Changed Your Life?' Bob Boilen on How Musicians Become Themselves." *NPR*, April 12, 2016. https://www.npr.org/2016/04/12/473953959/what-song-changed-your-life-bob-boilen-on-how-musicians-become-themselves.

Brown, Toni A. "Phish: No Fear of Flying: An Interview with Mike Gordon (Relix Revisited)." *Relix*, September 1, 2011. https://relix.com/articles/detail/phish-no-fear-of-flying-an-interview-with-mike-gordon-relix-revisited.

Budnick, Dean, host. *Long May They Run*. Produced by C13Originals. Released September–November 2019. Podcast. https://shows.cadence13.com/long-may -they-run.

Bush, Lawrence. "Judaism as a Counterculture." *Jewish Currents*, October 1, 2007. https://archive.jewishcurrents.org /judaism-as-a-counterculture.

Dawidoff, Nicholas. "Paul Simon's Restless Journey." *Rolling Stone*, May 12, 2011. https://www.rollingstone.com/music /music-news/paul-simons-restless -journey-240593.

Gloster, Rob. "How the Summer of Love Changed American Judaism in the Bay Area." *Jewish Weekly*, June 29, 2017. https://www.jweekly.com/2017/06/29 /how-the-summer-of-love-changed -american-judaism-in-the-bay-area -and-beyond.

Goodwin, Jeremy D. "Soapbox: Jews for Jerry." *Relix*, June 2012. https://relix .com/articles/detail/soapbox-jews-for -jerry.

9.

"Where the People Come to Pray"

SACRED PILGRIMAGE AND COMMUNAL REJOICING FROM THE ANCIENT TEMPLE IN JERUSALEM TO YEMSG

Jessy Dressin

I was standing barefoot in the sand with the sun shining, anticipating the first set of the first night of the first run of Phish in Mexico in 2016 when my friend Lisa joined my husband and me.[1] We were three seasoned Phish-seekers embarking on something new: Phish *en la playa*. Lisa is a unicorn in my life; it is unclear whether we connected first as colleagues or friends. I learned quickly that we were both passionate creatives in service to the Jewish people just a few minutes before the lights went down at a show in Hampton, Virginia, a few years earlier. Now in Mexico together, we filled the time before Phish took the stage by talking about the changing nature of American Judaism, the timeless need for deep human connection, and the power of a community rooted in shared, expressed values.

Immersed in the moment, I turned to Lisa and said, "I imagine this is what it felt like to make a pilgrimage to Jerusalem when the Temple was standing." Her eyebrows raised a little, as if inviting me to say more. "When I'm at a Phish show, descriptions of the Temple come to life. From the physical layout, to the different tiers of access and the varied functions performed by the band and showgoers. The vibe. The intention of transformation. Even Kuroda's light rig is set exactly where the ritual fire would be located in the Temple."[2]

Phish took the stage. The crowd erupted in ecstatic joy as my tribe expanded to all corners of the beach. Lisa turned to me and said, "You're on to something," as the band began to play "A Song I Heard the Ocean Sing."[3] The collective of individuals in the crowd traveled from different places to arrive at a perfect moment in time: Phish in Riviera Maya. After all the anticipation, preparation, and travel, pilgrims in bikinis and donut-patterned board shorts began to groove, hoping for transcendence, not unlike the ancient Israelites who made annual pilgrimages to the holy Temple in Jerusalem.

In Jewish tradition, three festival holidays required the entire community to make a pilgrimage to the Beit Hamikdash (the holy Temple). These festivals anchored the social, cultural, and religious experience of the ancient Israelites. As a rabbi and student of this tradition, I struggle to imagine the lived experience of these ancient moments. However, the emotions and experiences associated with attending a Phish show bring to life my understanding of the otherwise two-dimensional account of these sacred festivals.

In this chapter, I reflect on two components of the Jewish pilgrimage holidays—pilgrimage and communal rejoicing—and consider whether parallels exist surrounding the live Phish experience. The Phish experience, it seems, lends itself to a deeper understanding of the Jewish festival holidays and the aforementioned components necessary to their observance, just as reflection on ancient pilgrimage offers insight into the Phish phenomenon.

"I Feel the Feeling I Forgot": The Cultural Literacy of Membership

There are many who cannot understand why someone would see the same band 150 times. On the other hand, there are people, like my husband, who believe that 150 shows are not nearly enough. There is a term in Hebrew, *ha-mevin yavin*, which means "those who understand, get it." The term nods to a sort of insider/outsider experience that is also present in the context of cultural literacy in the Phish community. What does it mean to be part of a tribe? In an article for *Tablet* magazine titled "What Kind of Person Pays to See the Band Phish 150 Times?" Armin Rosen writes, "A Phish show is its own strange sort of spiritual community that exists for a few hours at a time and then dissolves with fearful instancy."[4]

In any culture—or tribe—those who identify as part of the community feel a sense of belonging because they share insider beliefs unavailable to those outside the group. For example, a person attending their first Phish show may not have the cultural literacy to know that when the band plays "Mike's Song," the crowd will soon also get to boogie to "Weekapaug Groove."[5] They won't know who Leo is.[6] They may not recognize a donut as a sign of affiliation with a tribe in the same way a mezuzah hanging on one's doorpost is a symbol of belonging for those who recognize it.[7] For those who can identify the symbols, the insider language connects an individual to both the group itself and to others who are fluent in a language reserved uniquely for its members.

Ha-mevin yavin—for those who get it—Phish is a way of life, the conduit for one's closest friendships. The music, both live and recorded, creates a rhythm by which people move throughout their lives. To outsiders, the connection between Phish experiences and the Jewish festival holidays may not be apparent. For those who get it, the exploration of the role that pilgrimage and communal rejoicing play in the festival holiday cycle can provide new nuance and language with which to describe the Phish experience for subscribed members of the culture.

"Where the People Come to Pray": Sacred Pilgrimage

The Torah prescribes, "Three times a year you shall hold a festival for Me."[8] Here, the Israelites are commanded to celebrate three harvest holidays: Passover, marking the redemption from bondage in Egypt and a new farming season; Shavuot, celebrating the reception of the Torah on Mount Sinai and the wheat harvest; and Sukkot, a harvest festival during which Jews build temporary booths to dwell in as a reminder of life's impermanence as the community prepares for winter. Furthermore, the Torah designates that these annual festivals take place in a specific location.[9] According to Jewish tradition, the Torah was given to the Israelite people while wandering in the desert on a journey to the Land of Israel after the Exodus from Egypt. Once settled in the land, they constructed a Temple that was the central location for worshiping the Divine.

During these designated festivals, Israelites brought offerings to the Beit Hamikdash. The festival holidays are explained in various Jewish texts, most notably in the rabbinic legal literature, which includes both the Mishnah and the Talmud.[10] It is in these texts that the rabbis outlined the framework of these celebrations and discussed the intricacies of how to properly observe a festival, in celebration of the Divine, where Israelites would engage in sacred ritual as a method of individual and collective transformation.

Mishnah 3:1 of Tractate Bikkurim of the Jerusalem Talmud instructs how a person should set aside a portion of the first fruits that "emerge each year" and designate them to bring to the Temple in Jerusalem as part of the pilgrimage festival.[11] The stages of fulfilling the obligation unfold in a series of three requirements: designating what to bring, the process of bringing offerings by way of pilgrimage, and the declaration one makes upon arrival at the Temple.[12] The tractate describes how preparation originates at home for a journey in which something wholly other is expected to occur. This rabbinic analysis begs an important question: What makes such a trip a sacred pilgrimage, in need of its own category and definition?

In his exploration of pilgrimage, anthropologist Victor Turner suggests it is possible "to envisage the social process, involving a particular group of pilgrims during their preparations for departure, their collective experiences on the journey, their center, and their return journey, as a sequence of social drama and social enterprises . . . in which there is development in the nature of intensity of relationships between the members of the pilgrimage group and its subgroups."[13] In other words, pilgrimage is a deeply personal endeavor shared alongside others, one that transforms the personal into something that is inherently and inextricably communal. The experience binds together those whose personal accountings can be exchanged with others, shaping into a shared history that can connect people who might otherwise be strangers. As a person embarks on a pilgrimage, they find themselves able to identify others set out for the same destination; they recognize symbols of membership that only those immersed in the culture can identify.

The ancient pilgrimage to Jerusalem brought together people in the same tribe who were otherwise dispersed and spread out during other times of the year. It was the occasion to experience a critical mass that only came together in certain seasons and for certain occasions, a time to encounter the power of their movement and culture. It just so happens that the mechanism for bringing people together was also an attempt to fulfill rites and rituals required for convening with the Divine.

Phish shows also involve pilgrimage. In December of 1999, I drove with my mother and sister from Washington, DC, down a long stretch of Route 95 to celebrate New Year's Eve at Disney World. As a new "phan," I was devastated that a family vacation prevented me from going to Phish's New Year's concerts at Big Cypress Seminole Indian Reservation, arguably the band's most ambitious festival to date.[14] I would miss an experience that so many others would share, moments that would be tucked away in time, available only to those present as Phish played to the sun rising over a new millennium.

As we got closer to our intended destination, I noticed an increasing number of phans making the pilgrimage to the Phish festival. At each stop, I felt a connection to fellow travelers while also yearning for an experience I was not on course to have. I was on a similar road but a completely different journey from those bound for the Everglades. Highways originating from various points began to merge as fewer roads led to their destination. I felt outside of the experience while also feeling like an insider to a culture expressed by travelers wearing patchwork, emerging

FIG. 9.1 Outside of Hampton Coliseum, known colloquially to fans as "The Mothership," Hampton, Virginia, October 21, 2018. Photo: Shaun Kessler (@shaunkess).

from vehicles adorned with stickers of antelopes blaring lengthy instrumental jams. I noticed the weird stares and glances of real outsiders who did not fully understand the masses of odd characters seemingly multiplying the farther south we drove.

Pilgrimage is an ascension of sorts and includes multiple stages of arrival. Each stage intensifies the elation, creating distance from one's daily routine, fostering the pilgrim's receptiveness to extraordinary experience. One may set out as a lone traveler or alongside a small group of companions. Along the journey, pilgrims become increasingly aware of others making their way to the same location, set out for similar purposes of celebration, ritual, and transformation. Those on the journey to Big Cypress knew exactly the path they were traveling and joyously connected with others bound for the same destination.

The physical journey mimics an internal one. Just as one must make a physical departure from her daily life to embark on a pilgrimage, so too must she orient herself to an openness, a vulnerability, a willingness to experience something truly apart from the limitations imposed by her normal, quotidian responsibilities. In the case of both pilgrimage to the Temple in Jerusalem and to a Phish festival, internal openness is essential for transformation. One embarks with the knowledge that the experience will be temporary and fleeting, and precisely for this reason may reveal a renewed sense of purpose and meaning to the life and circumstance she will return to when the journey concludes.

Earlier in December of 1999, Phish played two nights at "The Mothership" in Hampton, Virginia (fig. 9.1).[15] During the week before the shows, my friend Jeremy and I found ourselves debating whether we should sell our tickets for night 1, as both of us had a final exam the following morning. We could take our exams Saturday morning and leave promptly after, knowing that we had tickets for the second night. However, we felt that we had to be there for the first night as well—unable to reconcile the possibility that we could miss some major bust-out—something that felt much riskier than staying up too late the night before a college final.[16] So, we hit the road and drove four hours to Hampton Virginia, for two sets and an encore, then drove home to College Park, Maryland, to sit for our respective exams the following morning, only to drive back to Hampton the next day to pick up right where we left off.

Psychologist Robert Moore writes, "Spiritual masters of almost every tradition say that enlightenment must bring a return to the ordinary, and the enlightened person must return to the ordinary. You must be able to be ordinary, if you want to be enlightened."[17] To experience something different, one must consider something they have previously engaged with from a different vantage point, a result of transformation that took place between one ordinary moment and the next.

What is possible to experience in a period of twenty-four hours? A person can sit in her dorm room and study for an exam, combing her plant biology textbook for meaning that is already difficult to attain as an arts and humanities major trying to satisfy a basic science requirement. She can get a good night's rest, wake up the morning of the exam, and struggle to get a passing grade, knowing her future will not depend heavily on her knowledge of photosynthesis. Another option: adding another show to her list during the earliest days of her adventures to see Phish. In the same twenty-four hours, she can drive to a neighboring state, convene with friends, including the person who twenty years later will be her husband, spend an hour sitting in her car in the parking lot looking at that same textbook, furiously jotting down notes on flashcards that can accompany her inside the venue, eat a burrito in the lot, buy her first piece of patchwork clothing, figure out that her favorite song in the Phish canon is "The Moma Dance," consider the plant sciences connection to the song "Bug," drive home for a few hours of sleep, sit for a final, and get back in her car to attend a second show and the end of a college semester, making the otherwise ordinary into something truly extraordinary.[18] The twenty-four-hour period is a container of potential in which a person can remain in her typical routine or exchange that routine for something entirely different, resulting in something truly exceptional, but only if she is physically and spiritually open to the experience.

Songs of Ascent: A Soundtrack for Pilgrimage

The rabbinic writings of the Mishnah and Talmud differentiate offerings made during festival holidays from those brought as daily, more regular offerings to the Temple.[19] One distinction is the "great pomp and ceremony, by the multitudes of Jews traveling and singing together" on their journey from their homes to Jerusalem during these festivals.[20] The Talmud describes how people would travel, in groups, to Jerusalem. The Schottenstein commentary on chapter 3 of Tractate Bikkurim notes that "although one generally is not excited about visiting the same city numerous times, visits to Jerusalem are different," and so pilgrims would sing songs of appreciation for yet another chance to arrive in Jerusalem to participate in these sacred festivals.[21]

Family and friends of phans can be heard asking the following: Why do you need to see the same band three nights in a row? Didn't you go to Phish at Madison Square Garden last year? Don't you get sick of hearing the same songs? And yet, for many phans, the excitement to return to the same venues to see the same band year after year is a characteristic of the Phish experience. Phans return to places they've visited before to make new memories that can layer on top of those they've made in the same place previously, thereby mimicking the experience of Israelites who continually returned to Jerusalem.

Just as Phish's music drives that quest, music was part of all stages of the pilgrimage to Jerusalem, and the music changed as travelers reached different points along their journey. The shift in musical selection mirrored the building excitement and anticipation as the moment of arrival and ritual commencement drew nearer. The Hebrew term for psalm, *mizmor*, means "something sung."[22] The Book of Psalms includes 150 poems, often accompanied by instrumentation, and are often associated with praise and jubilation. Psalms 120–34 are known, uniquely, as the *shir ha-ma'alot*, or "songs of ascent."[23] These psalms were designed to accompany travelers during their final stage of pilgrimage—arrival—at "The (Original) Mothership," the Beit Hamikdash.

Daf 22a of Tractate Bikkurim describes the critical mass of pilgrims who would assemble to make the final ascent to the Temple Mount together, accompanied by music and joined by even the highest of community officials.[24] At this moment, I imagine the deeply personal elements of the experience and the collective, the proximity of the two levels of experience influencing the other with each step of ascent, drawing closer to the exact moment of arrival and sanctification. Proverbs 14:28 reads, "The multitude of people is the glory of the King."[25] The passage can be read as indicating that the holiness that emerges from fulfilling a sacred obligation is exponentially increased when performed in community. Phish's song "Strange Design," which asks, "Can I bring a few companions on this ride?" seems to reflect that sentiment.[26]

I imagine the moment of ascension as being like the point of entry at every Phish show when a crowded group of phans, densely packed together, are waiting to enter the venue. It is a moment of excitement, as an occasional pilgrim lets out a joyous "Wooo!" and hundreds of fellow phans echo the call. Smiles widen. A shared sense of purpose connects strangers who now recognize one another as comrades, even friends. Once inside, the energy throughout the venue increases to a point that feels impossible to contain. Finally, the lights go down, the crowd erupts in celebration, and the designated officiants of communal ritual ascend to the stage. Anticipation reaches its highest peak as the collective transitions from the mindset of "in pursuit of" to having "arrived." Within the fixed structure of two sets and an encore, anything seems possible. As Phish sings in one of their songs, "Let's get this show on the road."[27]

"We're All in This Together and We Love to Take a Bath": Communal Rejoicing

One of the most important functions of the Jewish pilgrimage festival is the sacred invitation to contribute to communal joy, an obligation commanded of every Israelite who journeyed to Jerusalem to participate in festival celebrations, something still required for holiday observance today. The preparations and rituals associated with these designated times for collective rejoicing required a cessation from work and other routine responsibilities so that the entire community could participate. Each person was to enter her observance with *kavanah*—sacred intention.

A person is commanded not only to appear at the Temple. Fulfillment of the religious obligation requires all members of the community to contribute offerings as part of their active participation in generating joy for the entire congregation. Chapter 3 of Tractate Bikkurim in the Jerusalem Talmud describes the pomp and ceremony by which individuals would bring their gifts and designate them for ritual use, transferring individual contributions into a collection of communal resources to achieve maximum rejoicing.[28] Once a community member made his offering, his primary obligation shifted to contributing to communal rejoicing.

Joy is everywhere at Phish, and it grows exponentially outward from groups of friends who planned to be together to those encountered because of vicinity. That joy is clear when cheers ripple throughout the crowd or an oversized balloon with glowsticks inside makes its way from the top tier of the venue onto the stage with the help of the multitude. My husband chased "Colonial Forbin's Ascent / Fly Famous Mockingbird" for 160 shows, and the moment he finally realized what he was hearing brought on him a feeling of ecstasy.[29] And we danced! When this unexpected, and yet highly anticipated, moment took place, it was an occasion for everyone around us, friends and strangers alike, to share in that joy.

Human beings require joy both to survive and to thrive. The lyrics to Phish's ballad "Joy" seem to convey this sentiment: "We want you to be happy / Don't live inside your gloom / We want to you be happy / Come step outside your room / We want you to be happy / Cause this is your song too."[30] Joy is something bestowed on each of us as a birthright, something we are all invited to engage with at Phish, just as ancient Israelites were tasked with experiencing joy on the pilgrimages.

What is different about joy when cultivated in community? Perhaps it is only alongside others that it is possible to amplify joy in ways that can ripple out into waves much more powerful than that which we cultivate on our own. As Phish sings in "Birds of a Feather," "It's not an experience if you can't bring someone along."[31]

"I Hope This Happens Once Again": We Will Return to You

In Jewish tradition, it is customary to utter the Aramaic words *hadran alach*, or "we will return to you," when completing a segment of Talmud study. It suggests an intention to return to the content again in the future, similar to phans shouting "See you next show!" to friends made during a concert.

For ancient Israelites, the festival holidays were a way of keeping track of time and a method of sustaining the communal structure. Members of the tribe would return to these celebrations year after year, through various stages of their lives, each cycle providing the opportunity to invoke memory and to imagine possibilities yet to occur. The act of showing up and participating served as a link to both the past and the future. The invitation is to return again and again, with an emphasis on active meaning-making, in hopes of capturing fleeting time in a capsule that will accompany a person long after the moment passed.

During the summer of 2009, I was a rabbinic student working at a Jewish summer camp in Malibu, California. Five senior staff members were phans, as was the camp director, whom I had met at my very first Phish show ten years earlier. Phish had returned from their hiatus and were slotted to play at Shoreline Amphitheater, a mere five-hour drive up the coast. The five of us decided that we could head up, see the show, and be back at camp the following morning.

We agreed that to get to the lot by five we would need to leave by noon, 11:30 if Nate could wrap up helping to belay campers on the climbing tower a bit early. We drove out of camp, turned right at the Pacific Ocean, and made our way inland for a straight shot to Mountain View. We took turns contributing to the soundtrack that accompanied us along the way, stopping only for a quick bathroom break in order to maximize hang time before going into the show. We exchanged stories of the last time seeing Phish before the band's hiatus. Bound by circumstance of a summer camp job and a desire to realize the opportunity to see our favorite band after a five-year break, we traveled as a pack, on pilgrimage together.

We arrived safely at Shoreline, reuniting with friends spanning every chapter of life before heading into the show. We danced as if the night would go on forever. The crowd released the power of all that had been pent up in the time since we had last been together watching the band—a sea of strangers entangled together in a life journey that dreamed of the next time we would see Phish.

As I drove home that night, the other four fast asleep preparing for a quick return to routine, I reflected on the power of the experience we had just shared. I laughed at the thought that five thirty-somethings would opt to drive through the night, only to show up the next day for a full day of working with children, just to see a Phish show. I knew then, as I believe now, that we had actually opted in to experience something much greater than just a concert. It was an occasion to leave our lives as they were, in their routine and purpose, and set out for something wholly different, an experience that would potentially transform us as individuals and in our connection to one another. We participated in a communal celebration, left feeling as if we had grasped something tangible, and would return back to life having a greater sense of fullness for having participated. The experience was our twenty-first-century ritual of sacred pilgrimage, one that we aim to repeat, year after year, whenever Phish is on tour.

Now, over a decade later, I reflect on the role that pilgrimage and communal rejoicing played in that adventure, along with so many others, seeing Phish. In the moments leading up to and during the shows I find myself thinking that these experiences might be a three-dimensional model of what it felt like to make a pilgrimage during the Jewish festival seasons when the Temple stood in Jerusalem. While it is impossible to know, the Phish experience, in its transformational power, provides the occasion to experience holy celebration in this lifetime. It is an invitation to celebrate in a framework worthy of Divine blessing that can accompany a person throughout her life.

NOTES

1. This chapter is dedicated in loving memory to Dov Wisnia z"l, who took the responsibility of communal rejoicing seriously and whom I still long to see whenever I attend a show. And for my husband, Mark, with whom sacred pilgrimage and communal rejoicing is a part of daily life.

2. Chris Kuroda is the lighting technician for Phish who is affectionately understood as the fifth member of the band.

3. Phish, "A Song I Heard the Ocean Sing," track 4 on *Undermind* (Elektra, 2004).

4. Rosen, "What Kind of Person."

5. Phish, "Mike's Song," track 5 on *Slip, Stitch, and Pass* (Elektra, 1997); Phish, "Weekapaug Groove," track 7 on *Slip, Stitch, and Pass* (Elektra, 1997).

6. "Leo" is a nickname for Phish keyboardist Page McConnell.

7. A mezuzah is a sacred object placed on the doorpost of a Jewish home that contains certain prayers.

8. Exod. 23:14.

9. Deut. 16:16.

10. The Mishnah (second century CE) and the Talmud (fifth and sixth centuries CE) are the basis for rabbinic legal debates about how to properly observe Jewish law and live out daily life in a Jewish framework.

11. Scholars of Jewish tradition will note that it is rare to seek the authority of the Jerusalem Talmud. The Babylonian Talmud is the preeminent source of Talmudic authority whenever the text is available. The first order of the Talmud is Berakhot, blessings. Due to the land-based nature of the majority of this section, there are a number of tractates in Berakhot for which the Babylonian Talmud did not expound. This is because the rules and instructions offered in these categories applied only within the Land of Israel, and the Babylonian Talmud was developed outside these geographic boundaries. The use of the Jerusalem Talmud as primary source text in this case is because these ideas were only developed in the Jerusalem version. Talmud Yerushalmi, Bikkurim 21b (Mishnah 3:1).

12. Chapter 2 of Tractate Bikkurim of the Jerusalem Talmud outlines the process of designating, bringing, and declaring the first fruits. The introduction to the tractate in the Schottenstein edition outlines these three stages of process in a simple manner for anyone who might wish to avoid the circular nature of conversation and tangents one encounters while reading the Talmudic text alone.

13. Turner, *Dramas, Fields, and Metaphors*, 167.

14. December 30–31, 1999, on Big Cypress Indian Reservation in southern Florida. "Phan" is another name for a Phish fan. The term will be used in context throughout this chapter.

15. "The Mothership" is a nickname for the Hampton Coliseum.

16. A "bust-out" is a song that the band has not played in a long period of time or that individuals are chasing to hear live.

17. Moore, *Archetype of Initiations*, 80.

18. I feel compelled to note that I passed the exam and my overall GPA was not negatively affected by my decision to attend both shows. Phish, "Moma Dance," track 13 on *The Story of the Ghost* (Elektra, 1998); Phish, "Bug," track 3 on *Farmhouse* (Elektra, 2000).

19. Page 19a of Tractate Bikkurim of the Jerusalem Talmud provides a few examples: a person who brings Bikkurim / first fruits to the Temple is required to stay overnight in Jerusalem, whereas a person bringing a daily offering is not required to do so; rejoicing is not regularly required for bringing daily offerings, while it is a central commandment for bringing of Bikkurim / first fruits; daily offerings do not require a complete cessation from work and are not deemed holy days in the same way the festival holidays are; daily offerings can be brought throughout the year.

20. Talmud Yerushalmi, Bikkurim 22a.

21. Talmud Yerushalmi, Bikkurim 22b.

22. Alter, *Book of Psalms*.

23. Ibid., 435.

24. "Daf" translates as "page" in reference to pagination of both the Babylonian and Jerusalem Talmud; Talmud Yerushalmi, Bikkurim 24a.

25. Rabbi Tamara Eskenazi teaches her students to degender references to the Divine Being. Though I would typically not use "King" to refer to the Divine Being, I have chosen to use the term in translation for the purposes of this chapter.

26. Phish, "Strange Design" (live debut 1995).

27. Trey Anastasio, "AC/DC Bag," track 12 on *The Man Who Stepped into Yesterday* (senior thesis, Goddard College, 1987).

28. The introduction to the Schottenstein Jerusalem Talmud on Tractate Bikkurim outlines the ritual by which a person contributes their offering for Temple use: The person arrives accompanied by great ceremony. The individual places the basket of Bikkurim on his shoulder and enters until reaching the Temple courtyard. A group of Temple officials commence in song. With the basket still on his shoulder, the pilgrim declares his offering of first fruits. He presents the basket to the priests, who participate in a waving ritual. He sets the basket down and then exits on his way to join other fellow travelers for the remainder of the festival celebration.

29. It also happened to be his birthday.

30. Phish, "Joy," track 3 on *Joy* (JEMP, 2009).

31. Phish, "Birds of a Feather," track 2 on *The Story of the Ghost* (Elektra, 1998).

REFERENCES

Alter, Robert. *The Book of Psalms: A Translation with Commentary*. New York: W. W. Norton, 2007.

Jewish Publication Society. *The JPS Hebrew-English Tanakh: First Pocket Edition*. Philadelphia: Jewish Publication Society, 2003.

Malinowitz, Chaim, Yisroel Simcha Schorr, and Mordechai Marcus. *Talmud Yerushalmi: The Schottenstein Edition; with an Annotated, Interpretive Elucidation, as an Aid to Talmud Study*. New York: Mesorah, 2007.

Moore, Robert L. *The Archetype of Initiations: Sacred Space, Ritual Process, and Personal Transformation*. Edited by Max J. Havlick. Philadelphia: Xlibris Corp., 2001.

Rosen, Armin. "What Kind of Person Pays to See the Band Phish 150 Times?" *Tablet*, January 3, 2019. https://www.tabletmag.com/sections/news/articles/what-kind-of-person-pays-to-see-the-band-phish-150-times.

Turner, Victor. *Dramas, Fields, and Metaphors: Symbolic Action in Human Society*. Ithaca, NY: Cornell University Press, 1974.

10.

"Pull This Timber 'fore the Sun Go Down"

THE JOYS AND QUESTIONS OF SHABBAT OBSERVANCE AT PHISH

Josh Fleet

After thirteen days and 2,362 miles of driving from Berkeley, California, we pulled into Big Foot Beach State Park campground in Lake Geneva, Wisconsin.[1] It was late Friday morning, July 12, 2019, and we had plenty of time to unpack the car, pitch the tent, and gather firewood before heading to the Phish concert at the Alpine Valley Music Theatre, which was just fifteen miles away in East Troy.

But as our neighbors zipped shut their own temporary tabernacles and headed to the Phish show, we settled into our campsite. My wife, Dori, lit candles for Shabbat, I turned east to pray, and our one-and-a-half-year-old got his first taste of the mosquito-thick midwestern wilderness. Later that night in our polyester taffeta palace in time, well after our dreams took flight, we woke to the sounds of revelers returning from the "circus of light" that is a Phish concert.[2]

My wife and I met because of a mutual love of the band. Even when we manage to catch ten shows in a tour, we want more. We had planned this whole summer around making it to Wisconsin for this one weekend to see Phish. So how could we come all this way and just not go? Judaism was the other shared interest that first brought Dori and me together, and since this concert occurred after sundown on

Friday and thus during the Jewish Sabbath—a different circus of light—we decided not to go to the concert in order to observe the rites and rituals of this special day.

"Our Intent Is All for Your Delight"

The Jewish Phish fan community is a microcosm of American Jewry; Jews of every level of religious observance attend Phish shows. And because Phish, like most bands, plays concerts on the weekend, Friday and Saturday shows raise a host of issues for the Jewish fan who wishes to honor and/or keep Shabbat. A wide range of otherwise normative Phish-related activities—travel, use of technology, exchange of money, consumption of food, smoking/vaping, listening to music played by Jewish band members, and more—as well as the musical substance of the concert itself, suddenly become complicated for the *shomer shabbos*, or Sabbath-conscious Jew.

In the Talmud, the rabbinic commentary on the Torah, there are thirty-nine Melakhot, the actions prohibited on Shabbat. These actions, based on the biblical narrative of the Israelites' sojourn in the desert after escaping Egyptian slavery, are general categories of work that religious Jews refrain from in order to observe the sacred day of rest. The goal of an observant Jew's life is to live in accordance with the Torah's laws, but it's not always clear how these ancient rules relate to modern existence. Since the most important thing for a religious Jew is to not break any of the commandments in the Torah, the rabbis instituted additional strictures as safeguards, known as "fences around the Torah," which are extra layers of law making it more difficult to break the initial commandment.[3] For example, fixing something is prohibited on Shabbat, therefore playing a musical instrument is forbidden lest you feel tempted to fix it if something breaks. Another example of a legal fence is the rabbinic perspective that discourages clapping and dancing on the Sabbath because these actions are associated with instrumental music.[4]

Though I am a longtime Phish fan, I only recently began contemplating the halachic implications (that is, the questions of Jewish law) raised by attending a Phish concert on Shabbat. My first show took place on a Saturday in the summer of 2003, but my memory of making that pilgrimage includes no notion of Shabbat. I was fifteen years old and had been hooked by Phish a few years prior, not long after my bar mitzvah, during "the hiatus."[5] At the time, nothing would stop me from catching a live show.

I grew up having Shabbat dinner with family on Friday evening and going to shul (synagogue) on Saturday mornings. But challah, roasted chicken, and all the fixings were often followed by the night's TV lineup; we drove to synagogue the next day because our house was several miles too far to walk, and it was not uncommon to pay for a plate of food at a diner after services ended if the postprayer luncheon was lacking. Dinner and a movie, shul and a show—*zakhor* but not *shamor*.

Besides the eating and the praying, many of these activities are verboten on Shabbat. The Torah contains 613 commandments, including 248 "positive" directives that tell Jews what to do and 365 "negative" strictures indicating what not to do.[6] Keeping Shabbat is a twofold mitzvah—a scriptural commandment containing both positive and negative legal components—embodied by the guidance to *shamor* (observe, keep, guard) and *zakhor* (remember, commemorate, cherish) the holiness of the day.[7]

My family's emphasis on remembering the importance of Shabbat over strictly following traditional rabbinic rules about proper observance of the Sabbath felt like normative practice. And in my Conservative Jewish community, it was.[8] We kindled the Shabbat candles and gathered to eat a special meal every Friday night, but we might go to the movie theater after dinner and had no problem driving around town on Saturday after attending synagogue services. My family's perspective reflects an interesting trend in American Jewish identity. Less than one-fifth of Jews in America believe following halacha is an essential component of what it means to be Jewish, and a slightly larger portion (23 percent) typically light candles on Friday night.[9] Even a simple gesture acknowledging Shabbat may be considered exceptionally religious in the American Jewish milieu.

From a young age, I felt drawn to Jewish practice. At some point in elementary school, my sister and I convinced our parents to keep a kosher kitchen at home, and my interest in religious observance has been evolving ever since. Just as my desire to keep mitzvot—as exemplified by my weekly return to sacred rest—has grown, my relationship with the music of Phish, too, has taken different forms and reached varying levels of intensity as I've matured into adulthood. And the space in my heart and in my life for both Shabbat and Phish has only expanded exponentially. It's impossible to know why (perhaps, as the song Phish has covered eighty times since the late 1990s says, "it's my soul!"), but I think it has something to do with the notion of delight, which is bound up in the bonds of both Phish and the Sabbath.[10]

In the morning liturgy found in many Jewish prayer books, each day of the week has its own particular "song of the day," or "Shir Shel Yom," that was sung by the Levites in the ancient Temple in Jerusalem, and each of these has a special introduction.[11] Before reading Sunday's unique psalm, for instance, we say, "Today is the first day of Shabbat." The point is that each day of the week points to the culmination and essential aspect of that week—the Sabbath—which itself contains every particular manifestation of weekly time and yet somehow transcends it. Drawing Shabbat awareness into the week elevates the mundane, adding an element of delight to day-to-day drudgery. Similarly, the knowledge of an approaching Phish show raises the spirits of many fans, infusing purpose, focus, and excitement into the monotony of workaday routine.

The Hebrew prophet Isaiah said, "You shall call the Sabbath a delight."[12] Building on this prophetic statement, Abraham Joshua Heschel wrote, "To observe the Sabbath is to celebrate the coronation of a day in the spiritual wonderland of time, the air of which we inhale when we 'call it a delight.'"[13] Just as Shabbat is the essence of the week, a Phish festival is the essence of that band's live music experience, reaching beyond other, "regular" shows. When Phish plays in your town on a Wednesday night, or even on the weekend, you can still go to work or run errands in the daytime before the show starts. The music is a momentary escape from the daily grind. And though there's always a possibility the band will discover new musical frontiers while improvising, there's still a predictable, familiar structure to the ceremony of a typical concert.

A Phish festival, on the other hand, creates an elevated space that defies expectations. More destination than escape, one must travel far from the familiar comforts of modern existence, leaving behind work and home to get to the festival. The words "Our intent is all for your delight" are often inscribed high above the hallowed gates of a Phish festival, and once you arrive, there's no way to predict what will happen.[14] The band has the time to let their art unfold organically—there's no venue curfew, nowhere else to go, nothing left to do. For fans, it's a chance to revel in the gift of existence, to be deeply in the moment, to dance and to delight.

"Sometime After Sunset"

There's a lot to do before one is ready to head to the parking lot outside of a Phish show, just as there are massive preparations of the body, mind, and home before lighting candles on Friday evening and the beginning of Shabbat.[15] At home or the campsite, one must cook, clean, arrange Shabbat-friendly lights and appliances, bathe, and take care of any number of tasks that otherwise can't be done on Shabbat. No matter how far down the list one gets, the sun eventually disappears behind the horizon and the mundane world is seen in a new light. At Phish, this pregnant instant arrives well after the official showtime listed on your ticket when the collective buzz reaches an unspoken peak and you'd better get in the security line near the venue's entrance or risk missing the opening notes. No more searching the scene for friendly faces, mind-altering substances, or fan-made crafts—it's time to go inside the venue and "get this show on the road."[16] Similarly, there is a precise minute of the day when one should kindle the holy flames to mark the beginning of Shabbat.[17]

On Shabbat, as well as at a Phish show, we mark the separation between the sacred and profane. When we light the Shabbat candles, just as when the lights go down for the show to begin, we enter into the extraordinary, a special moment in time.

Back at the campsite in Wisconsin, we chose to cross the threshold of Shabbat instead of the show. That choice was the culmination of years of my religious evolution. Every Phish show I attend is a spiritual laboratory. The communal gathering and collective listening, the space to dance and scene to dream, the intimate familiar comingling with transcendent unknown—it kindles an internal, alchemical process, clarifying what is true and foundational in my life.[18] As I look back on the eighteen years I've been following this band, I can easily trace my own path of Jewish observance, using notable improvisations, resonant lyrics, and consequential showgoing experiences as signposts along the way. For me, Phish shows and Shabbat practices are opportunities for renewal. Whether it's listening closely enough to hear the band stumble onto a novel musical phrase or reading intently enough to come to a new understanding of an ancient biblical story, Phish and Shabbat are about striving for growth—and noticing when you fall.

There was the time in the summer of 2014 when I convinced my sister and mother to attend a show in Charlotte, North Carolina. It took place on a Friday night. Getting to the venue was no problem. The sun still hasn't set when most summertime shows begin. So we grabbed our tickets and hopped on a shuttle to the amphitheater with plenty of daylight left to get from the parking lot to the lawn before the band walked onstage. Our hotel was too far from the venue to walk, so after the show ended, with much reluctance on my part, we boarded the return shuttle. The pit in my stomach on the way back to the hotel told me that, despite the fact that this ride was not arranged specifically for my benefit (it was a hotel service for all guests requiring no money that would come and go with or without me) and that the driver was probably not Jewish (and therefore not herself violating the rabbinic interpretation of combustion engines as violating the scriptural prohibition against kindling fires on Shabbat), I would not again go to a show on Shabbat to which I could not walk because I realized that my Shabbat observance was more important than going to a Phish show.

In July 2013, Dori and I traveled to the first five shows of Phish's summer tour but skipped a Friday-night performance on Long Island and detoured to Columbia, Maryland. We found a hotel near the Merriweather Post Pavilion, aiming to attend the shows there on Saturday and Sunday. The walk was two miles of sunbaked highway shoulder, but there was no eruv encircling the area of our hotel and the amphitheater, so we faced one of the primary issues confronting any observant Jew who hopes to attend a Friday-night show: the prohibition against carrying things on

Shabbat.[19] We had nothing with us—no phones, no money, and, critically, no tickets. Our pockets were empty and the road was clear, but given the heat and the walk, carrying was unavoidable. I must admit, I felt a little uneasy setting out with a water bottle in hand, but before reaching the edge of the hotel's property (the issue of carrying only comes into play when transferring objects between private and public domains), all apprehension had already left my body as sweat. This was a matter of *pikuach nefesh*, or "preservation of life," a supreme value that always supersedes the laws of Shabbat. Arriving on the lot in such brutal heat, we had little time to recuperate in the less-than-cool shade. The show was sold out, and we needed two miracles.[20] Other fans were holding $100 bills in the air with no luck, but we didn't have any money to offer.

We were thrilled when, after an hour of walking around with fingers in the air, we heard, "Hey, are you looking for a ticket?"

As we're walking to the gentleman's car, my then fiancée said, "Do you know anything about the Jewish faith—"

He cut her off: "Yeah, of course. I saw the *hamsa* on your necklace."[21]

"Well, the thing is," she continued, "we keep Shabbat and so we don't have any money so we can't pay you for a ticket."

"Oh, it's cool," the mensch said. "I was just going to give you the ticket anyway."

One ticket down. We set out to find its pair. Several hours passed with no success. "Showtime" had long since passed and we heard the collective fever pitch indicating that the first set loomed. Just as I told my fiancée where to meet me after the show—a certain patch of venue fence where I have resolved to dance alone to muffled jams—a man approached asking if we needed a ticket. "Yes!" I said. "But do you happen to know anything about the Jewish faith?" The guy stares back like he's got a blank space where his mind should be. "Well, so, today is our Sabbath and part of observing the Sabbath is not using money, so I don't have anything to give you, but I could try to remember your name. Come back tomorrow and I'll find you."

"Let me go to talk to my girlfriend about this," he said with a skeptical look. "Wait right here."

After a few breathless minutes the guy returned and said, "Here, take it. It's yours. Don't worry about paying."[22]

Needless to say, the two-mile walk back to our hotel that night passed like a glorious breeze. But on Shabbat, even walking a few steps with a ticket stub in your hand is fraught with implications in Jewish law.

On Shabbat one week prior to the show at Merriweather, we were in Saratoga Springs, New York, for the shows at the Saratoga Performing Arts Center. Dozens of friends and acquaintances from around the country (and even a few from Israel) set up tents at Lee's Campground, a few miles from the venue. We planned to attend all three of the shows that weekend, but others were content and committed to spending Shabbat at the campsite. They would join us at the amphitheater for Sunday's festivities. One of the people in our group, Mendel Karp from the Chabad Hasidic community in Crown Heights, Brooklyn, said, "I had no intention of going on *motzai shabbas* [Saturday night after Shabbat]. I was camping at Lee's and walked over to the gate because I was bored (hour-plus walk). While I'm standing there, I'm miracled a ticket, and I realize I can't move because there is no eruv. I stood there staring at the ticket for an hour unable to walk anywhere [because it was still Shabbat]."[23]

When an observant Jew discards the typical conundrums associated with going to a show on Shabbat—no money for beer, no lighters for joints, no phones for communication, no cameras for documentation—the only significant issue is what to do with your ticket. You have to carry the thing. At most shows, you would need to ask a non-Jewish friend prior to Shabbat to hold the ticket for you. But in certain circumstances, walking while holding a ticket on Shabbat isn't problematic. Some consider the island of Manhattan to be a distinct enough domain to constitute an eruv, which makes attending a show on Shabbat at Madison Square Garden a possibility for many. Better still, the venue could be adjoined to a campground, all of which is surrounded by a fence, like at the Gorge Amphitheatre in Washington State.

A festival is an ideal setting for seeing Phish on Shabbat. The concert and the campgrounds are located in one contiguous area. Large groups of friends can gather and set tents up near one another, forming a kind of pop-up community, which enables the sharing of food and groove alike. A number of grassroots religiously oriented Jewish organizations have, over the years, traveled to Phish's official festivals to hold sacred space. I first met people from JamShalom (formerly PHIShalom) at Lee's Campground. Some had traveled significant distances to attend these shows and to create a Shabbat-friendly, judgment-free space featuring ample kosher food and wine along with words of Torah and endless banter. This was a practice inspired by the group's founder, Rabbi Shu Eliovson, who regularly hosts large and diverse groups of Jewish fans at his house in the Negev for Shabbat. At Phish festivals, fans might also seek out the Shabbat Tent, an organization now led by Rabbi Yonah Bookstein, which grew out of the "holiest of holy music moments" that was Big Cypress (see fig. 8.1).[24]

"There's nothing like davening Kabbalat Shabbat and that night or the next day or the next night being able to see Phish," Adam Weinberg, a Shabbat Tent founder, told me before Super Ball IX in 2011.[25] Some who join in Friday-night prayers at the Shabbat Tent walk over to the stage afterward to hear Phish's set. Others wait to formally join the audience until three stars are visible in the sky the next day, which, according to the Talmudic rabbis, is the official endpoint of Shabbat.

Rav Shmuel and the Gefilte Phish crew joined the scene in the late 1990s. On a Friday evening in 2004, the Gefilte Phish RV got stuck in the legendary traffic that stretched twenty miles from the site of Phish's festival in a rain-soaked mud field in Coventry, Vermont.[26] With the sun setting, the halacha-bound drivers got out, gave the keys to a stranger, and walked to the festival grounds as Shabbat settled in. The RV was found Saturday morning in the festival's parking lot with a guest book signed by the righteous non-Jewish shepherds who guided the holy wagon to its destination. One of the ex-drivers explained how they'd convinced the rotating cast of chauffeurs to drive the rest of the way: "We told them they could have all the fried chicken and marijuana they wanted."[27]

Another fan at the festival in Coventry, Ben Dreyfus, davened Kabbalat Shabbat on Friday night with friends, ate dinner, got a heavy dose of Shabbat rest, and then joined Rav Shmuel and the Gefilte Phish team for a kosher communal meal the following day. Dreyfus contrasted this experience of connection and spiritual camaraderie with his Shabbat-honoring attempt at the previous year's IT festival in Limestone, Maine.[28] He recounts being stuck in traffic on the road to the festival grounds as the sun set on Friday. Though he had no qualms about driving on the day of rest, he wanted to honor the Sabbath nonetheless. While the other people in the car happened to be Jewish, Dreyfus was the only one determined to ritually honor Shabbat, so he planned to celebrate with any like-minded Jews he could find at his campsite. Around midnight, however, the car was at a standstill. Conceding that he wouldn't make it into the festival anytime soon, Dreyfus opened a bottle of grape juice and made hamotzi, the blessing over challah—and then, finally, the cars began moving. "God appreciates the gesture," one of his car-mates commented.

Me Enjoy Yourself?

Major sages of the Talmud, including Rav and Rava, prohibit Jews from playing and hearing music following the destruction of the ancient Temple in Jerusalem. One Talmudic rabbi even claims that listening to song is a form of spiritual self-harm.[29] Such an outright ban on music could not endure. Maimonides, a significant medieval authority known as "the Rambam," who claims music should not be played at all after the Temple's downfall, nevertheless permits music as a cure for depression.[30] And, writing in the 1500s, Joseph Karo, the noted Jewish legal authority, acknowledges that music is permissible for the sake of a mitzvah.[31]

FIG. 10.1 A remix of the traditional page layout for the Talmud by Josh Fleet (@PhishTalmud) featuring lyrics to "Run Like an Antelope" and commentary from Jewish sources related to different concepts in the song.

When the Temple was destroyed in 70 CE, altar-based worship disappeared. In its place, the sages codified the liturgy and set times for daily prayer. They tried to institute silence in place of song, but that didn't stick. Today, music is an essential element of Jewish cultural and religious life that transcends denomination and observance levels. In reality, it has always been this way. In the Jerusalem Temple, the music of the Levites accompanied all offerings on the altar, whether land animal, bird, grain, wine, or water. Live instrumental music was an integral component of Jewish worship in the Temple era; Shabbat, too, had a soundtrack.[32] The Levites sang a special song for the day, and we in turn find this text repeated three times in the traditional liturgy invoked on Shabbat.

While liberal Jewish denominations, such as the Reform, Renewal, and Reconstructionist movements, generally embrace instrumental and sometimes electrified music as a potent communal worship tool on Shabbat, you won't find a guitar in an Orthodox synagogue on Friday night. Setting aside the issues of amplification and repair, or tuning a string, all of which are problematic in the rabbinic tradition, there's even a concern about simply listening to and appreciating music played by a Jewish person on the Sabbath. Talmudic authorities explain that *hana'ah*, translated as "benefit" or "enjoyment," can only legally be derived from something tangible.[33] Music seems to be an exception—song certainly isn't a physical phenomenon—and there may be room to say it is not prohibited to receive *hana'ah* from the "scents and subtle sounds" of a Phish show on Shabbat.[34]

Despite this legal ambiguity, I have consistently heard Shabbat-conscious fans raise the issue of benefiting from the sound of music as a reason to not attend Phish shows on Shabbat. There are at least two sides to this fillet. When you buy a ticket for a Phish concert that falls on Friday or Saturday, the band members benefit. You are paying them to play music on Shabbat. Looking at it from another angle, Mike Gordon and Jon Fishman, the two Jewish members of Phish, do not actively keep Shabbat, and whether you buy a ticket doesn't really determine whether they will play the gig. Thousands of others will go to the concert regardless, and the show will happen without you. So, the benefit they receive from your one ticket is essentially nullified in relation to the total proceeds the band receives from all the tickets, merch, and concessions combined.[35]

But what about the enjoyment, the *hana'ah*, you receive from the band's Jewish bassist and drummer? I'm not sure there's any single approach that will release the tension of this concern, but this is something I've tried: When seeing Phish on a weekday, focus on Mike's bass playing or listen for Fishman's contribution to the group improvisation; then, at a show on Shabbat, try instead to listen only to how Trey plays or filter out Page's effects from the rest. This way, the *hana'ah* is from a person who is not Jewish—someone who is not subject to the laws of Shabbat as traditionally understood.

As I get deeper into both Phish and Jewish observance, it makes less sense for me to go to a show on Shabbat, the ideal circumstances becoming increasingly rare. Chasing shade, evading mosquitoes, and eating out of a cooler at our Wisconsin campground in the summer of 2019 while our neighbors let loose at two shows down the road without us, it was at times difficult to remember why we chose Shabbat over Phish. But not being in the pit on Shabbat meant I had no pit in my stomach, no sense of doubt, no need to rationalize or self-justify. The delight of the ideal Shabbat experience, which is mirrored at the best of Phish concerts, is one where there's no need to be or do anything else other than exist in the moment. "Happiness is how rooted in the now," sing Phish in "Everything's Right," and their words reinforce my decision to prioritize Shabbat.[36]

Each fan must walk their unique path. Observing Shabbat at a Phish concert has the potential to facilitate a state of spiritual equanimity. But the balance is delicate.

In the face of halachic uncertainty, the "beautiful buzz" can suddenly turn into a spiritual hangover.[37] In Wisconsin in the summer of 2019, despite the heat and the pronounced feeling of missing out, not going to the Phish show on Shabbat meant I could truly delight in the day.

On Sunday, we brought our one-and-a-half-year-old to his first show. At the top of the vast lawn early in the first set, he noticed a cluster of balloons bouncing around to the groove. He *really* wanted those balloons. And sure enough, as they bopped and floated and eventually landed at his feet, the notes of "The Man Who Stepped into Yesterday," a rarely played song from Trey Anastasio's senior thesis, fluttered our way, and then the band played "Avenu Malkenu," a funk rendition of the melody and prayer heard around the world every year during Rosh Hashanah and Yom Kippur services. Originally a spontaneous supplication for rain in a time of drought, this prayer was composed by first-century sage Rabbi Akiva not long after the ancient Temple's destruction.[38] Nearly two thousand years later, how do we give thanks for the blessing of such a song falling from the sky? By offering ourselves, limb by limb, on the altar in dance.

NOTES

1. The title of this chapter contains lyrics from Josh White, "Timber (Jerry the Mule)," track 5 on *Josh at Midnight* (Elektra, 1956). Cowritten with Sam Gray in the 1930s, Phish has performed this song nearly one hundred times since 1987.

2. Phish, "Roggae," track 11 on *The Story of the Ghost* (Elektra, 1998).

3. I think the sages would recognize truth in Phish's verse "Fences are filters that purify our souls" from the song "Light," track 7 on *Joy* (JEMP, 2009).

4. See Mishnah, Beitzah 5:2.

5. On September 30, 2000, Trey Anastasio announced during Phish's show in Las Vegas that the band would soon embark on an indefinite hiatus. This break ended unofficially less than two years later when an animated version of the band performed on an episode of *The Simpsons* ("Weekend at Burnsie's," episode 285, April 7, 2002), followed by an announcement a few months later that they would play live on New Year's Eve at Madison Square Garden.

6. See Rabbi Simlai's teaching at the end of Babylonian Talmud, Makkot 23b.

7. These orientations are derived from the two times the Torah mentions the Ten Commandments, Exod. 20:8–17 and Num. 5:12–15.

8. Broadly speaking, Conservative Jews value the Jewish legal tradition while believing it can and should adapt to the shifting dynamics of modern society and the needs of its communities. Levels of observance vary by communities and households.

9. Translated as "the way," *halacha* is the Hebrew term for Jewish law derived from the Bible and interpreted and adapted through the ages by rabbinical authorities of the Talmudic era until today. See Pew Research Center, "Portrait of Jewish Americans."

10. Clifton Chenier, "My Soul," track 2 on *Bajou Drive* (Checker, 1959).

11. See Babylonian Talmud, Rosh Hashanah 31a.

12. Isa. 58:13.

13. See Heschel, *Sabbath*, 8. Heschel's description of time and Shabbat are cited in an unofficial Phish documentary from 1999 by an unnamed scholar-fan, who implies that Phish creates the same spiritual conditions at their shows. See thirty-two minutes into the film *Circus of Light*, directed by E. R. Silverbush.

14. Based on a line from Shakespeare's *A Midsummer Night's Dream*, this statement of intent has welcomed fans at two Phish festivals—the IT festival in Limestone, Maine, in August 2003 and in August 2015 at the Magnaball festival in Watkins Glen, New York—as well as at the destination vacation Phish shows at a resort in Cancun, Mexico, in February 2020.

15. Trey Anastasio, "Sometime After Sunset," track 1 on *Paper Wheels* (Rubber Jungle, 2015).

16. Phish, "AC/DC Bag," track 4 on *The White Tape* (self-released, 1984).

17. This time is based on your precise location on earth and changes weekly.

18. Phish, "Rift," track 1 on *Rift* (Elektra, 1993).

19. One of the Melakhot prohibited on Shabbat is the simple act of carrying an object. A distinction is made between carrying in a private domain (like in a house) and in a public domain (like on the sidewalk). Carrying inside a building is permitted, but one is not allowed to carry something outside on the street. An *eruv* (literally meaning "mixtures") is a conceptual and physical boundary that joins together many small private domains into a larger collective area within which carrying is allowed. In simplest terms, imagine a complete fence—an unbroken chain, if you will—surrounding all the disparate campsites and stages at a large music festival. Without it, a Shabbat-keeping festivalgoer would not be able to leave their tent while holding anything. Carrying a ticket, therefore, is problematic.

20. A "miracle" is a free ticket given as a surprise gift or act of charity from one fan to another. The term is a holdover from the Grateful Dead's fan culture.

21. A hand-shaped amulet with shared significance for Muslims and Jews.

22. Use of money is not explicitly included in the thirty-nine categories of prohibited work. However, its association with business and the fact that monetary transactions may involve writing or require carrying means that having to pay for something on Shabbat is a no-go according to interpreters of Jewish law.

23. Mendel Karp, Facebook Messenger message to the author, May 27, 2020.

24. Gensler, "Coachella or Passover?"

25. Fleet, "Shabbat Tent at Phish."

26. The festival was billed as Phish's last performance. See Rosen, "Phish, the Shas, and God."

27. Dreyfus, "Look Back on Those Days When My Life Was a Haze."

28. See Dreyfus, "Cars Trucks Buses."

29. See Babylonian Talmud, Sotah 47a. Rav is Abba Arikha (175–247 CE), a first-generation amora ("one who says")—that is, an early expounder of the codified Oral Law found today in the Talmud—who founded a center of Torah study in Sura, Babylonia, that endured for nearly eight hundred years. Rava is Abba ben Joseph bar Ḥama (ca. 280–352 CE), a fourth-generation amora, who lived in Babylonia and, along with his study partner Abaye, is one of the most commonly cited sages in the Talmud.

30. See Mishneh Torah, Laws of Fasts 5:14, as well as Eight Chapters 5:2, where he says, "One who suffers from melancholia may rid himself of it by listening to singing and all kinds of instrumental music, by strolling through beautiful gardens and splendid buildings, by gazing upon beautiful pictures, and other things that enliven the mind, and dissipate gloomy moods. The purpose of all this is to restore the healthful condition of

the body, but the real object in maintaining the body in good health is to acquire wisdom."

31. Shulchan Aruch, Orach Chayim, Siman 560:3.

32. See Tucker, "Musical Instruments."

33. Babylonian Talmud, Pesachim 26a, explains, "Didn't Rabbi Shimon ben Pazi say [that] Rabbi Yehoshua ben Levi said in the name of Bar Kappara: The sound [of the musical instruments in the Temple, and] the sight and smell [of the incense] are not subject to [the prohibition of] misuse of consecrated property?" Translation is drawn from the Sefaria digital library.

34. Phish, "Scents and Subtle Sounds," track 11 on *Undermind* (Elektra, 2004).

35. Ways to avoid this altogether are to get a miracle, to buy a friend's extra, or to utilize the virtuous secondhand CashorTrade online community.

36. Phish, "Everything's Right," track 3 on *Sigma Oasis* (JEMP, 2020).

37. The Rolling Stones, "Loving Cup," track 9 on *Exile on Main St.* (Rolling Stones, 1972). Phish has covered this song more than 130 times since the early 1990s.

38. See Babylonian Talmud, Ta'anit 25b.

REFERENCES

Dreyfus, Ben. "Cars Trucks Buses." *Mah Rabu* (blog), June 12, 2006. http://mahrabu.blogspot.com/2006/06/cars-trucks-buses.html.

———. "Look Back on Those Days When My Life Was a Haze." *Mah Rabu* (blog), December 26, 2006. http://mahrabu.blogspot.com/2006/12/look-back-on-those-days-when-my-life.html.

Fleet, Josh. "A Shabbat Tent at Phish." *Jewish Week*, June 29, 2011. https://web.archive.org/web/20110703061453/http://www.thejewishweek.com/arts/shabbat_tent_phish_concert.

Gensler, Andy. "Coachella or Passover? Matzahchella Lets You Do Both." *Billboard*, April 22, 2016. https://www.billboard.com/articles/news/7341567/coachella-passover-matzahchella-seder.

Heschel, Abraham Joshua. *The Sabbath: Its Meaning for Modern Man*. Boston: Shambhala, 2003.

Pew Research Center. "A Portrait of Jewish Americans." October 1, 2013. https://www.pewforum.org/2013/10/01/jewish-american-beliefs-attitudes-culture-survey.

Rosen, Armin. "Phish, the Shas, and God." *Tablet*, January 14, 2020. https://www.tabletmag.com/sections/news/articles/phish-the-shas-and-god.

Silverbush, E. R., dir. *Circus of Light*. 1999; 40 Years and a Desert Productions. YouTube video, June 22, 2017, 1:04:11. https://youtu.be/VKImxu2JzZo.

Tucker, Ethan. "Musical Instruments on Shabbat and Yom Tov." Mechon Hadar. https://www.hadar.org/torah-resource/musical-instruments-shabbat-and-yom-tov.

11

Phish Jews

IMPROVISATION AS RELIGIOUS ORIENTATION

Joshua S. Ladon

In the fall of 2003, I moved to Jerusalem to study in yeshiva, having just finished university. When I arrived for the opening night barbeque at the small postcollege program, I didn't know anyone, so I sat down next to the guy wearing a Phish shirt and we began to trade stories. Both of us had grown up involved in the Jewish community. We both attended Jewish day school and overnight summer camp and traveled to Israel on organized trips. Both of us thought that we might want to become rabbis one day, and both of us liked the band Phish. Frankly, I was unsurprised to meet someone else who liked Phish in this deeply Jewish setting.

Phish and Judaism have been two of the most constant features of my life. It was at Jewish summer camp that I was introduced to Phish and went to my first show. When my family moved across the country the summer before I began high school, it was a fellow Phish fan who invited me to a Temple youth group event, a social experience that would come to define my high school years. While Phish and Judaism had often acted as social connectors for me, it was only in Jerusalem that I started to develop a mature vocabulary to describe my own spiritual journey and reflect on the ways that my experience with Phish shaped my yearning for a deeper, more consistent encounter with Jewish tradition and observance. While Phish was perhaps not the primary agent guiding my spiritual progression, Phish provided (and continues to provide) unique outlets for spiritual growth, facilitated both by the band's rich and layered music and the surrounding fan culture, tradition, and lore.

I am far from the only religious Jew who finds Phish integral to their spiritual maturation. *The Newish Jewish Encyclopedia: From Abraham to Zabar's and Everything in Between*, a brash and flippant introduction to Jewish concepts, starts the authors' definition for *ba'al teshuva*, or a Jew who becomes newly religious, with the line "The proper term for your friend who was super into Phish in college and now sports a long beard and a black hat."[1] This tongue-in-cheek definition picks up on something quite profound: the Phish community includes fans who find Phish concerts and all that surrounds them as potential sites for Jewish spirituality and even spiritual progression.

How, if at all, do other self-identified religious Jewish Phish fans reflect on the role of Phish in their spirituality? To find out, I designed an informal survey addressing questions of spirituality and Phish fandom and then shared it widely online.[2] As expected, many religiously active Jewish Phish fans find opportunities for spiritual growth at Phish; those opportunities most frequently occur during what I call "connective encounters." These moments of transformative experience brought on by an encounter with Phish's music and/or the scene surrounding it typically assume three forms: mystical encounters with the Divine, reflective encounters with oneself, and radical connection with other humans.

Phish, as the paradigmatic jam band of the late twentieth and early twenty-first centuries, creates, for some Jews, an arena for encountering and expressing Jewish spirituality. For many of these Jews, experiences of connection—or "connective encounters"—at shows have led to the adoption of a religious orientation of improvisation.[3] This religious orientation prizes the flexibility, responsiveness, and possibility of improvisation and sees such elements as offering much to personal practice and communal worship. For that reason, some religious Jewish Phish fans in leadership positions draw on Phish's improvisational playing and their experience of that improvisation when they articulate a vision for their spiritual communities, especially as it relates to communal prayer. These connective encounters may resonate with the experiences of the broader community of Phishheads. Nonetheless, that some religious Jews find religious meaning in their involvement with Phish and that some bring that meaning to their Jewish communities broadens our understanding of modern Judaism and religious practice in the twenty-first century.[4]

Jewish Phishheads, Religious Phans, and Phish Jews

While many Jews like the band Phish, this chapter is not about all Jewish "Phish-heads."[5] Instead I focus here on Jews who have rich identities as religious Jews and who find in Phish something concomitant with their spiritual lives. These Jews, a number of whom are in positions of Jewish communal leadership, are rabbis and lay leaders who draw on their Phish experiences as they design religious worship for others. These Phish fans are self-identified, religiously active Jews who find spiritual relevance through their participation in the Phish subculture. I refer to them as "Phish Jews." These Jews are different from religious Jewish "Phishheads," observant Jews who like the band but do not ascribe any spiritual significance to their experiences with Phish.

"Phish Jews" are part of what might be called "normative" synagogue-centered religious Jewish communities and active participants in Phish subculture. Their experiences with Phish have led them to a deeper interest in Judaism, and further, many see these experiences as mutually constitutive. As Ben, a Reform rabbi, explained, "Most of the people I seriously discuss my Judaism with also listen to Phish, and many defining conversations have taken place on the way to shows, at shows, or with recordings in the background." An investigation of Phish Jews and their experience of seeing the band live offers insight into how religious Jews integrate spiritual experiences from outside the tradition. Additionally, given the robust spiritual vocabulary of Phish Jews, such a study might provide a window into the spiritual experience engagement with Phish and jam-band music can offer any listener. While my focus is on Phish Jews, many of the experiences described in this chapter are not exclusive to this community. Reflection on their experiences, however, can help illuminate how lived religion functions in a concert setting and how Jewish practice can integrate spiritual experiences from its broader cultural context.

David, a Modern Orthodox Jew in his forties who grew up in a Conservative home, offers a snapshot of a Phish Jew's experience. He tells the story of his attempt, at age seventeen, to convince his father to allow him to see Phish's four-show New Year's Eve run at Madison Square Garden in New York City. His father could not understand why he wanted to see a band four nights in a row. The ensuing debate, he recalls, "involved . . . comparisons to learning a *sefer* [holy book] or listening to a Rabbi's *drasha* [homily] multiple times looking for new meaning and inspiration." The pair began to study Torah together, leading to a conversation about "the power of improvisational music and how it was similar to the early Hasidim and their desire to use more personal or improvisational prayer for more intense connections." David compares Phish's improvisational style, commitment to deep practice, and willingness to try new things to the dawning of the eighteenth-century Hasidic movement, which aspired to breathe life into rote forms of Judaism, not by rejecting Jewish observance but by finding ways to infuse it with meaning and purpose. Eventually, his father relented and "encouraged" him to attend the shows.

For David, the conversation became paradigmatic of the way Phish and Judaism took on a mutually supportive symbiotic relationship throughout his studies and his continued fandom. Coincidentally, when he found his way to a yeshiva in Jerusalem in his early twenties, the rabbi he connected with had spent time touring with Phish. One summer, when he himself toured with Phish, he helped create an avenue for religious Phishheads to keep Shabbat. He went on to share that a "deep connection to Phish's music and interest and practice with Judaism went hand in hand for a long time. These two things helped me transcend who I am by providing similar avenues towards holiness in this world." For him, Judaism and Phish both offered formative spiritual experiences that were mutually constitutive. David's story is just one account of many Phish Jews who integrate two cultures rich with tradition, lore, and spirituality, one ancient and the other decidedly modern. And many Phish Jews point to the band's extended jams and experiences of connectivity and oneness encountered during them as deeply impactful in their spiritual lives. These musical moments of experimentation lead many Phish Jews to a sustained religious orientation of improvisation. But ritual and order are necessary to facilitate these instances.

The Ritual Foundations of Improvisation

These connective encounters, these instances that are instructive and valuable for so many Phish Jews, are born out of the consistencies of the ritual practices—the range of activities, behaviors, and norms—of the Phish fan experience. From the intense planning required even before Phish tickets go on sale to the less than orderly entry into a venue, and through the concert itself as fans listen for the expected first set, second set, and encore, Phish fans engage in ritual behavior. Phish Jews join other fans in Phish-bound ritual, whether they are writing down set lists in notebooks, searching out a preferred location in a venue, or wearing a favorite show outfit. These familiar and orderly rituals associated with Phish fandom create an environment that Adam Seligman, Robert Weller, Michael Puett, and Bennet Simon would call a subjunctive world of "as if." In ritual, they note, "getting it *right* is not a matter of making outer acts conform to inner beliefs. Getting it right is doing it again and again and again—it is an act of world construction."[6] When Phish fans engage in these shared acts, they express their commitments to the Phish community and they ready themselves for the newness of each show, a novelty that keeps them coming back for more.

It is precisely in the repetition, of going through the motions of the show, of the known music heard anew, that participants simultaneously replay past experiences and project possible futures. Seligman et alia observe that "repetition circumscribes the future in and by the past. It limits an otherwise infinite and uncontrolled set of all possible future events within the frame of a known, specific, particular and felt (past) experience. . . . It creates community and union by replicating precisely delineated actions, words, and gestures."[7] They go on to note that repetitive involvement in the defined and controlled elements of Phish create community. As a fan learns the flow of the show experience, they become an insider. And perhaps that fan, too, prepares for the sometimes-intense improvisational journey enabled by the predictability of the show's rituals.

Because Phish has performed for nearly four decades without repeating a set, their shows always promise something new. Consequently, every show is an event not to be missed. The element of surprise presented by a Phish show is always embedded in a network of familiar practices and rituals. This balance of the "unpredictable and familiar" draws the audience into a partnership with the band, one rife with excitement and possibility.[8] Upon hearing the first note or two of a song, the crowd erupts with excitement and approval.

Attendees at Phish shows, like regular synagoguegoers, know the rich repertoire of signals and signs the band uses to telegraph to attendees what will happen next. They know the unspoken rules for participation. So too for some Phish Jews, the moments of spiritual connection emerge from these more mundane practices. Phish can serve as a model. Yehezkel, who is both liberal and Charedi (ultra-Orthodox), remarks, "The same way the music is so tight and so well coordinated, I want to find balance and harmony in my life of observance, study, *avodah* [worship], *shmiras habris* [channeling male sexuality], and of course *simcha* [joy] and *dveykus* [clinging to God]." For Yehezkel, Phish's music presents an aspirational balance between order and play, between idealized ritual performance and the realities of living a life of observance. For many other Phish Jews, the balance of order and free expression at Phish shows offers opportunity for intense religious experience. Jamie, a Reform Jewish educator, shares, "The experience of a Phish show allows for the combination of fixed practice and improvisational intention that creates the kind of spiritual expression and release I look for. The Phish community offers me both a subset within the larger Jewish community, as well as something beyond its traditional institutions and boundaries."

Ariel similarly ties the notion of improvisation specifically to prayer and the need to navigate fixed liturgy with an eye toward spontaneity. Ariel, who grew up in a Yeshivish Orthodox home and now identifies as "just Jewish," reflects, "Phish taught me to prize improv as a necessary element of authentic devotion. . . . Phenomenologically, my liturgical prayer experiences and [my] experiences listening and dancing to Phish share structural components. Both are woven around structure (liturgy/song structure) but from there anything might happen." For Ariel, the order of the band's shows creates a sense of familiarity and attests to a ritual regularity. A range of possibilities emerge from there.

For Jamie, Yehezkel, Ariel, and many more, the repetition of the rituals of Phish in conjunction with the newness of each concert experience leads to a professed religious orientation of improvisation wherein innovation serves as a model for modern religiosity. The consistent order of a Phish show mirrors that of a prayer service, and yet Phish's creativity and inventiveness offers something radically different than many traditional synagogue services. That improvisation fosters spiritual growth both during Phish shows and when what is learned at Phish is introduced to the ritual and order of synagogue communities. Phish offers access to ecstatic release on a scale unparalleled in Jewish institutional life. And during these moments of ecstasy, brought about by extended jams, participants are invited into a revelatory experience that, for Phish Jews and others, can lead to a religious orientation of improvisation.

Perhaps Phish Jews easily integrate lessons learned from Phish's exploratory jams and improvisational approach because improvisation has roots in the Jewish literary genre of midrash, a form of commentary that explicates a verse of scripture and often interrogates breaks in text or linguistic anomaly. The midrashic condition begs playfulness and sees tradition as something to build with, appropriate, and make one's own.[9] Kabbalah scholar Melila Hellner-Eshed explains that both improvisation and midrash "require the total presence and profound mutual attunement of the participants. Yet, above all else, what is required is something less tangible: neither the musician nor the instrument nor even the melody, but rather the tension and play among the players, the eros of the improvisation."[10] Hellner-Eshed uses the metaphor of improvisational jazz to describe her analytical lens of Zoharic midrash, the mystical text at the center of Kabbalah, going so far as to insert a break, or "jazz interlude," in her book.[11] As Hellner-Eshed notes, great midrash is attentive to detail and adheres to structures while creatively building on them. The same certainly can be said of Phish's approach to improvisation. The fact that the band executes improvisational musicianship at the highest level creates a model to be pursued. While this offers an intellectual ideal, it is through ongoing engagement with Phish performances that Phish Jews adopt an improvisational attitude.

The Jam and Connection

To attend a Phish show is to bear witness to the coordinated efforts of master musicians and their lighting artist.[12] But, according to the band (and to many fans), the audience plays a significant role, too. Guitarist Trey Anastasio describes the act of live performance as one of communication with bandmates and the audience: "The music exists in the universe and if you're lucky enough, or strong enough to get your ego out of the way, the music comes through you. The audience that we have is open to that. They understand that conversational transfer of energy."[13] For him, the audience's presence facilitates musical flow. Anastasio sees this as a spiritual experience of oneness. Describing a particular performance of "Tweezer," he recalled:

> It occurred to me that the conscious thinking minds of everybody in this room, as individuals, had momentarily vanished. And whoever was in line for the bathroom or getting a beer was equally affecting the vibration of this jam. No one's leading or following—it's this unified moment. Then, I thought . . . "Everyone is affecting the twists and turns of this jam." . . . In that sense, it's the physical embodiment of what I consider to be spirituality, which is that we're all connected. We are absolutely intertwined. I'm not a molecule floating freely around the universe. I'm part of a collective consciousness, like a ray of light from the sun.[14]

Anastasio uses Durkheimian language of collective consciousness to explain the feeling of connectivity and flow during a particularly powerful jam.[15] During the jam, he experiences a moment of alignment between the musicians, the lights, the receptivity of the audience, and the environment, in which all the parts are greater than the whole.

Many Phish Jews echo Trey's description of collective consciousness when describing their connective encounters with other human beings, moments brought on by an interaction with Phish's music that foster a sense of oneness with other people. Saul, for example, who identifies as a Neo-Hasidic rabbi, describes "feeling at one with twenty-five thousand people." And Yael, a Conservative Jew in her thirties, explains, "A long jam can fill my heart the same way a powerful *niggun* [traditional melody without words] can." She goes on to compare this feeling to visiting an unfamiliar synagogue and to hearing a piece of liturgy sung in a beautiful, harmonious way. It is both new and old: "That feeling like your heart will overflow from love and connection to the past and future. Many Phish shows have given me that same feeling." It is in getting lost in the music that Yael found love and a connection to Jewish people across time. Of course, Phish Jews are not the only fans to experience this sense of collectivity and oneness when listening to and, according to Anastasio, participating in Phish's improvisational jams. Nonetheless, Phish Jews find the occurrence both spiritually significant and transformative.

The Jam and Self-Reflection

While some Phish Jews recount connective encounters of oneness with others fostered by the band's improvisational style, others find in that innovative playing the space for reflective encounters with the self. Such connective encounters often seed deep self-knowledge. Jack, a Reform Jew, reflects on the impact of Phish's music on his spiritual path. He notes, "Improv encompasses so many parts of life—connecting with / listening to and reacting to others, tapping into and getting lost in a moment, making mistakes, learning about yourself, learning about others, going to dark and light places, et cetera. All of which, for me, tap into a higher appreciation, understanding, and exploration of my own spirituality." Like Jack, Yoav, who grew up Reform and now identifies as Neo-Hasidic, ties Phish's approach to his own religious attitude: "Phish always toes the line of sacred and profane, secular and religious, silly and serious. The 'Yes-And' approach of improvisational mastery. It's how I hope to live a life of authenticity and curiosity and growth," he notes. While Phish Jews describe their experiences of Phish in a variety of ways, many claim that their experiences at Phish lead to moments of self-reflection. These moments of self-reflection, in turn, impart an open and flexible religious orientation and lead to the adoption of improvisation as an orienting value in religious practice.

For Michael, a rabbi in his forties, "Divided Sky," a long, composed epic with multiple movements and a long silent pause in the middle, offers an opportunity to reflect.[16] Because it is a song he knows well, it draws him into a personal accounting:

> "The Divided Sky" is my favorite Phish song, and they played it the first time I had gone by myself to a show. Having just celebrated my first son's first birthday just days before, I was reflecting on much of my life from the first time I heard and fell in love with the song around 1996 up to the present day. I thought about the heartbreaks and tough times I'd gone through and was going through the past sequentially. As I got to a part in my own reflection where I thought, at that time in my life, that I had arrived at a good place, but knowing that I in fact had not, it was just then that Trey messed up a crucial transitional part and key riff of the song. He was very funny and played it off by saying something like "I did that on purpose." At first, I was upset that he flubbed such an important couple of notes, but

then I laughed as I realized how perfectly it mirrored my reflective journey. He recovered and finished the song beautifully, which also felt very apropos of what I was feeling in that particular moment as well as that point in my life.

Seligman et alia observe that in repetitive ritual, "the self is left more 'room to wander' (perhaps also to wonder) than in one where the self has to be firmly identified with its role."[17] Michael's reflection is born out of his familiarity with "Divided Sky." Because he knows its form, he can allow himself to go places he otherwise would not. When guitarist Anastasio flubs a major transition, Michael is jolted. But he also finds comfort. Despite mistakes, one can recover. The proverbial show must go on. And it will. More shows will happen, the song will be repeated. It is exactly this opportunity—this coming back to the song—that gives it its power. The ritual of the Phish show, its planned atopy, and the material experience of long, melodic jams paired with stellar light shows (and for some, drug use) provides an opportunity for reflective wandering and wonder.

The Jam and Mystical Encounters

Some Phish Jews experience mystical encounters in these moments of wandering and wonder at Phish shows. Eliezer, an Orthodox rabbi, claims that these moments offer "prophetic experiences and spiritual clarity," and Dan, a Reform rabbi, shares that such moments during shows made him "more aware and conscious of [his] relationship with God." Brad, a Conservative rabbi, describes the moment as an encounter with the Divine influenced by the overpowering force of the music, the lights, and the use of mind-altering substances, which led, for him, to a "redefinition of beauty in the world." Through the encounter he was "able to transcend [his] body with a soulful experience." Eliezer, Dan, and Brad find the Divine in the Phish experience, in moments of revelatory encounter. They are moments shared with the Divine and spent in reflection of holiness.

Such connective encounters offer Phish Jews something that exits the arena and travels home with them, as do community-focused or inward-facing transformative moments. These three types of connective encounters—mystical encounters with the Divine, reflective encounters with oneself, and encounters of radical connection with other human beings—are not unique to the experience of Phish Jews. However, the fact that a community of self-identified religious Jews finds meaning in these experiences at Phish concerts offers insight into a facet of modern Jewish spirituality.

FIG. 11.1 Rabbi Yehoshua "Shu" Eliovson embraces Rabbi Moshe "Mickey" Sher while Rav Shmuel Skaist looks on after a set break minyan. Photo: Rachel Loonin Steinerman.

Phish in Religious Communities

Phish Jews draw on these connective encounters when imagining and fashioning their religious communities. Steven, a Conservative rabbi, describes a sacred energy at shows, something he has referenced "multiple times in sermons and [in describing his] approach to creating holy communal space." Some Phish Jews include a Phish tune when leading prayer services or reflect on Phish lyrics in sermon. But most focus on capturing and re-creating the improvisational spirit, energy, and intensity of community at Phish shows. Alex, a Reform Jew, writes, "As a *sheliach tzibbur* [service leader], my understanding of what communal prayer can be at its best is strongly influenced by my experiences with Phish: the way that the whole *kahal* [community] is fully engaged with the music (even if the four people at the front are "leading"), and the balance of *keva* (the fixed elements of each Phish song) and *kavanah* [intention] (the space for jamming). I'm only half joking when I say that I think High Holiday services would be better if everyone had glowsticks."

For Alex, the model of great prayer services is informed by his encounters with Phish. Yehezkel offered a similar reflection, connecting Phish to the recently developed Hasidic custom of celebrating Rosh Hashanah in the Ukrainian city of Uman.[18] He explains, "Phish set a high standard that I now long for during davening. Rosh Hashanah in Uman is meant to be a derivative of my earlier experiences worshiping the idea of mindfulness and respecting unity and song. Obviously, I am way past that stage of life but it opened me up past services that were dry and rote and empty." For Yehezkel, Phish is his reference point for highly engaged prayer services. This type of comparison was echoed by several clergy. Avi, a Reform rabbi, explains that the power of Phish's music and the community it engenders has led him to try "to replicate them at the synagogue to the extent possible." These rabbis see their Phish experiences as inspiration for molding their ideal prayer communities.

Phish shows replicate elements of great prayer experiences and offer moments of connection—with community, with the Divine, and with the self. In those moments of connectedness, brought about by the ritual of the show, Phish Jews find space to wonder, reflect, and encounter. These moments become models that some Phish Jews aspire to re-create in their own communities.

Conclusion

The study of Phish Jews locates Jewish religious practice in a new setting. Phish Jews, who share a language rooted in the rituals and behaviors of Judaism, find deep parallels between their Jewish ritual lives and their Phish lives. Phish Jews use the language of Judaism to articulate their Phish experiences, and their Phish experiences shape their Jewish experiences and sometimes prayer communities. For some, the study of self-identified religious Jews and their involvement with the band Phish reeks of gimmick. Such scholarship may appear a glorification of the hedonistic pursuits of upper-middle-class Jews of privilege. But the music, the culture of touring, the altered states (some drug induced), are a version of the many rejections of the staid, dry, suburban intellectualism of late twentieth-century Judaism.[19] It should be no surprise that Phish Jews find in Phish spiritual experiences that supplement their existing schema and, for some, offer a model for Jewish institutional and communal practice. Phish Jews offer a model for understanding twenty-first-century religious integration in a globalized world. Through the rituals of fandom, the larger Phish community sets the stage for improvisation and the transformative experiences that accompany it. Phish Jews find great meaning in Phish's improvisational jams and the connective encounters brought about by the band's creativity. Indeed, Phish's jam-filled playing has encouraged many Phish Jews to adopt a religious orientation of improvisation defined by a deep comfort with possibility, flexibility, and imagination.

NOTES

1. Butnick, Leibovitz, and Oppenheimer, *New Jewish Encyclopedia*, 24.

2. This chapter is based on this mixed quantitative/qualitative survey, which

allowed participants to self-identify as religious Jewish Phish fans. The survey was shared broadly online, resulting in a sample size of 333 respondents. It was designed to differentiate between clergy and general respondents. Names of participants have been changed.

3. Blau, "Phan on Phish."

4. This study relies on a bounded notion of Judaism and an expansive notion of religion. It draws on understandings of lived religion found in Asad, *Genealogies of Religion*, and Orsi, *Between Heaven and Earth*. Additionally, this study relies on ideas of religious experience. See James, *Varieties of Religious Experience*, and Taves, *Religious Experiences Reconsidered*. While this study looks at religious Jews' activity, it finds them in new places, contributing to the growing literature about lived American Judaism. See Eichler-Levine, *Painted Pomegranates*, and Gross, *Beyond the Synagogue*.

5. Lawton, "Jewish Deadheads."

6. Seligman et al., *Ritual and Its Consequences*, 24.

7. Ibid., 120.

8. Rome, "Unpredictable Phamiliarity."

9. Gruenwald, "Midrash and the 'Midrashic Condition.'"

10. Hellner-Eshed, *River Flows from Eden*, 203.

11. Ibid., 202.

12. Chris Kuroda, Phish's light designer, is often described as the band's fifth member.

13. Silberman, "Happy Birthday Trey Anastasio."

14. Budnick, "Trey Anastasio."

15. Durkheim, *Elementary Forms of the Religious Life*.

16. Phish, "Divided Sky," track 7 on *Junta* (Elektra, 1992).

17. Seligman et al., *Ritual and Its Consequences*, 24.

18. The tradition of pilgrimage to Uman, Ukraine, among Breslover Hasidim to catch sight of Rebbe Nachman of Breslov's grave, known as the Rosh Hashanah kibbutz gathering, has increased in popularity since the fall of the Soviet Union.

19. See Sleeper and Mintz, *New Jews*; Danzger, *Returning to Tradition*; Prell, *Prayer and Community*; Magid, *American Post-Judaism*.

REFERENCES

Asad, Talal. *Genealogies of Religion: Discipline and Reasons of Power in Christianity and Islam*. Baltimore: Johns Hopkins University Press, 2009.

Blau, Jnan A. "A Phan on Phish: Live Improvised Music in Five Performative Commitments." *Cultural Studies ↔ Critical Methodologies* 10, no. 4 (2010): 307–19.

Budnick, Dean. "Trey Anastasio on the Power of Live." *Relix*, July 1, 2020. https://relix.com/articles/detail/trey-anastasio-the-power-of-live.

Butnick, Stephanie, Liel Leibovitz, and Mark Oppenheimer. *The Newish Jewish Encyclopedia: From Abraham to Zabar's and Everything in Between*. New York: Artisan, 2019.

Danzger, M. Herbert. *Returning to Tradition: The Contemporary Revival of Orthodox Judaism*. New Haven, CT: Yale University Press, 1989.

Durkheim, Emile. *The Elementary Forms of the Religious Life*. Translated by Joseph Ward Swain. Mineola, NY: Dover, 2008.

Eichler-Levine, Jodi. *Painted Pomegranates and Needlepoint Rabbis: How Jews Craft Resilience and Create Community*.

Chapel Hill: University of North Carolina Press, 2020.

Gross, Rachel. *Beyond the Synagogue: Jewish Nostalgia as Religious Practice*. New York: New York University Press, 2021.

Gruenwald, Ithamar. "Midrash and the 'Midrashic Condition': Preliminary Considerations." In *The Midrashic Imagination: Jewish Exegesis, Thought, and History*, edited by Michael Fishbane, 6–22. Albany: State University of New York Press, 1993.

Hellner-Eshed, Melila. *A River Flows from Eden: The Language of Mystical Experience in the Zohar*. Stanford, CA: Stanford University Press, 2009.

James, William. *The Varieties of Religious Experience*. Cambridge, MA: Harvard University Press, 1985.

Lawton, Leora. "Jewish Deadheads: A Cultural Demographic Story." *Journal of Popular Music Studies* 27, no. 1 (2015): 69–89.

Magid, Shaul. *American Post-Judaism: Identity and Renewal in a Postethnic Society*. Bloomington: Indiana University Press, 2013.

Orsi, R. A. *Between Heaven and Earth: The Religious Worlds People Make and the Scholars Who Study Them*. Princeton, NJ: Princeton University Press, 2013.

Prell, Riv-Ellen. *Prayer and Community: The Havurah in American Judaism*. Detroit: Wayne State University Press, 1989.

Rome, Kristine Warrenburg. "Unpredictable Phamiliarity: Atopy Performance Art and the Fourth Persona." Paper presented at the Phish Studies Conference, Oregon State University, Corvallis, May 17, 2019.

Seligman, Adam B., Robert P. Weller, Bennett Simon, and Michael J. Puett. *Ritual and Its Consequences: An Essay on the Limits of Sincerity*. Oxford: Oxford University Press, 2008.

Silberman, Steve. "Happy Birthday Trey Anastasio: Fall 1994 Interview with Steve Silberman." *JamBase*, September 30, 2018. https://www.jambase.com /article/phish-trey-anastasio-interview -fall-1994-steve-silberman.

Sleeper, James A., and Alan L. Mintz. *The New Jews*. New York: Vintage Books, 1971.

Taves, Ann. *Religious Experience Reconsidered: A Building Block Approach to the Study of Religion and Other Special Things*. Princeton, NJ: Princeton University Press, 2011.

12.

Tour and Torah

JEWS AND CREWS FROM THE SAGES OF THE GEMARA TO THE RAGERS ON THE RAIL

Noah Munro Lehrman

> When the children of Rabbi Gamliel returned home from a House
> of Drinking they asked their father what to do. He said, "If the 'pillar of
> dawn' had not risen, the *Shema* must still be performed."
> —BABYLONIAN TALMUD, BERACHOT 2A

Mesechta Berachot, the traditional starting point of the Talmud, opens with Rabbi Gamliel's sons, young spiritual seekers, returning to their father's house after a long night of revelry celebrating a wedding, an event full of music, dance, and drink.[1] It was an ecstatic union of two individuals as a married couple, a transcendence of self and other that the guests experienced through the raucous, joyful, and intoxicating festivities. Upon their return well after midnight, they asked their father if they should still say the evening *Shema* prayer—an obligation they neglected to fulfill at the party. Although it was past the appointed hour, Rabbi Gamliel told them they could say the *Shema* until dawn's first light, reconciling their revelries with their communal and spiritual responsibilities.[2]

For many, this effort to reconcile ecstatic transcendent experience with the obligations and structure of everyday existence is born anew with every Phish tour. Young students must balance the desire to follow the band with the demands of their academic schedule. Middle-aged parents must balance travel for Phish shows with family responsibilities and the rigor of their careers. Orthodox Jews must find ways to navigate the technical aspects of tour schedules, venue operations, and ticketing procedures while maintaining traditional religious observance that forbids the use of electrical devices and carrying objects in public on Shabbat, the Jewish day of rest.

It was in my own efforts to reconcile my religious observance, my obligations to my work, to my friends, and to my neighbors, and my love for the band that I recognized how the Phish show phenomenon emulates certain ethical lessons found in the study of Torah and Talmud. Over my many years as both an avid Phish fan and a practicing Jew, I have come to see both Phish tour and studying Torah as pathways for spiritual growth and the reconciliation of ecstatic personal experience with communal care and responsibility. Through text and song, dance and drink, fun and friendship, both Judaism and the Phish community balance personal inspiration with communal obligation. Examining the parallels and interplay between Phish fandom and Jewish religious observance—between tour and Torah—can simultaneously enhance the appreciation and understanding of the experience of both Phish shows and Jewish spiritual engagement.

Jews and Crews

I experience Jewishness on Phish tour in both explicit and implicit forms. Jewish fans regularly hold religious services during set breaks and Torah readings take place at many festivals.[3] At Phish's Super Ball festival in July 2011, fans set up no less than three kosher Shabbat hospitality tents, and there were two Torah scrolls on site in the camping and RV areas, with each group conducting its own full, public Sabbath celebrations, allowing fans to be both observant Jews and committed "Phishheads."[4] In addition to Jewish worship and practice among fans, on stage Phish plays explicitly Jewish songs—including "Avenu Malkenu" from the High Holy Days liturgy—and mentions explicitly Jewish names in their original compositions such as "Suzy Greenberg."[5]

So too, much of the material and social substance in both Jewish and Phish cultures find parallels in the other. Hasidic Jews and Phishheads distinguish themselves and identify each other by the shape of their hats—fedora or derby, flat brim or curved.[6] Jewish fans rush to prepare for the Sabbath, as well as for shows, and

<figure>**FIG. 12.1** Jewish concertgoers laying tefillin in a parking lot before a Phish concert. Photo: Leib Meadvin.</figure>

find relaxation and joy as the Sabbath candles are lit or the lights go down and the concert begins. Some wish each other "Good Shabbos" when they enter their sacred, set-apart ritual time and space, while others say "Have a good show" as they enter a venue. When I'm in a public space, I scan the crowd for signs of a kippah or flat-brim hat, tzitzit or Phish socks, *peyot* or Phish "donut" attire to find other members of my tribes.[7] Whether tefillin straps and boxes or pit bracelets and hat pins, you "bind these as a sign upon your arms and let them be a symbol above your eyes"—signs and symbols to remind both myself and my fellow Jews and Phishheads that we have key commonalities that enable us to identify as part of a tribe (fig. 12.1).[8]

Phish shows feel like Jewish spaces to me because I can go to concerts alone, with no plans for food or housing, yet find welcoming hospitality. On Shabbat I can announce that I need a place to stay within walking distance of the Phish venue and feel confident that both Jewish and non-Jewish fans will provide shelter and sustenance. As a young student traveling from yeshiva in the mystical city of Tzfat to Jerusalem to spend Shabbat at the Western Wall, I would arrive without plans for the night and invariably a member of the local community would offer an evening meal and a warm bed.[9]

The community surrounding Phish also feels Jewish to me because when I'm dancing with my crew at shows the only word to describe the thoughts flowing through me is "Torah." As I dance, the music and lights engage my senses, and my mind opens to inspired interpretations of quotes and concepts from Jewish texts and how they reflect and integrate with one another as well as with circumstances and relationships in my own life. Like Phish's famous group improvisation, it is an exercise in the creative synthesis of free-flowing inspiration and the structures of communal interplay.[10] This is akin to the process of learning, interpreting, and living out the lessons of Torah. The music the band generates arrives at the listener as an external flow that the mind synthesizes with the structures and discernments of its own cognitive forms. Phish shows and after-parties are spaces where friends—inspired by the revelation of the music and often enhanced by drink, herbs, and one another's company—come to contemplate the substance of their lives. Like the study and practice of Torah and the performance of meditative Jewish prayer, the Phish experience is one of intellectual, spiritual, and emotional catharsis. As a dear friend who is a rabbi, a religious school head, and a Phish fan once said to me, "the best davening is in your seat during the music."[11]

Books and Peoples

Sacred texts are central to both the Jewish and Phish communities, and the concept of community is fundamental in both textual traditions. Jews are known as "the People of the Book," a moniker that highlights that the community is centered around a commitment to the Torah, Judaism's most sacred text. Phish's song catalog also contains a literary sacred text, the "Helping Friendly Book."[12] Guitarist Trey Anastasio introduced the "Helping Friendly Book" in his "Gamehendge" saga, and Phish fans often reference it as a guide for life.[13] The revered text is described in song as "possess[ing] the ancient secrets / Of eternal joy and never-ending splendor / The trick was to surrender to the flow."[14] While I excitedly find parallels between lines, themes, and maxims of Torah, Talmud, and Phish lyrics throughout the band's broad oeuvre, I also note explicit plot parallels between the Book of Exodus and Phish's Gamehendge rock opera.[15] Moses, born a Jew but raised Egyptian in Pharaoh's palace, returns to Egypt from exile in Midian as an outsider and becomes the Jewish people's redeemer.[16] In Gamehendge, the hero Colonel Forbin enters the land of the people known as "the Lizards" both as an outsider and as their potential redeemer.[17] Moses ascends Mount Sinai to receive the Torah from HaShem as the Jews' spiritual and moral guiding text in their ultimate step to freedom from Egyptian bondage.[18] Colonel Forbin also ascends a mountain to receive the Lizards' sacred text, the "Helping Friendly Book," from its divine author Icculus so that it can free the Lizards from enslavement to the cruel tyrant Wilson.[19] Both sacred texts are revelations that inspire their people to form ideal communities of responsible relationship and ethical interaction.

The Lizards' quest for freedom is presented in song, as Lizard Rutherford sings, "They would be saved . . . if they could be enlightened / By the writings of the Helping Friendly Book."[20] Similarly, when ancient Israelites achieved freedom, they sang about their experience: "In Your love You lead the people You redeemed; In Your strength You guide them to Your holy abode."[21] Expanding beyond the "Helping Friendly Book," the entire Phish songbook can serve as a sacred text and communal guide for their fans in their quest for transcendence. Ultimately, Phish fans and Jews live in relationship to, and dialogue with, text— be it Jews and Torah, Phishheads and lyrics, or even Gamehendge's Lizards and the "Helping Friendly Book."

In the Talmud, sages seek appropriate verses from the Torah to apply to both real and hypothetical situations as means of identifying modes of Jewish law and practice. Likewise, Phish fans delight in perfect references to Phish lyrics and covers. When Phishheads discuss directions, invariably one quotes the lyric "Left is where I always turn" from Phish's song "Limb by Limb."[22] A fan having trouble finding his sandal after dancing barefoot at a show is met by his friends with a hearty "Whatever you do take care of your shoes" from the song "Cavern."[23] And when someone is late, a Phishhead quotes "still waiting" from the band's beloved cover of the Talking Heads classic "Crosseyed and Painless."[24] This last lyric has additional meaning for some Jewish fans who wait for the Messiah and ultimate redemption.[25] And at sunset after every Shabbat when reciting its parting blessings to the divine "creator of light and dark," I recall Phish's line from "Roggae," "I can't forget to turn the earth so both sides get their share / Of darkness and of light."[26]

Ethics and Empathy

For many Phish fans and Jews, sacred texts—be it Torah or the "Helping Friendly Book"—encapsulate the ethical imperatives that drive everyday life, such as the question of what to do with discovered property. A significant section of the Talmud, which interprets and expounds on the Torah, is indeed devoted to the laws of "found and abandoned property." Sages debate the obligations, entitlements, and acceptable assumptions surrounding items encountered in their owner's absence. According to the Talmud, the status of an item changes based on the circumstances of its discovery, including where it is found or if it has any identifying marks. One particular passage asks whether one can assume that "a person would agree to have his property used to perform a mitzvah," even in his absence or without his knowledge.[27] Such seemingly mundane and civil matters and their implications are considered fundamental to Jewish practice and moral responsibility to humanity and to the Divine. The teachings we learn from the Talmud manifest in lived experiences on Phish tour with surprising frequency.

For example, one summer at a Phish show at the Saratoga Performing Arts Center, I noticed a fan unsteady on his feet. Before I could step forward, a nearby Phish-head steadied him as another stranger also rushed to help. They asked if he needed water, then discussed what to do.

"I don't have water, do you?" one asked.

"No, but I see a bottle on the ground," the other said, then called out to those nearby, "Is this anyone's water?"

"Whose is it?"

"There's no name, but I'm sure the owner wouldn't mind under the circumstances."

Hearing them debate whether they should take the water bottle to help the needy fan reminded me of the debate in the Talmud, as the laws of found objects and abandoned property were rederived from moral necessity by Phish fans inspired to ethical action, and played out among the mounds of belongings and ground scores on the venue's lawn.[28] One reveler's excess led to the community's spontaneous ethical response, echoing principles derived by Jewish sages millennia ago. Even as sacred texts themselves can inspire moral behavior, so too does the natural interplay within ethical communities form the basis of much of the content recorded therein.

For me, literary and mystical examples of individuals' ethical trials also seem to emerge from the Talmud's pages and manifest at Phish shows. The Talmud describes the Prophet Elijah taking on profane, non-Jewish guises—an Arab trader, a repulsive person, or other forms—in encounters with Jews to test their mettle.[29] At a show, when an unknown "wook" barrels through my row and I can choose to box him out or dance around his movements instead, I wonder, "Is this Elijah, and will I meet his challenge to embrace community amid my revelry?"[30] And so a "wook," the symbol of Phish fan excess par excellence, becomes an invitation to ethical reaction (fig. 12.2).

The biblical patriarch Abraham was known for the hospitality he gave to strangers—angels disguised as fellow travelers—in his wall-less desert tent, by dint of which the Jews were later able to receive the Torah.[31] The matriarch Rebecca was recognized as the righteous soulmate for Abraham's son Isaac when she offered water unbidden to a wanderer and his camels.[32] So too, when Phishheads welcome new friends to their open-sided EZ-UP shelters in the parking lots at shows and share water from camelbacks on the dance floor, they create and reveal the community ethos and ethics central to both the Phish and the Jewish experience.

Yet, even as the free flow of generous hospitality and loving-kindness is essential to the sense of ethical community at the heart of my understanding of both Judaism

FIG. 12.2 Poolside between sets during a Phish festival in Riviera Maya, Mexico. Photo: Danna Numerow.

and Phish tour, so too is the need for individual self-discipline to create space for others, both physically and metaphorically. The sage Hillel distilled the Torah to the maxim "Don't do to others what you would not have them do to you—the rest is commentary."[33] Loving one's neighbor requires self-restraint. Phish tells fans, "Try not to step on your best friend's feet."[34] It is a precept I try to practice both literally and figuratively when dancing at every show.

Tunes and Teachings

For millennia, the Talmud, or the Oral Torah—the tradition passed down verbally from teacher to student across generations—has served as the key interpretation of the Written Torah, the Pentateuch. The Talmud is a record of discussions deliberating on the interpretations of the Torah. Originally an oral record, the Talmud should be sung in order to understand the flow of the discourse, which is absent of punctuation. When handed down orally, singsong melody also functions as a mnemonic device, making the words easier to remember. Ancient Jewish sages initially forbade writing down the Oral Torah, a prohibition that ensured that it was passed in an unbroken chain of nuanced personal transmission from generation to generation.[35] However, in the aftermath of the Roman destruction of the Second Temple in Jerusalem and the forced dispersion of the Jewish people from the Land of Israel almost two thousand years ago, the Oral Torah was begrudgingly set down in writing amid fears that the oral tradition would be lost. Still, the Talmud's rising and falling tones and tempo variations impart meaning to vague or ambiguous text. Similarly, the Written Torah is sung to precise tunes recorded in ancient notations as part of Jewish services where congregants sing quietly and sway along to prayer.

At Phish shows, fans sing in undertones along with the band, hopefully soft enough not to disturb neighbors. Fans, too, often turn to friends during lyrics that are personally pertinent. As with verses of Torah, Phish lyrics form intricate and interwoven texts out of existential images and insights that can stand on their own and are open to alternative interpretation. Torah, Talmud, Jewish prayers, and Phish lyrics are the songs of their peoples that they sing to one another. In Judaism and in the Phish world, song and music are quintessential acts of cultural transmission and cohesion, fundamental to the process and impartation of spiritual understanding.

During evening study sessions, my rebbe from yeshiva in Tzfat used to say, "The music of the Talmud comes out at night," and would then rise to lead us students in dance as he sang melodies from Talmudic passages. Phish, too, sings for their audience while imploring them to "Read the (Helping Friendly) Book."[36] When fans dance and live together as a community at Phish, the Talmud of music comes out on tour.

Pirkei Avot, a Talmudic collection of rabbinic ethics and practical advice, acknowledges that a friend affords opportunities for spiritual growth even beyond that of a religious leader. The sages teach that one should "make for yourself a rabbi" but "acquire for yourself a friend."[37] Indeed, fellowship is a foundation of traditional Jewish life. Similarly, friendship is featured in the lyrics and themes of many Phish songs.[38] Phish compels us to "keep what's important and know who's your friend" in their song "Theme from the Bottom."[39] And in "Strange Design," they rhetorically advise us to "bring a few companions on this ride."[40]

Tour and Torah

One of the central elements of both Jewish life and the Phish world is an emphasis on community and friendship even in the quest for personal revelation. On Phish tour, fans gather in groups of friends called "crews"; Jews gather in *chevrahs*—Hebrew for "groups of friends"—for Torah studies and meals. Even Rabbi Shimon Bar Yochai, a prominent figure in the Talmud known as the "Revealer of the Hidden Torah," is described in song as "fortunate to be dabbed with joyful oil from your *chevrah*," to whom he gives his holy secrets.[41] In contemporary Phish tour parlance, "dab oil" is high-potency cannabis concentrate, a substance often shared with friends. Interestingly, the Hebrew word for the promised redeemer/messiah who will usher in an age of transcendent consciousness, Moshiach, also translates as "dabbed with oil."[42]

Indeed, there are biblical and rabbinic traditions that this messianic heir to King David will be recognized by his own fragrance and will discern the true nature of others by their smell.[43]

Phish parking lots and festival grounds before and after shows are filled with tailgating fans grilling and sharing food and drink, and vendors offering culinary lot specialties, Phish-themed souvenirs, and glowsticks. Whenever walking through the rows of fans and vendors, I am reminded of the annual festivities celebrating Rabbi Shimon at his mountain tomb in Meron, Israel, on the anniversary of his passing, where refreshment stalls are set up outside as part of the ceremony. Inside Phish venues lights flicker and flash to the beat; around Shimon's tomb bonfires and live music fill the air in unrivaled revelry. Both at shows and on Mount Meron bearded men with flowing locks and women in swirling skirts dance with abandon, just as King David did when he threw off his regal garb and danced exuberantly before HaShem in the Tabernacle.[44] David danced not as king but as an ecstatic worshiper, as Trey often does during the song "You Enjoy Myself" when he sets down his guitar and dances just like any other fan.[45] For me both are visions of the Temple, and the image of redheaded David composing redemptive Psalms on his lyre resonates with that of redheaded singer-songwriter-guitarist Trey and his transcendent music.

The Talmud says that during each Temple pilgrimage festival in Jerusalem, the city's inns miraculously had room for everyone.[46] No one was ever turned away. Phish crews pray for such a miracle every time tour dates are announced and hotel reservations fly. The Talmud also recounts that when all the Jewish nation came to fill the Holy Temple, they fit exactly while standing, yet again miraculously had room without touching when stretching out fully in prostration as well.[47] At Phish shows, when ten friends dance within the confines of five seats without colliding, one similarly witnesses that Talmudic miracle in our time.

Revelation and Return

Even as the experience of transcendence leads to ethical interaction at Phish and in Judaism, returning from the venue of revelation to the routines and requirements of communal life within a greater society can be a challenging reintegration—both for Phishheads with jobs and families and for mystical Talmudic sages. The Talmud describes Rabbi Shimon and his son Eleazar's flight from Roman persecution.[48] They hid in a cave revealing hidden secrets of Torah day and night while buried naked in sand, rising and dressing only to pray, and sustained by a flow of water and a carob tree that mystically appeared. After twelve years, when the danger passed, they ventured out and saw people engaged in the everyday agricultural activity necessary for life. After so much time steeped in esoteric revelation, the two sages couldn't accept how others spent life in mundane pursuits. The fire of their perturbed gaze burned the landscape until a heavenly voice called, "Have you come out of the cave in order to destroy My world? Go back to your cave!" So they did and hid for one more year. Upon reemerging again, they met an old Jew carrying home two fragrant myrtle bundles to honor Shabbat. When they asked why one bundle was not enough, he replied that one was for where the Torah says "remember" Shabbat, the other for where it says "keep" Shabbat.[49] "Remember" alludes to the divine revelation, while "keep" alludes to human responsibility and self-restraint. When Rabbi Shimon and Eleazar realized how this simple Jew integrated both concepts in his weekly observance, they were ready to rejoin the world.

When leaving the revelry, revelation, and relationships of tour to return to my everyday life—like Rabbi Shimon and Eleazar, or Rabbi Gamliel's sons—I sometimes ask myself which, in fact, is "real life." But are these two parts of my life truly in opposition? Or can it be, as Phish describes in the eponymous line, "we find ourselves in the show of life"?[50] Can it be, as Phish sings in "Sigma Oasis," that "you're already there"?[51]

Phish and Judaism present both deeply personal and profoundly communal experiences. Tour and Torah are vessels for both revelation and loving one's neighbor, and what lovely vessels they are. May the vessel and the flow always be worthy of each other, and may Jews and Phishheads always be worthy of them. Yet they are not an end but a means. Phish and Judaism plant the seeds, which then must be nurtured. The band sings that "the Tree of Knowledge in your soul will grow, and the Helping Friendly Book will plant the seed," while the Jewish mystics tell us the shoots must be tended and the fields must be watered for the trees to grow.[52] What tour and Torah engender can be made manifest only through our own actions in our own lives and communities.

NOTES

1. Dedicated to my Rodeo Crew, JEMP, and my holy parents, who taught me by example to love music and people. "Whatever you do, take care of your crew . . . and your Jews!" This dedication is a reference to the lyric "Whatever you do, take care of your shoes" in Phish's "Cavern," track 3 on *A Picture of Nectar* (Elektra, 1992). The Talmud comprises the traditional interpretation and commentary on the Torah, and its core is regarded as having been revealed orally on Mount Sinai.

2. Reciting the *Shema*, the personal affirmation of revealed divine oneness addressed by the individual to the Jewish people collectively, is itself an act of engagement with one's spiritual community. Deut. 6:4.

3. Observant Jews recite certain prayers three times a day, preferably in a quorum of

ten. Jewish fans regularly organize quorums for afternoon prayers before shows and evening prayers at set breaks inside venues. At festivals, fans organize additional Sabbath prayers, including post-Shabbat *havdalah* ceremonies.

4. Scrolls are required for formal ritual Torah reading during Sabbath services. "Phishheads" are fans for whom the band and Phish community are primary parts of their cultural identity.

5. Phish, "Suzy Greenberg" (live debut 1987).

6. Different sects of Jews wear different hat shapes and brim styles, while flat-brimmed caps are popular among a certain subset of Phishheads.

7. A kippah is a Jewish skullcap. Tzitzit are ritual fringes on certain garments. *Peyot* are devotional sidelocks worn by some Jews. Phish's drummer Jon Fishman wears a donut-patterned muumuu.

8. Tefillin are ritual boxes filled with Torah passages worn during some services. Bracelets are distributed at shows to access preferable venue areas, which some fans collect and wear, and enamel pins with Phish-related images worn on hats, bags, or jackets are popular fashion accessories among fans as well. The quotation is drawn from Deut. 11:18.

9. A yeshiva is a religious seminary. The Western Wall is the last remaining structure of the Jerusalem Temple.

10. Both the creative tension between metaphysical flow and form, and the synthesis of flow and form, are central concepts in Jewish mystic thought.

11. Davening is the traditional mode of Jewish prayer, an embodied meditation as one sways while singing and contemplating texts.

12. Trey Anastasio, *The Man Who Stepped into Yesterday* (senior thesis, Goddard College, 1987).

13. The Gamehendge saga is Phish guitarist Trey Anastasio's senior thesis song cycle completed at Goddard College. Trey Anastasio, *The Man Who Stepped into Yesterday* (senior thesis, Goddard College, 1987).

14. Trey Anastasio, "The Lizards," track 3 on *The Man Who Stepped into Yesterday* (senior thesis, Goddard College, 1987).

15. Phish seems to hint at these parallels by repeatedly transitioning from Gamehendge's opening song "The Man Who Stepped into Yesterday" into the traditional Jewish liturgical "Avenu Malkenu" and back again in live performances.

16. Exod. 2–3.

17. Trey Anastasio, "The Man Who Stepped into Yesterday," track 2 on *The Man Who Stepped into Yesterday* (senior thesis, Goddard College, 1987).

18. HaShem, Hebrew for "The Name," signifies the tetragrammaton, the Hebrew four-letter name that is one of the Divine appellations used in the Torah. Exod. 19–20.

19. Trey Anastasio, "Colonel Forbin's Ascent," track 11 on *The Man Who Stepped into Yesterday* (senior thesis, Goddard College, 1987); Trey Anastasio, "Fly Famous Mockingbird," track 12 on *The Man Who Stepped into Yesterday* (senior thesis, Goddard College, 1987); Phish, "Icculus," track 14 on *Junta* (Elektra, 1992).

20. Phish, "The Lizards."

21. Exod. 15:13.

22. Phish, "Limb by Limb," track 7 on *The Story of the Ghost* (Elektra, 1998).

23. Phish, "Cavern."

24. First performed by Phish at their iconic 1996 Halloween show homage to the Talking Heads' *Remain in Light* album at the Omni Coliseum in Atlanta, Georgia, and performed over fifty times since then as a fan-favorite dance anthem; Talking Heads, "Crosseyed and Painless," track 2 on *Remain in Light* (Sire, 1980).

25. It's a mitzvah, or religious imperative, for Jews to await the Messiah's arrival.

26. Phish, "Roggae," track 3 on *The Story of the Ghost* (Elektra, 1998).

27. Babylonian Talmud, Baba Metzia 29b. See also Babylonian Talmud, Pesachim 4b.

28. In general admission areas at shows fans pile their bags, water bottles, and the like into "mounds" for safety and to clear dance space. "Groundscores" are forgotten, lost, or abandoned property found at venues.

29. Babylonian Talmud, Berakhot 6b; Babylonian Talmud, Ta'anit 20b.

30. "Wook" or "wookie" is a *Star Wars*–derived slang term for a long-haired, bearded fan, used for Phishheads who celebrate exuberantly at shows and in life.

31. Gen. 18:1–8. There is an oral tradition that when Abraham fed the disguised angels, their angelic countenance was bestowed on him and passed down to his descendants. Later, when the Torah was to be given to the Jews through Moses, other angels rebelled, declaring that its holiness was only fit for the angels themselves. But as the Jews had gained an angelic countenance through Abraham's hospitable act, they were thus able to receive the Torah on Mount Sinai.

32. Gen. 24:10–20.

33. Babylonian Talmud, Shabbat 31a.

34. Phish, "Everything's Right," track 3 on *Sigma Oasis* (JEMP, 2020).

35. Babylonian Talmud, Gittin 60b.

36. Phish, "Icculus."

37. Pirkei Avot 1.6.

38. Phish, "Lizards"; Phish, "Theme from the Bottom," track 7 on *Billy Breathes* (Elektra, 1996).

39. Phish, "Theme from the Bottom."

40. Phish, "Strange Design," (live debut 1995).

41. Shimon Bar Yochai is the central figure of the mystical work the Zohar.

42. The Torah lists cannabis as one of the ingredients of this sacred anointing oil. See Exod. 30:23.

43. Lamentations 4:20; Babylonian Talmud, Sanhedrin 93b.

44. The Tabernacle was the Temple's tent-based precursor. See 2 Sam. 6:14.

45. Phish, "You Enjoy Myself," track 2 on *Junta* (Elektra, 1989).

46. Babylonian Talmud, Yoma 21a.

47. Ibid.

48. Babylonian Talmud, Shabbat 33b.

49. Exod. 20:8; Deut. 5:12.

50. Phish, "Show of Life" (live debut 2010).

51. Phish, "Sigma Oasis," track 1 on *Sigma Oasis* (JEMP, 2020).

52. Phish, "Colonel Forbin's Ascent."

ENCORE

"ALL THINGS RECONSIDERED"

Reflections on Phish and Jewishness

13.

"Yerushalayim Shel Zahav" Comes to Phish

AN INTERVIEW WITH SHIRLEY HALPERIN

SHIRLEY HALPERIN is Executive Editor of Music at *Variety* where she spearheads music coverage. She is the author of *Pot Culture: The A–Z Guide to Stoner Language and Life* and *"American Idol": The Official Backstage Pass* and coauthor of *Reefer Movie Madness: The Ultimate Stoner Film Guide.*

OREN KROLL-ZELDIN AND ARIELLA WERDEN-GREENFIELD: As Executive Editor of Music at *Variety*, you certainly have an insider's view into the music scene. Can you tell us a bit about your relationship to Phish? How did the band capture your interest?

SHIRLEY HALPERIN: I listened to pretty early stuff from the first two albums, anything off of *Lawn Boy* or *Junta*, and I just completely fell in love with their music.[1] It just resonated. It was weird and smart playing and I sort of gravitated toward Phish. And then I just fell into it hardcore, I just loved everything they did. I went to a show and saw that it was a community. I felt at home.

I always know when I discovered Phish because I was finally allowed to drive my senior year, I had a car, and I put stickers on the back that a friend had made for me. And one of them said, "Reba sink a boulder in the water, Reba tie a cable to a tree."[2] It didn't say Phish or anything. And I would drive around and people would be like "What the hell is up with your weird bumper stickers?" And then I'd say, "It's a Phish song." I was in on it so early and I was so into it. Once I got a car I would go to as many shows as I could.

Then I started getting into music journalism. And one of the things that got me into it was wanting to write about Phish. I was pretty crafty about getting interviews with them when I was in college. I think I got myself invited to their record release party when they were just signed to Elektra. It's not like they had a big press following in 1991. We could probably count it on two hands. And I was one of them. So they let me come to a record release party.

Somehow at the H.O.R.D.E. tour in the summer of 1992 I saw Jon Fishman just walking around the lawn seats.[3] So I just went up and started talking to him. I was about to leave for Israel for my year abroad, so I mentioned that I was leaving and going to Israel for a year. He was strangely interested in Israel, fascinated I would say. He asked me a lot of questions about growing up there, what it was like, the political situation. And of course, me being a huge advocate for Israel, I probably played it up like it was the greatest place on earth, telling him that he needed to go and that every Jewish person should experience it. And that was that.

Then I swapped a ticket with my friend who was also at the show who was more interested in seeing Blues Traveler. He had front-row seats. And I said, "Can I have your front-row ticket stub for the Phish set?" And he said, "Yeah."

We swapped places and I went to the front row and Fishman saw that I was there and had Brad come and pull me out of the audience.[4] "Here's a backstage pass, come after the set and come meet the band," he told me. "Jon wants to hang out" or whatever. I was nineteen. My little brother was with me. He was probably fifteen. So we went backstage and I'd never been in a situation like that before. And I was really wowed and felt super special and got to meet Trey and Mike and all the guys really. Brad was super nice and to think about it now, it's like, "There's a nineteen-year-old backstage at the concert with her little brother, how weird," but it actually wasn't because they were so hospitable. They were so nice and so caring.

That was really my first experience with the music world and being behind the scenes. It really motivated me. I went to Israel and Fishman and I stayed in touch and I convinced him to come and visit during my spring break. We talked all the time. We were kind of pen pals, phone pals, and sure enough, that spring, he came to Israel! I know it sounds so crazy. Even when I say it, it sounds crazy. But yeah, he came to Israel in 1993. I have some pictures of him at Masada and in Tel Aviv and my grandparents' house. I don't know. I guess maybe he was kind of interested in me, but we never hooked up or anything because it really wasn't like that. We just had really good conversations. I was very interested in music and I was very interested in the music business and he was more than happy to tell me how they got their record deal and how touring works and how the promoter gets paid. And this was my education because it's what I do for a living now.

We had this amazing trip in Israel. I planned the whole thing. We rented a car, we went to the South, we went north, we stopped at all the important places. I don't remember if we made it to Jerusalem because it might have been dangerous at the time. I'm going to put my bet on there was a problem in Jerusalem because I don't remember being there.

I took Fishman to the top of Masada.[5] There's a photo of it. (fig. 13.1) We did that thing where you wake up at four o'clock in the morning and you fucking do it, get up it. We made it. I think we went to the Dead Sea, definitely went up to the Galilee, did a little bit of a northern tour because I was living on a kibbutz and I was studying at the University of Haifa. I knew that whole area really well. I think Fishman even came to visit the kibbutz where I was living. I'm sure Israelis, their minds will be blown if they knew how much of the country he had actually seen and just how into it he was. We had this amazing ten-day trip together. He taught me so much about the music industry. I think I taught him a lot about Judaism and being Israeli and Zionism. And we remained friends.

I returned home to the States and one random day I got a call from someone in the Phish camp asking if I could get on the phone with Mike and talk him through the song "Jerusalem of Gold," which is a very well-known Israeli song.[6] Not that I knew the lyrics, because I didn't really. I knew the melody, obviously, but I said yes. I pulled up the lyrics somehow. I remember that my mom was in Israel at the time, so I called her and said, "I might need your help getting the right pronunciations of some of these words and the right meanings." I think because of the time zone I ended up talking to one of my mom's friends to walk Mike through the pronunciation of the words. They wanted to include it on the *Hoist* album, which they did. And I think I have a "thank you" in there somewhere.

It was so bizarre. It was hours on the phone, line by line, very difficult to enunciate a lot of those words and explain them. For me to be on the phone, explaining how to sing "Jerusalem of Gold" was something else. Sometime around then, they performed "Avenu Malkenu" and that was it.

That was my forever bond with Phish. It was like, "Their music in general sounds like klezmer and almost something that I would sing at the synagogue." I spent a lot of time in the synagogue because my mom taught at a Hebrew school and so those melodies were very familiar to me. I remember telling my grandparents and my mom about them playing "Avenu Malkenu" and explaining why this group was so special. Then I got back to school at Rutgers. I was working at the school paper and I wrote an article. And I kept this relationship with Phish going. I also had my own magazine called *Smug*. I put them on the cover and wrote the cover story. This was August 1995. And like I said, I really took advantage of that relationship as much as I could.

I got an internship at *High Times* because I was coming in to interview Phish and my interview was scheduled right after the *High Times* interview. So when I walked in, there were magazines everywhere. And it smelled like amazing weed. There were rolling papers everywhere. And I was like, "Oh my God, you guys didn't just do an interview with *High Times*." And they were like, "Yes we did." I met Steve Bloom, who was the music editor there. I just said, "I want to intern for you." He said, "Okay, call me on Monday." So I did, I called him and ended up going into New York for an internship at *High Times* and helping them get Phish into the pages of the magazine regularly.

I ended up getting a job there. I was the photo editor and then I was the managing editor. I spent a few years there and again, just kept that relationship going. But I would say by the end of the '90s, I was kind of exiting the scene. It was a little too much. And I had too much going on. I was way involved in the pop world and I couldn't really give the band the attention that it needed.

OKZ AND AWG: Those are really incredible stories. We would love to return for a moment to that unexpected phone call. Do you have a sense of why Mike Gordon wanted to play "Yerushalayim Shel Zahav"?

SH: It is a really beautiful song, really iconic, moving. I have a feeling that Mike is a bar mitzvah kid, he would have known that song growing up receiving a Jewish education. It wasn't a pop hit. It was always a traditional sort of patriotic song. I thought it was completely random when I got the call. I was like, "Really? Okay."

Some of the language is very complicated and very pretty, which is why I reached out to my mom for help. Because that is what she does, she teaches Hebrew literature and language. In a way it kind of bonded us, even to this day she's like, "How are those Phish guys doing?"

OKZ AND AWG: You also mentioned "Avenu Malkenu," which Phish started playing before "Yerushalayim Shel Zahav." They still play "Avenu Malkenu" even though they never recorded it on an album. But they don't play "Yerushalayim Shel Zahav" anymore. Why do you think the band continues to play one of them but not the other?

FIG. 13.1 Jon Fishman atop Masada, Israel. Photo: Shirley Halperin.

SH: I think "Avenu Malkenu" fits in stylistically and musically with the Phish repertoire. "Yerushalayim Shel Zahav" feels like a departure. That's not to say that it couldn't be a great sendoff song, end of the night, let everyone go in peace kind of thing. But I don't know politically, inside the band, how they feel about being affiliated with something so Jewish. Yes, half the band is Jewish. Fishman's adopted, but he's Jewish, and Mike is obviously Jewish, and some of the management is Jewish, too. I just don't know that they would want to be the poster boys for northeastern Jews.

OKZ AND AWG: Can you share your experience of hearing Phish play a song in Hebrew live for the first time?

SH: "Avenu Malkenu" is something I have a personal connection to. It is something that I've heard every year, my entire life. It's iconic. Being Israeli and having to explain to my Israeli grandparents who escaped the Holocaust why I'm spending all this time driving around America following some band, to be able to say, "Well, they sing 'Avenu Malkenu,' that's part of their repertoire." My grandparents were like, "Oh, okay." All of a sudden they approved of Phish. I think that was part of it. I didn't want them to think that I was just crazy and had just gone off the rails and was out there, smoking a lot of pot and being silly. It was still basically something of my foundation, my heritage. I'm sure they loved that a decent amount of the fan base was Jewish kids like me. It probably felt like I was in a safer environment in that sense. But really it was the music that stood out to me.

OKZ AND AWG: We're going to be very direct with this question. Why do so many Jews like Phish?

SH: Well, first of all, I think you have to connect it musically. Phish's melodies are similar to Jewish melodies, traditional Jewish melodies. Maybe they connect to it because it's a safe scene. I don't want to generalize, but I want to say it's for good kids, it's for smart kids, college-bound kids. I can only speak from my tiny little myopic view, which is, I lived in a town that I think was 40 percent Jewish. My parents moved to this area specifically because they knew that there was an Israeli community and that there was a Jewish community around them. There were synagogues, there were Hebrew schools, it was very Jewish. But that's just my situation. I can't speak for other kids. I do think the band being half Jewish is a big part of it. Because there just aren't that many in popular music. And so to legitimately be able to say "50 percent of that group is Jewish" is a big deal.

OKZ AND AWG: It's not just that two of them are Jewish, but that they have incorporated these two distinctly Jewish pieces of music into their catalog.

SH: For sure. But take that out of their catalog, I still think Jews would be pulled toward Phish. The "Helping Friendly Book" feels a little Talmudic, a little Torah-like, a little bit of fables with morals and stories that go beyond human interactions to something a little more spiritual.[7] I think that's part of it, too. In their shows there are all those prompts and all those things that are very inside. There's something about that, too. It might be synagogue-like as well, the getting up, the sitting down, the bowing, all of those things, which I hate now, but when I was a teenager, I was really into it. I was very spiritual, and faithful in that way. So maybe that's it, too.

OKZ AND AWG: We would love to talk a bit about cannabis and the Phish community. What is your perspective on the relationship between cannabis and the Phish universe?

SH: That's such an excellent question. And it is always good to remember that marijuana is kosher. I use cannabis as a creative juice, and I always have. I never looked at it as like, "I'm going to get so fucked up or whatever." It was always about opening up my mind and absorbing music, art, entertainment, in a different way, it's like a different lens. I do believe that the Phish scene and pot go together; you can't have one without the other. They are so integral to each other. I think, musically, there are so many long jams and long interludes of music that the pot really helps take it in. Some people do criticize Phish: "Those jams are so long." Well, if you're really focused and smoked some really good stuff, that is not too long for you. It really takes you into some other world of your brain, which I love.

NOTES

1. Phish, *Lawn Boy* (Absolute A Go Go, 1990); Phish, *Junta* (Elektra, 1992).

2. Phish, "Reba," track 2 on *Lawn Boy* (Absolute A Go Go, 1990).

3. The Horizons of Rock Developing Everywhere tour, otherwise known as the H.O.R.D.E. tour, ran from 1992 through 1998. The 1992 lineup featured Blues Traveler, the Spin Doctors, Widespread Panic, Aquarium Rescue Unit, and Phish.

4. Brad Sands worked as part of Phish's crew from 1991 through 2004.

5. Masada is a mountain in southeastern Israel and the site of an ancient fortress built by Herod the Great in 30 BCE.

6. Phish, "Yerushalayim Shel Zahav," track 12 on *Hoist* (Elektra, 1994).

7. The "Helping Friendly Book" is a mythical guidebook that plays a significant role in Phish's lore. A selection of Phish's songs, many of which originated with Trey Anastasio's senior thesis at Goddard College, tell the story of Lizard people who depend on the Helping Friendly Book, written by their supreme leader, Icculus, for survival; Trey Anastasio, *The Man Who Stepped into Yesterday* (senior thesis, Goddard College, 1987).

14.

Bringing Phish to the Holy Land

AN INTERVIEW WITH RACHEL LOONIN STEINERMAN

RACHEL LOONIN STEINERMAN is a blogger known online as "The Phunky Bala-busta."[1] Her blog, *Whole Phamily*, addresses everything from Jewishness to parenting and rock and roll. She is also the creator of the "OhKeePah," a yarmulke made with the same fabric as Phish drummer Jon Fishman's signature muumuu (plate 4). Rachel dreams of seeing Phish play in Israel and has made it a personal mission to make that a reality.

OREN KROLL-ZELDIN AND ARIELLA WERDEN-GREENFIELD: How did the OhKeePah come to be?

RACHEL LOONIN STEINERMAN: When my first child was born in the mid-2000s, I started a blog called *Whole Phamily*. It was a blog about the things that were in my life at the time: parenting, Judaism, and a whole lot of rock and roll. I wanted to do something to contribute to this incredibly special music community. I then came up with the idea of producing a Phish kippah, a Phish yarmulke.[2] I'd never successfully sold anything on lot, so I thought, "Oh, that'll be fun, to produce this Phish kippah and sell it before a show."[3] I wanted to connect with people, but also make some money to cover the cost of my ticket. It would give me something meaningful to do before a show, rather than just sitting around in lawn chairs or playing Frisbee, and it would help me build community. And that is what happened. Selling the OhKeePah created an opportunity for me to connect with other fans, and now I vend at PhanArt shows when my schedule allows.

OKZ AND AWG: Why did you start making the OhKeePah? Why does the Phish community need a Fishman donut kippah?

RLS: I thought to myself, "Well, I really believe that Phish should play in Israel, so if that's the case, there should be a Phish yarmulke, an OhKeePah." #PhishInIsrael is printed in the inside of every OhKeePah. Once I started selling OhKeePahs and people would wear them to shows, people responded in incredible ways. One guy came up to me and said, "Hey, I bought one of those from you and now people come up to me and say shalom. It's really awesome." Another person told me, "I went to pick up my daughter from school and I got the 'hey' head nod from another Jewish fan who knew what the kippah symbolized." From the people crawling out of the woodwork to people who would otherwise have no clue that they were also Phish fans, the OhKeePah gives people the chance to connect. What I started taking away from this as people were buying them was that it gives people a way to connect with their Judaism through the music that they love. I often hear from people, "I'm not religious" or "I don't wear a yarmulke. I would only wear it once a year." But then these same people say, "When I wear it, it's really great." There is something, whatever it might be, that makes some people want to conceal their Phish love "in real life," as it were. They feel the need to be stealth, to be low-key about their fandom when they're out in the world. I think that's part of the reason why the donut explosion has been so successful. You can somewhat pass by wearing Fishman donuts, and if you don't know, you don't know. But if you do know, it's like your little way to identify yourself.

People love the OhKeePah. I've produced them for weddings and bar mitzvahs (plate 10). I did a wedding last year where the groom passed them out to all of his buddies just as the party started. We gave Trey an OhKeePah when he played that acoustic "show in a shul" in Washington, DC, at the synagogue and performance space at Sixth & I (plate 2).[4] My friend and I signed the inside of it, and at the end of the show, my friend who was sitting in the front row handed it to Trey. It was so nice that Trey received it in a synagogue.

By the way, that name "OhKeePah" came to me via my friend Josh Fleet.[5] He heard the word "OhKeePah" being used to refer to a Phish yarmulke, and I'm like, "Well, can I use that name?" And he gave me permission.

OKZ AND AWG: Wearing a donut kippah is like a secret handshake, a visible marker that informs other fans of your dedication to Phish. Can you tell us about how your dedication to the band led to your embrace of the nickname "The Phunky Balabusta"? What does the name mean and how was it inspired?

RLS: My nickname, The Phunky Balabusta, is inspired by the fan group The Phunky Bitches, a group of female fans who leave items including feminine hygiene products and Advil in the women's bathrooms at shows. I think it's great. They take care of other women. It's a sisterhood. I always liked the song "Funky Bitch," but there's the word "Bitch" in there, which isn't the most dignified choice of words to use. Also, I don't go to shows on Friday night or Saturday night in the summer because Shabbat is not over until 9:30. I also don't go to shows during certain times in the Jewish calendar year because of my religious practice, times when observant Jews don't see live music.[6] What am I doing during those times? I am being the *balabusta* that I am grateful and honored to be. Generally, I am serving my "loaves of love," the challah that I bake every week. I'm serving the healthful and delicious meals that I cook. I'm hosting guests. I'm having people in my sukkah.[7] I'm making a seder.[8] I'm playing games with my children. I unplug and don't have any screen time for twenty-five hours on a weekly basis. I'm doing a lot of things in the home. I am there for my family on a consistent basis, trying to bring peace into my home. That's the definition of a *balabusta*.

So I was like, "Let me transform the 'Funky Bitch' and turn it into 'Phunky Balabusta.'" Then there's the Shabbat candles. To lead a more meaningful life, one ought to live their truth. And when you are true to your real self, you should share that with the world because your own inner light could make the world a better place. The Lubavitcher Rebbe teaches that every single person has their special, unique qualities, innate talents, and gifts that they can and should share with the world. The goal is to reach a certain point to figure out what that is, your own personal mission in life. For a long time, I shied away from doing anything Jewish at Phish shows, but then I realized that is part of my mission. I've been seeing Phish the whole time I've been leading a committed Jewish lifestyle. So when I came up with this whole Phunky Balabusta thing, I would start talking about the idea of Shabbat candles at Phish shows. I would talk with other Jewish women I'd meet at shows. In December 2019 I began handing out "Love and Light on Friday Night" pouches, which include candles, a thoughtful card, and a small gift.

Once I started, living and speaking my truth at Phish shows actually made things better for me. I don't know if it's connected, but a couple of years ago a ticket fairy reached out and offered me industry seats for sale at face value. I like to believe this is because I was putting out my good energy to the community. I would point out how awesome Chris Kuroda's lights are. And I would point out that once the show is over we all go back to our lives. So I started to say to people, "I just want to share one thing with you. When you go back to your life, I really encourage you, if you don't already, to light Shabbat candles on Friday night, and you can bring in a different type of love and light into your life. It's different than being at a Phish show, but I hope you can carry the energy of being at the show into your life." Because it's such a downer when a show is over and you're like, "Oh, now I've got to go back to work tomorrow."

OKZ AND AWG: Your religious practice requires you to make selective choices about attending Phish concerts. How do you reconcile that with whatever fear of missing out might exist internally?

RLS: Of course I wish I could go to shows on Friday night, or on Tisha B'Av. I never saw Phish on Shabbat, even in the 1990s when I first started seeing the band. I accept the fact that I can't go to every show. While it is challenging, I know that my traditional Shabbat observance also brings ecstatic joy and meaning to my life. But that's my choice. I choose to have a lovely Shabbat experience, in my tent, at my campground, away from the stage, away from the music, or I could choose not to.

Because I can't get to every single show, I am even more grateful and appreciative for those I can attend. I'm not going to go to a three-night Dick's run, for example.[9] I was going to go to Dick's in the summer of 2020 but then COVID hit. I had tickets for Sunday night. I was going to try for Saturday-night tickets and just go to the second set and encore. It felt completely worth it for me to fly out to Colorado from Philly even if was only going to go to one and a half shows because I would make the most of what I could see.

When I go to just the Sunday night show of a three-night run in the summer, especially with social media when you see photos, I do have that feeling of missing out. I will say, the thing that I feel that I have lost out on is the opportunity of not even missing the music, but of the social opportunity to develop my real relationships with people in a stronger way.

OKZ AND AWG: How do you find other observant Jews who are Phish fans or other Phish fans who are observant Jews? Is connecting with similarly minded fans a significant part of that social aspect?

RLS: We connect through friends of friends mostly. It's a little bit through the Heady Jew Tribe.[10] Social media really keeps you connected these days. Observant Jews have always been going to shows, but it seems to me that since 2010 there's been a stronger and more open display of their connection to their traditional Judaism at Phish. You hear about groups of people gathering in the parking lot, things like, "Oh, those guys down at row E, they're having a kosher barbecue." In the 1990s it was like, how would you find out about stuff? Maybe you'd get an email, if you were on email in '95. The way that information was disseminated was obviously very different. Now there's a Facebook group called Gefilte Phish. But before it started, there was this group called Heady Jew Tribe.

OKZ AND AWG: How do you negotiate your halachic practice when you are at a show? Have there been instances where halacha has led to questions? Have you had any halachic concerns while attending Phish shows?

RLS: Yes, but only recently. I don't touch guys who I'm not married to.[11] I only touch my husband and close family. But at shows, I was not always so careful about it. Phish is a huggy community. I've been observant for twenty-five years, but for a long time I still would give my guy friends hugs. Even most of my guy friends are like, "I'm not really sure. Are you hugging guys now, or are you not?" But I made a conscious decision at Phish to not hug or touch guys. It's been interesting, because most Jewish people have never heard of this practice, let alone non-Jewish people. People are confused that I won't hug them. They say, "That's what we do at Phish. We give each other big bear hugs. What do you mean, you're not going to hug me?" But when I just say that it's a Jewish thing, most people are respectful, and usually say it's news to them. I don't want to be that person to have to explain, that Jewish person where people say, "Oh yeah, ask Rachel." I don't want the conversation to always turn to that. I'd rather talk about the "Tweezer" that they played over the New Year's run.[12] I don't always want to talk about Jewish stuff. But of course you can't *not* talk about it.

A rabbi, or somebody who interprets halacha in a stricter way than I do, might say to me, "Well, you're putting yourself in an environment where there's mixed dancing to begin with. So how do you justify that?" Because if you're putting yourself in an environment where there's mixed dancing, then you should expect that people should be able to give you a hug, and you never know where that can lead. I'm there for the music first and cannot imagine my life without it. It's very interesting that just as I have chosen to keep a stricter level of *shomer negiah*, an organization called GrooveSafe has taken hold in the scene to prevent unwanted touching and create a safe space for people at shows. They are building a community based on exactly what I'm talking about, which is, "Do not touch me unless I say it's okay."

Forget about the *shomer negiah* angle for a moment. This is about personal space. And it has been well received. It's very nice because it's showing that you can still have a very strong connection to another human being without touching. It's interesting how I'm finding that my religious practice is validated by other things happening in society which are not specifically Judaic, religious, or halachic in nature.

There is also, as I mentioned earlier, the issue that I am placing myself in an environment where everybody is dancing and the question of whether I preemptively avoid the situation in the first place. A fine line exists between dancing with yourself and sharing in a groove with the guy next to you. The question is: Can a woman dance a groove, or a man dance a groove near another person, and it just be that? Ideally I would be at a show with my husband, with whom I love dancing, or surrounded by good girlfriends. The sisterly connection I feel when I'm at a show is unparalleled. I go into a show with the intention to connect with the band and their music, and it's a bonus when I see friends and we exchange a smile during a show. I view the music as not just something nice to listen to but as essential to my soul. So when I'm dancing and grooving, I'm doing it because that's part of me getting to that space of joy, happiness, whatever it is that's necessary for my existence.

OKZ AND AWG: Is attending Phish important to your Jewish existence?

RLS: My Jewish existence is just part of me. I would say yes, because my Jewish existence is essential to who I am, and my Phish existence is essential to who I am because that's me.

OKZ AND AWG: Your example of *shomer negiah* is interesting to think through in terms of how religiously observant women show up on tour as opposed to religiously observant men. This speaks to the issue of gender more broadly in Phish. Are women involved in some of the more visible Jewish ritual activities or expressions at Phish shows, such as the set break minyan?

RLS: Phish is by and large more of a guy space. In the Jewish world there aren't huge numbers of observant women who see Phish. I have some girlfriends who are connected Jewishly and who are specifically very connected Jewishly to Shabbat. Yet I wouldn't say that there is any infrastructure of observant Jewish women at shows. There is definitely, however, an unspoken code of "hey, we're in the same club" when you see another outwardly *frum* woman wearing a skirt and a *sheitel* or other Jewish head covering at any jam-band show, and often you will smile if you see her.[13] Maybe even start chatting.

The only really ritualistic thing I have encountered at Phish is the set break min-yan. Bystanders are so fascinated with it. People love the ritual after *Maariv* when the guys do a circle dance and sing a *niggun* or two.[14] This past New Year's run, I saw a group of super-cool Jewish women looking at the guys dancing and were genuinely interested. A girlfriend came up to me and said, "I want to just get into that hora. Will the guys hate me if I just did that, just went into the circle?" Another girl was like, "No way am I going in there." So I just busted into the middle of the circle and then the guys disbanded! I wouldn't have done that during the davening itself but during the *mitzvah tantz* I thought it was okay.[15] Maybe so or maybe not. People are very curious. They're like, "What is that?" And then certainly, non-Jewish peo-ple have asked me if it was a Jewish holiday. I will say, "Oh it's just men doing their daily evening Jewish prayer with a quorum of ten men. They have the opportunity to meet at Phish, and they love it."

There's no organized infrastructure. It's impressive in and of itself that you get, at set break, a bunch of guys to come together for a *Maariv* minyan at a specific loca-tion.[16] What a feat! One thing I do want to add regarding these set break minyans is that even though it is very grassroots, I noticed that they are happening at shows more frequently and that more people know about it. It just attracts people. The con-nections that end up happening because of this minyan are tremendous. It's always like, "Oh, wow. I haven't seen you in a long time." It's also a great time for me to sell OhKeePahs.

OKZ AND AWG: That brings us back to message etched onto each OhKeePah: #PhishInIsrael. Why do you want Phish to play in Israel? What are you doing to try to make that happen?

RLS: Seeing that band playing the music that touches my soul so deeply, in a loca-tion that has such a deep meaning to me and, of course, to many people, would be an ultimate convergence of good energies. It would infuse the Phish community with a wonderful sense of goodness. Maybe it's a kabbalistic connection to some-thing deeper.[17] It would be good for the Jewish people. It would be good for Phish fans, and that would be good for the world. Would seeing Phish in Israel be a spiri-tual or religious experience for all? I don't know, but I feel that it would be an expe-rience that would enhance people's lives in a very significant way. It could be this incredible experience of going to the Promised Land and seeing your favorite band, and it's not just your favorite band, it's Phish who has played "Avenu Malkenu" and who has this tribal thing going. Recently I spoke with Big Steve Parish on his show on SiriusXM radio, where he shared with me about the deep levels of what it was like going with the Grateful Dead family to the pyramids in Egypt in 1978. I want that legacy to continue with Phish in Israel.

OKZ AND AWG: How do others react when you tell them your goal? What are you doing to make it happen?

RLS: Across the board people say that they would go. A very unscientific study and data collection on my part over the past eight to ten years has shown that every single person would go to see Phish in Israel. What am I doing to make it happen? I'm trying to use the power of social media. I wrote about it on my blog. Also, through selling the OhKeePah I spread the idea just by writing #PhishInIsrael underneath the OhKeePah. I've also written to the band numerous times. I mentioned it directly to two of the four band members. I mentioned it to Fishman. I have a picture of that. And he said to me, "Oh, yeah. Sounds like a great idea. Yeah, that sounds good. I'll go anywhere they tell me to set up my drum kit." Then he's like, "Whoa, whoa, whoa. I'm not the one who's going to make that happen." I also mentioned it to Mike Gordon, probably more than once. He read my Hebrew name necklace and said, "Oh Rachel (in Hebrew), that's nice." I gave Tom Marshall an OhKeePah once, and I said to him, "Yeah, I really want Phish to play in Israel."[18] He snickered and said, "That'll never happen." But you know what? You can't let one person, even if it's Tom Marshall, deter you from your dream.

NOTES

1. *Balabusta* is a Yiddish term referring to a skilled homemaker.

2. A kippah or yarmulke is a ritual skullcap worn by religiously observant male Jews.

3. The phrase "on lot" refers to the parking lot outside of Phish shows where fans congregate.

4. This was a Trey Anastasio solo acoustic show on February 4, 2018. Sixth and I is a synagogue and community space in Washington, DC.

5. The product's name references the Phish song "The Oh Kee Pa Ceremony," track 5 on *Lawnboy* (Absolute A Go Go, 1990).

6. In addition to avoiding concerts on Shabbat, many observant Jews do not attend concerts in the three-week mourning period that concludes with Tisha B'Av.

7. A sukkah is a temporary structure built during the festival of Sukkot.

8. A seder is a ritual meal that entails a retelling of the Passover story.

9. Dick's Sporting Goods Park in Commerce City, Colorado.

10. Heady Jew Tribe is a Facebook group.

11. Someone who is *shomer negiah* restricts themselves from physical contact with the opposite gender with the exception of a spouse or close relative. Spousal contact, too, is restricted based on a woman's menstrual cycle and the laws of Niddah.

12. Phish, "Tweezer," track 11 on *A Picture of Nectar* (Elektra, 1992).

13. *Frum* is the Yiddish word for religious and refers to a religiously observant Jew. A *sheitel* is a wig worn by religiously observant married women.

14. *Niggun* means melody.

15. *Mitzvah tantz* refers to a custom in Hasidic communities at weddings where men dance in front of the bride.

16. A *Maariv* minyan is an evening prayer service.

17. Kabbalah is an ancient Jewish mystical tradition.

18. Tom Marshall is a lyricist for Phish and Trey Anastasio's longtime collaborator.

PLATES

PLATE 1
"I Prayed a Prayer into the Tide," Madison Square Garden, New
York, December 31, 2017. Photo: Andrea Z. Nusinov.

PLATE 2
Trey Anastasio performing at Sixth & I, Washington, DC,
February 14, 2018. Photo: Andrea Z. Nusinov.

PLATE 3
In the parking lot at Dick's Sporting Goods Park, Commerce City, Colorado, 2014. Photo: Kristina Canfield, Show of Life Photography.

PLATE 4
Before the show, Madison Square Garden, New York, December 2019. Photo: Rachel Loonin Steinerman.

PLATE 5
"Donuts Are Everywhere," Madison Square Garden, New York,
December 31, 2018. Photo: Andrea Z. Nusinov.

PLATE 6
"Looks Too Obscure to Me," North Charleston Coliseum, North Charleston,
South Carolina, December 2019. Photo: Andrea Z. Nusinov.

PLATE 7
MGM Grand Arena, Las Vegas, October 28, 2021. Photo: Shaun Kessler (@shaunkess).

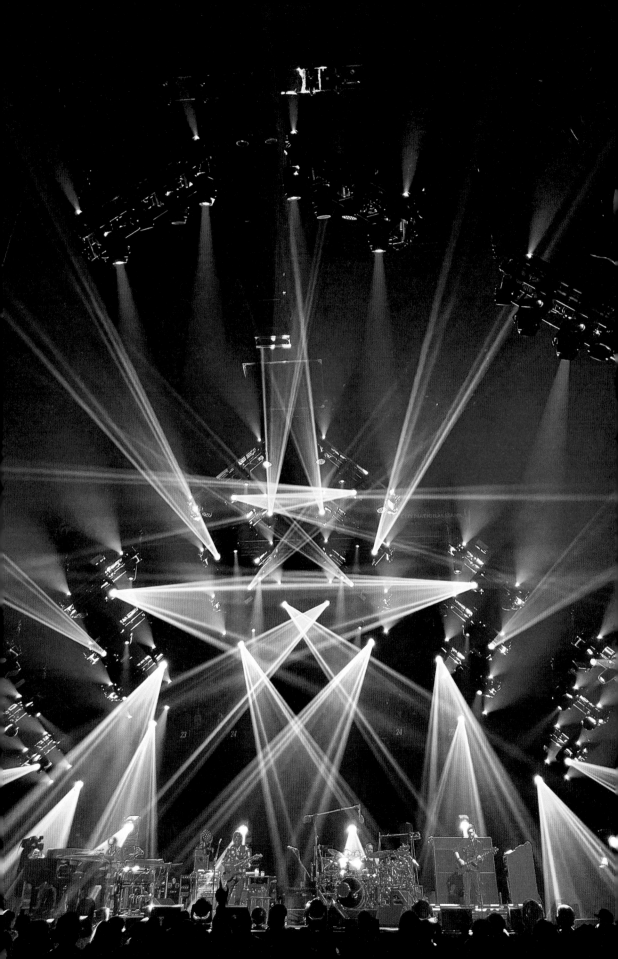

PLATE 8
North Charleston Coliseum, North Charleston, South Carolina,
December 7, 2019. Photo: Shaun Kessler (@shaunkess).

PLATE 9
Madison Square Garden, New York, December 31, 2019. Photo: Matt McGlone.

PLATE 10
Phish-inspired kippahs at a wedding. Photo: Boris Shvartsman.

PLATE 11
Underneath a wedding canopy that includes Phish and Grateful Dead logos.
Photo: Jessy Gross Dressin, Mark and Jessy Dressin's wedding, 2018.

PLATE 12

Ketubah (marriage contract) designed by renowned artist and
poster designer Jim Pollock. Photo: Bari Epstein.

PLATE 13
Jim Pollock and the happy couple stand with the "Pollocketubah." Photo: Bari Epstein.

PLATE 14
Poster design for Mia's Lot Mitzvah, a bat mitzvah celebration that took place in
the parking lot of a Phish show at Dick's Sporting Goods Park, Commerce City,
Colorado, September 1, 2019. Design by Alexis Braun (@unbreakablenet).

rachel's
bat mitzvah

10.07.17
odysea aquarium
SCOTTSDALE, ARIZONA

PLATE 15
Bat mitzvah invitation inspired by the band. Photo: Rob and Dani Mattisinko.

PLATE 16
A Phish-inspired first night of Hanukkah. Photo: Jeremy Mittman.

PLATE 17
"Treydel." Design by Ari Stein.

PLATE 18
A candid photo from the World's Biggest Cowbell Ensemble, organized by Ben & Jerry's and
hosted by Jon Fishman, Burlington, Vermont, April 14, 2012. Photo: Christopher Cousins.

PLATE 19
"Hampton Golden Age 2013," Hampton Coliseum, Hampton,
Virginia, October 20, 2013. Photo: Andrea Z. Nusinov.

15.

Blessed by Bass

AN INTERVIEW WITH MARC BROWNSTEIN

MARC BROWNSTEIN, a pioneer of live, improvisational electronic rock music, is the bassist for the Philadelphia-based rock band the Disco Biscuits. He is also the founder and cochair of HeadCount, a nonprofit organization that uses the power of music to register voters and promote participation in democracy.

 OREN KROLL-ZELDIN AND ARIELLA WERDEN-GREENFIELD: Can you tell us your Phish origin story? How did you first learn about and come to love Phish?

MARC BROWNSTEIN: I started to hear about Phish while growing up in New York City, but it was when I got to college at the University of Pennsylvania in Philadelphia that I started to get into the band. There was a whole segment of the population at Penn that came from northeastern boarding schools and they all had Phish tapes. I remember I was in the quad one day and somebody said, "Listen to this song," and then they played "Fee."[1] And I was like, "Okay, this is cool sounding. This is catchy. I think I get it." And then from there, I was driving on a road trip in the summer of '92 and we had a tape in the car of Phish from Broome County Forum in '92.[2] It had the song "Wilson" on it and I connected with the song.[3] There are sets of chord changes through "Wilson" and they're all three-chord changes. But they're continuously changing. And it caught my attention that they had a chance to take any one of these three-chord changes and write a whole song over just that and it would be fine. Phish has done that many times as you dive deeper into their catalog. But what caught me was they didn't sit there, they went to another and then there was another section and every section was as catchy as the previous section. And it was just hook, line, and sinker. From that moment I delved deep into the band's music.

I had a moment where I was like, "Whoa, every song is good. Every song is a hit." It's funny to say that every song is a hit for a band that's had zero hits. But that's the thing. In our world we call them "jam-band hits." A jam-band hit is a song that the fans accept as one of their own. And it doesn't ever have to be on the radio. It could be twenty minutes long. It doesn't have to have any of the other characteristics of a hit song. But songs that "hit" with the fans make it into the repertoire. That's a jam-band hit. You write 300 songs, and 180 of them "hit" and 120 of them kind of fall by the wayside. But if you're Phish, every song is a hit. They're all hits. They all stayed in the repertoire for the most part. I started to recognize that on this road trip in the summer of '92. I was like, "Man, this band, they're all hits. Every song is a hit." When I dove deeper into the music, I had a feeling that every note was right. It went from "Here's one song that I like" to "Whoa, every song is great" to "Every note that they hit is perfect."

I don't feel like I've ever heard another band where I had that moment when I thought every single note is intentional and perfect. The band has an intention that they put into their improvisation where they start to set up what's going to happen three or four minutes down the line and you can start to hear it developing. You can hear them developing the theme, but you know that it's all going to peak at this one moment. And you hear that moment coming from so far away. To have a band that had intention to their music and their improvisation—they were developing things so far out and taking you on this journey—it almost makes you feel like you are making it happen yourself. Actually, it's common for Phish fans who take acid (and some who don't) to feel like they're controlling the band. There's that moment where you're on psychedelics and you're like, "I am making this happen." That is the magic behind Phish and improvisational music in general. But it's not just Phish that can do this. JRAD does it and the Biscuits do it and the Dead did it.[4] There's a lot of bands that have that intention. But Phish was where I discovered it.

OKZ AND AWG: How did that road trip in the summer of 1992 change your life?

MB: After that trip I realized that I had found my scene, my people. I started looking for Phish fans around campus. I was looking for Phish shirts. Over time, I developed a little group of friends and fans. A couple of us even played music. And then it is November of '92 and Phish is playing at the Keswick Theatre for Thanksgiving.[5] I had really screwed up at school that semester. I basically had withdrawn from all of my classes and was just hanging out and playing music and not going to school. My mom was so put off and upset by my performance at school that she came and picked me up from Philadelphia on the day that I was supposed to go see my first Phish show at the Keswick. My punishment was to not go to the show. As soon as I got home to New York I got an apartment and applied for music school. I had met Jon, the guitarist of the Disco Biscuits, and Sammy, the drummer of the Disco Biscuits, that semester at school.[6] We had started to jam, but they were so far ahead of my level that I needed to accelerate at a really high pace.

I intentionally went into music school to catch up. It was a conscious effort. I was like, "This is what I want to do with my life." I had met a couple of people who are genius musicians at Penn, but I couldn't be at the school. Instead, I decided to use my time really well. I practiced music eight hours a day, every single day for the next year. I said to myself, "I'm going to go back and start a band with Jon and Sammy in the vein of the Grateful Dead or Phish. I'm going to go start a jam band."

On February 5 and 6, 1993, Phish was playing two nights at the Roseland Ballroom in New York City. All of my friends from Penn drove up, the whole crew. I finally got to see Phish for two nights. It was great! On February 6, John Popper from Blues Traveler came out and played the encore. Noel Redding from the Jimi Hendrix Experience came out to play bass on "Fire."[7] They did a little shtick where they started the song and Mike Gordon botched it. Then they started over and Mike botched it again. Then they're like, "Mike, what's wrong?" He replied, "I don't know, I can't play the song. Maybe we should bring up Noel Redding from Jimi Hendrix." They brought him out to play the song. It was an excellent combination of the music being perfect and the shtick being perfect. I was like, "Where do you find shtick in a band?" It was funny and cute and warm and it felt like home. And I've been going to see Phish ever since.

Even before I saw my first show, in the fall of '92 I felt like I had found my scene for the first time in my life. I felt for the first time that I belonged somewhere, which is a profound thing to find at the age of nineteen just as you're coming into your own as an adult. I found a scene where I felt comfortable, where I felt like myself and where everybody shares something special.

Phish has this incredible talent of making you feel like you're in on a secret. Even with millions and millions of fans, you still feel like it's all an inside joke. Phish integrates things that were specifically aimed at that, like the secret language.[8] I just was getting into Phish when they gave language lessons to introduce their fans to the secret language. It was a brilliant tactic of making everybody on the inside feel like they were a part of something. I guess that's my origin with Phish. Like most people, I heard it, I loved it, and I stuck with it forever.

OKZ AND AWG: Phish sparked your interest in playing intentional improvisational music. Has your relationship to Phish inspired your journey as a professional musician in other ways?

MB: Oh, of course it has. I felt like I was home and I felt like I had finally found a place where I fit in. Phish forged a path for me to follow as a musician. When people say you're a trailblazer, it means that you forged a path. Before Phish, the Grateful Dead forged this path for many years. And then Phish forged this path for so many other young jam bands to come along and just to kind of get on and ride the wave with them.

There's also something significant about the fact that I look at Phish and I see myself. It is important to be able to see yourself in something that's happening on stage in front of thousands of people. That is very inspiring. It's like when people talk about Hollywood and inclusivity, you look at Marvel and *Black Panther* and see how there's a whole generation of young kids who are now finally getting to see people that look like themselves as superheroes.[9] Well, that's what it was for me seeing Phish. I was able to see myself as a superhero. You know, I looked up on stage and I was like, "Here's superheroes and it's just a couple of nerdy Jewish kids and a couple of their friends." I deeply value the concept of inclusivity and I deeply relate to the importance of seeing yourself in roles on TV or in rock bands, as that experience was significant for me as a Jewish kid from New York whose dream was to be a musician and a rock star.

OKZ AND AWG: Was it impactful for you as a bass player to know that Mike Gordon, the bass player in Phish, is Jewish? Did it matter for you as a Jewish kid from New York who plays bass that it was the bass player in Phish who is Jewish? Or would it have impacted you equally if other band members were Jewish?

MB: Well, Fishman is Jewish, too, right? It was both Gordon and Fishman, the drummer, being Jewish that was important for me. It was important in subtle ways though. It's something that I discovered later on about myself that I recognized why I connected so deeply with these guys. Look, it was not subconscious with "Avenu Malkenu." It was celebratory. We were in an arena and they were playing "Avenu Malkenu" and it meant a lot. I'm a secular Jew. I identify as Jewish despite the fact

FIG. 15.1 Madison Square Garden, New York, July 21, 2017. Photo: Shaun Kessler (@shaunkess).

that I'm not a religious Jew. It is my identity. And it meant a lot to me that the Beastie Boys were Jewish.[10] It meant everything as a kid from Brooklyn.

OKZ AND AWG: Members of both the Beastie Boys and Phish are Jewish musicians creating music in a predominately non-Jewish space. Whether that music is explicitly Jewish, like Phish's rendition of "Avenu Malkenu," or not so explicit, Jews seem to connect with it for a number of reasons. Have Jewish Disco Biscuit fans ever shared connections to the music that you are creating directly because of your Jewish identity?

MB: It's funny. Now that I'm a Jewish musician who's had a modicum of success, people have flipped the scenario around on me. Actually, a lot of people connect with me. Of course I respond when other Jewish Phish fans or Jewish Disco Biscuit fans reach out. There is a segment of the Disco Biscuits population that come to shows on Saturday nights but not on Friday nights, and we've come to understand that there's this small segment of our fans that are hyper-religious. There are some hardcore religious Disco Biscuits fans and they pop back up on Saturday. They're not there on Friday and it's part of the culture.

This thing keeps happening to me where Electron or Star Kitchen, my side projects, keep getting booked at the Ardmore Music Hall and for some reason it's continuously falling on a Friday.[11] I live in a predominantly Jewish neighborhood out in Philadelphia's Main Line and there are a lot of religious jam band fans there.[12] I know a lot of them. And I get a lot of crap. Every time that one of these shows get booked on a Friday I'm conscious of it. I'll call the Ardmore and be like, "Hey, I want to play on this weekend." They'll be like, "We have Friday." I'll respond, "No, I need a Saturday. I really need a Saturday." Because there are a lot of religious Jewish fans here in the neighborhood. We're not being inclusive of all of our fans by putting this show on a Friday if there's only going to be one night and we're going to drop it down in Ardmore, which is in the middle of a particularly religious area. It comes up multiple times a year. Where does Judaism intersect with booking music gigs for us? It comes up on Rosh Hashanah and Yom Kippur and Passover. And we have to work around this. Why do we have to work around it? Because we're in a scene with a disproportionately large Jewish fan base compared to how many Jews there are in the United States.

OKZ AND AWG: What about you? Do you mind playing on Rosh Hashanah, Yom Kippur, or Passover?

MB: I have played shows on Yom Kippur that have been booked without forethought. I have done it. I've done it when we're on tours. But I'd say nine times out of ten we're taking Yom Kippur and Rosh Hashanah off and we try to take Passover off. You have to take them off.

OKZ AND AWG: Beyond their Jewish heritage and their schtick, what else about Phish intrigued you as a young aspiring rock star?

MB: If I'm going to be a rock star and I'm growing up in the '80s and '90s, I'll tell you what I'm not doing. I'm not putting on shiny tights and growing my hair out. The thing about Phish is they're just regular guys dressed like regular guys and they made it okay to be regular guys on stage. Okay, they did have a fashion renaissance over the last ten years. Sure. But they've got crazy money so they can go spend ten grand at G-Star RAW and wear jeans that have wax on them or whatever. Looking at you, Gordo![13]

OKZ: The Jews are fashion-forward.

AWG: Yet one of the Jews in Phish wears a muumuu.

OKZ: The same one for thirty years. The other thing you're saying, Marc, is that you found your people through Phish. You also spoke of becoming an insider, of being in on a secret. Can speak more to what that experience is like?

MB: First of all, my early group of Phish friends came from this boarding school culture into Penn. Most of them were not Jewish. The kids that I was going to see Phish with were not a Jewish crowd. They were boarding school kids from Rhode Island and Massachusetts and New Hampshire. Second, I grew up in Flatbush, Brooklyn. So I didn't feel like an outsider growing up. I grew up in New York where there really isn't such a thing as an outsider. It truly is a melting pot. I felt like an outsider in high school, where I felt I didn't fit in among the cool kids. I wonder if you can go back and look at the demographics of the cool kids versus the uncool kids and how it would relate to the Jewish kids and the non-Jewish kids.

But I did feel like an outsider. I wasn't from the one Jewish family in a non-Jewish town or something. You know what I mean? There were Jews everywhere. But maybe where I did mostly feel like an outsider was in private school. And maybe part of that did have to do with the fact that I was the Jewish kid and I never really did make that connection. Because there weren't a lot of Jewish kids actually looking back. There were only ninety kids in my class and not a lot of them were Jewish. So yeah, it probably was connected. When I did find Phish, though, it was like, "Oh my god, there's people that are like me, and who like the same things as me." And Phish just made everybody feel warm and loved and happy. Whatever was missing at home, you found in Phish.

NOTES

1. Phish, "Fee," track 1 on *Junta* (Elektra, 1992).

2. March 20, 1992, at the Broome County Forum in Binghamton, New York.

3. Trey Anastasio, "Wilson," track 7 on *The Man Who Stepped into Yesterday* (senior thesis, Goddard College, 1987).

4. Joe Russo's Almost Dead, or JRAD, is a successful Grateful Dead cover band.

5. The Keswick Theatre in Glenside, Pennsylvania.

6. Jon Barber and Sam Altman. Altman left the Disco Biscuits in 2004. He was replaced by Allen Aucoin in 2005. The band also includes founding member and keyboardist Aron Magner.

7. Jimi Hendrix Experience, "Fire," track 8 on *Are You Experienced* (Track, 1967).

8. Phish's secret language includes a series of signs or signals that are meant to trigger a crowd response.

9. Marvel Studios released the movie *Black Panther* in 2018.

10. Michael "Mike D" Diamond, Adam "MCA" Yauch, and Adam "Ad-Rock" Horovitz of the Beastie Boys share Jewish heritage.

11. In addition to Brownstein, Electron features Mike Greenfield, Aron Magner, and Tom Hamilton, while Star Kitchen features Marlon Lewis, Rob Marscher, and Danny Mayer. The Ardmore Music Hall is located in Ardmore, Pennsylvania.

12. Philadelphia's Main Line area comprises primarily affluent suburbs.

13. "Gordo" is a popular nickname for Mike Gordon.

16.

Becoming the General of Jam

AN INTERVIEW WITH JONATHAN SCHWARTZ

JONATHAN SCHWARTZ is an on-air host at SiriusXM radio (Phish Radio, Jam On), founder of General Musica LLC, and manager for the Grammy-nominated artist Southern Avenue. He has been working in the music and media industries for over twenty years and listening to Phish for close to thirty.

OREN KROLL-ZELDIN AND ARIELLA WERDEN-GREENFIELD: As the on-air host of SiriusXM's Phish Radio, you are one of the foremost public experts on Phish's music. How did first you discover the band?

JONATHAN SCHWARTZ: I grew up in the Northeast in Westchester County, New York, and attended college at the University of Missouri in Columbia, Missouri. Interestingly, it wasn't until I went to the Midwest that I really fell in love with Phish. I had to go to the Midwest to discover a northeastern band.

In college, I lived in a Jewish fraternity house with seventy other Jewish guys. I remember walking down the hallway one day and I heard "Esther" coming out of my fraternity brothers' room.[1] It sounded like circus music, and I was like, "What the heck is this?" Jordy and Howie, who were playing the music, answered, "Oh, this is Phish." I immediately thought, "This is the band that my friend, Francisco, was trying to get me into at camp in '91." I couldn't believe that an actual rock band made music that sounded like this, and that it was on an actual compact disc that you'd buy in a store. I was totally blown away by that fact and it sucked me in. I think the next thing that we heard was "Icculus."[2] I'm like, "Really? This is also on this CD?"

That is kind of how I was hooked—by those two random songs. It was "Esther" and "Icculus." I'm like, "Can I borrow this album?" And then I heard "Fluffhead" and it changed my life.[3] That's how I first got into Phish. I needed to hear more. They then they started spinning tapes for me . . . this was '92.[4] My first opportunity to see them was in 1993. It was April 14, 1993, at the American Theater in St. Louis. My third show was August 16, 1993, also at the American Theater in St. Louis. Both of those shows were released a couple of years ago as the St. Louis '93 box set. I was very lucky that those two shows were my first and third Phish shows ever. My second show was August 14, 1993, in Tinley Park, right outside of Chicago, which was released as one of the original live Phish CDs. My first three shows were so good that the band commercially released them.

OKZ AND AWG: Those are pretty incredible first shows! How did your initial interest in the band translate into a career in the music industry? Your professional journey seems to have taken you to some interesting places.

JS: When I graduated from college in '95 I really didn't know what I wanted to be when I grew up, as most people don't. My first job out of college, I actually worked for the Hillel at Queens College.[5] I was very active in Hillel as a student at the University of Missouri. My second day home from college, I went to go meet with my new boss, a rabbi who was a musician and used to be a hippie, and we connected instantly. He was like, "Listen. I'm leading a tour to Israel with a bunch of Jewish college students from the New York City schools that leaves in a week. I know you're not a student, but it's a really cheap trip. We've got room. You want to come? We'll hang out in Israel for the summer." I went on this trip and had the best time. Then I went to San Francisco for a couple of weeks. Every night my college friend and I would drive around on his motorcycle and see two, three, four different bands.

Then I got back home to New York. I would open up the *Village Voice* and I saw I could do the same thing in New York City. There's so much music going on. I would go out three, four, five nights a week to see a ton of bands. This went on for months. Then I realized I was running out of money. I needed to figure out how to continue seeing as much music as I wanted without having to pay for it. I thought, "How do I do this and not have to spend all the rest of my bar mitzvah money?"

I was living in Manhattan at this point. There was a classic rock bar that had live music on the Upper East Side called Crossroads. They held some early Disco Biscuits shows there, a lot of Dead cover bands. It was my neighborhood watering hole. I would go and hang out, and they would give me pints on the house. The venue hosted live bands about three nights a week. I was twenty-four years old and living the dream. I was there one day at like five in the afternoon, hanging out with the bartenders, drinking a Guinness, and I saw this dude who is the lead singer and guitar player of this band that I used to go see around town there, just putting up posters. I introduced myself to him and said, "What are you doing?" He's like, "I'm putting up posters for our show." I was shocked and responded, "Yeah, but you're a rock star." He responded, "Somebody's got to do it." That's when a little light bulb went off. I told him, "I have a college degree. I can put up posters. I can even go to Kinkos, take that poster, and make them into four little postcards and give them out to people." He's like, "If you do that, I'll put you on the guest list for our shows." Shortly thereafter, they had their first headlining show at the Wetlands, which was the mecca of everything jam in New York City.[6]

OKZ AND AWG: What band are you talking about?

JS: They were called Inasense. They morphed into a band called Soulfarm. They were a very spiritual Jewish band. Their lead guitarist actually toured with Shlomo Carlebach for twelve years.[7] The singer grew up on the Carlebach moshav, moshav Mevo Modi'im, in Israel.[8] That's a whole separate Jewish spiritual thing going on. Anyway, maybe it was God that had me in that bar, drinking a Guinness at that moment in time. I think there's something there. The other guy in the band, who was the guy who played guitar for Shlomo Carlebach for years, he basically says, "Listen, we just got a call. We're headlining the Wetlands. It's our first headlining show there. They told us that if we don't bring two hundred people there, we're never going to play there again. Can you help us?" I'm like, "I can help you."

I realized that, not only could I get to see their shows for free, but if I went to the Wetlands with a stack of flyers for one of their shows, they would let me in any night of the week because I'm helping them get business. No one likes to give out flyers, it's the shittiest job on the planet. But I was twenty-three, twenty-four years old. I had just moved to the city. I didn't have a lot of friends yet. Basically, I would go every night of the week that there was a band that was sort of relevant, and I would just go up to every cool person and would say, "You have to come see this band." Every night. Every night I would go, and I treated it like a job. I was professional about it.

I wasn't annoying, but I did the job and it was a ton of fun. I saw amazing music and met a lot of interesting people.

A few weeks go by, and it's the night of the big Inasense show. It was on Motza'ei Shabbat, because they had religious fans.[9] There is a line out the door, and over six hundred people were waiting to get in. The owner of the club, Pete Shapiro, was like, "What the fuck?" He wasn't even planning on going. He's like, "How is this sold out? Who the fuck is this band?" The doorman said, "They have this guy coming every night promoting their show." They're like, "Find us that guy." They brought me in to the office in the basement of the Wetlands. "Did you do this?" they asked me. I'm like, "What are you talking about?" I was nervous. They're like, "How did you do this?" So I told them. They said, "Now you're doing that for us." That was my first real job in the music business. The Wetlands made me their grassroots promotions guy. From there, I got a job at a record label doing that for all of their artists. Then from there I got a job at *Relix*, and I was there for almost nine years. I built their marketing department, and their circulation, and their events.[10] I worked with Pete Shapiro. I was his coproducer on the Jammy Awards for eight years. That's basically how I started in the music business.

OKZ AND AWG: What a fascinating story. How did you go from there to working with Sirius as an on-air personality?

JS: Flash-forward to 2000, 2001, maybe, when I was working at *Relix*. I was at the 9:30 Club with Andy Bernstein, now of HeadCount and formerly of *The Pharmer's Almanac*, which was the unofficial guide to Phish.[11] He and I we were driving back to New York the next day when we saw the XM building on the side of the road. No one knew what XM was in 2001. No one knew what Sirius was. No one had satellite radio. It wasn't a thing. We just started riffing the whole drive up. We may or may not have been partaking in herbal refreshments at the time. We just started riffing about satellite radio as a concept, and how, if one of these companies had a jam-band channel, they could potentially get tens of thousands of fans for this one channel alone, because there really wasn't a home for the jam-band community. It's not on MTV, it's not on commercial radio.

We basically put a plan together. As the marketing guy at *Relix*, I thought it was a really good opportunity to have a *Relix* channel. It was purely a marketing play from my viewpoint. I knew a guy at Sirius. We went and met with him. He introduced us to his head of programming, who couldn't have cared less. It was just not happening. Then we met the chief programming officer at XM, who is a radio legend named Lee Abrams. Very interesting, bright, and polarizing guy in the world of commercial radio. He gave us a tour. We ordered in lunch. He's like, "Listen. I get it. My kid is a fucking Phishhead. He just left for three weeks to go see shows. But we're not adding any new channels now."

At this point Andy was like, "Listen, man, I've got other shit going on. If you want to keep focusing on this, go ahead, be my guest, but I'm out." But for me it was just part of my job. Every few weeks I would follow up with one of the guys at Sirius. Flash-forward to 2003, I've been doing this for two years. The guy at Sirius calls me back, and he's like, "We have a new head of music programming. I think he gets it. Will you come and give him your spiel?" I went to this guy's office. His name is Joel Salkowitz. I literally give him my ninety-second elevator pitch about what jam radio could be on Sirius. He leans across his desk, takes off his glasses. He goes, "Dude, I went to Hartford. Max Creek was my band. Let's do this! We'd love for you to be on air. You'll do this many shifts a week." I'm like, "I'm not really looking to get on air. I've never DJ-ed in my life." He's like, "That's why we want you. We don't want a standard jive-talking DJ, we want someone who sounds like they're sitting on their couch, pulling bongs with their buddies." I'm like, "I could do that!" We launched the channel two weeks later. That was in March of 2003.

OKZ AND AWG: Let's talk a bit more about the industry. Why do you think so many Jewish people are beacons of the Phish community and leaders of the jam-centric music industry?

JS: I've had different thoughts about this over the years. I don't think there's any way to really know. I mean, if you look back at like the original jam-band scene, you're looking at Jefferson Airplane and the Grateful Dead, and the biggest proponent of those guys was Bill Graham, the big promoter. He was a New York Jew, who is from the Bronx, who really got his start promoting card games in the Borscht Belt, the Catskills. I'm just riffing here, but a lot of industries were shut off to Jews early on. You couldn't join certain clubs, you couldn't go to certain schools, you couldn't do certain jobs. The world of entertainment was something that Jews could do on both sides of the stage, so I think there are a fair number of Jewish people that got involved in entertainment because that was one of the industries that they could do. Fast-forward forty years, Jews have just been doing this for a long time because it's one of the fields of industry that they were allowed to participate in and they did well.

OKZ AND AWG: What about Phish fans? Why do you think there are so many Jewish Phish fans?

JS: A good question. One, half the band is Jewish. That doesn't happen with all bands. Half of Pearl Jam or Metallica or Destiny's Child are not Jewish. For a young fan getting into music, when you see four dudes on stage, and half of them are Jews, I think people feel a connection with that that you don't normally see in rock bands. I think that might be part of it, but also the fact that they've incorporated Jewish liturgy and Jewish songs into their repertoire. Nirvana never played "Yerushalayim Shel Zahav" or "Avenu Malkenu," arguably the most holy piece of Jewish liturgy. The fact that Phish plays these songs is significant. They're playing the most spiritual, maybe most important song or prayer. I think that's pretty heavy. There's something there, so I think that's definitely a reason why Phish may resonate with Jews. Also, Phish was a northeastern band and there are so many Jews in the Northeast, so I think that definitely plays a role.

I also think that there's a tribal thing going on. Phish fans and the Phish community are a tribe to a certain degree. They're an underdog community. I mean, Phish is arguably the largest underground band in the history of popular music, you know? Yeah, they may sell out thirteen nights in a row at Madison Square Garden, but if you walked down Seventh Avenue any day of the week and ask fifty random people, "Hey, do you like Phish?" I would say probably forty-eight of them would not have any idea what you're talking about, even though their name is on the marquee. Phish is an underdog band and Jews are underdogs by definition. We're a minority. Phish is sort of in the minority in the large-scale music world, so I think there's some sort of connection there, between the tribal thing and the fact that Phish is kind of an underdog. It's kind of like Phish against the world. Remember, was it fall '97? It was like, "Phish Destroys America."[12]

OKZ AND AWG: How has Jewishness factored into your personal and professional journey?

JS: I grew up in a conservative Jewish household. My mom was very active in the shul and B'nai B'rith, as was my dad.[13] We were very Jewishly connected and kept a kosher house.[14] We were not *shomer Shabbat*, but my mom lit candles every Friday night and we went to synagogue most Saturday mornings.[15] I also went to after-school Hebrew school three days a week—I hated it. It was terrible.

I had a bar mitzvah, too. It's funny. I never really considered myself super Jewish or anything, but when I went to college, I realized that I definitely had more of a background than most typical American middle- and upper-middle-class Jews. I wouldn't say I had more of a spiritual connection, but I knew how to daven.[16] I knew how to do stuff, even though my knowledge of Hebrew was nonexistent. I joined a Jewish fraternity when I went to college because I was in the middle of Missouri with so few Jews. People often ask what it was like going to the University of Missouri in the '90s and if there were other Jews there. I tell them I lived with seventy Jewish dudes from the North Shore of Chicago and St. Louis. I lived in the Jewiest place ever. No wonder I got into Phish.

But it's funny. At the frat they would say "Someone's got to make kiddush."[17] All right. Call Schwartz. Schwartz is the guy. Bring him in. He'll do it." Even in college, I barely did shit Jewishly, but I was definitely connected. I was also the only one from New York, so from the perspective of my fraternity brothers I was practically from Israel.

OKZ AND AWG: Now that you mention Israel, do you currently live there?

JS: I do. My first time in Israel was in '95. I got hit with the bug. Not the Jewish bug, but definitely the Israel bug. I definitely remember my dad picking me up at the JFK airport after being in Israel for four or five weeks and driving through shitty neighborhoods in Queens. I'm like, "This is what I came back for? I should have stayed in Israel." Then, four years later, I met an Israeli woman. We got married and lived in New York together for about twelve years. By 2010 we had two young kids and another on the way. I was self-employed. I was working at SiriusXM and I was managing a few artists, and we figured, why do we need to be stuck in the US? Let's try living in Israel to be closer to my wife's family. If SiriusXM is cool with me doing my show remotely, then why not? So we moved to Israel, and that was ten years ago. I commute back and forth, and I do the Phish Radio thing and did the Jam On thing at SiriusXM, but I also manage a band called Southern Avenue that just got nominated for their first Grammy. I've been doing that for four years, so I commute back and forth a lot. I would say, until coronavirus, every other month I was back in the US for ten days to two weeks. My wife says I have the world's longest commute. Most people don't realize that I live in Israel.

OKZ AND AWG: Can you tell us what the Phish scene is like in Israel?

JS: There is no Phish scene in Israel. There are Phishheads, but not too many. Most of them are expats from the US. I haven't met any native Israeli Phishheads. One, but he's actually my neighbor. He's one of my Phish friends who is also a Deadhead. His son went to school with my son. But he doesn't count, because he grew up mostly in Italy, which is also a weird place to become a Deadhead and a Phishhead. There are some Phish fans in Jerusalem, some in Tel Aviv. They may have had several hangouts on occasion. I know a pretty fun hippie rabbi, Rabbi Shu, who lives on a kibbutz in the desert in the South who's an enormous Phish fan. He'll go on Phish tour. He's a righteous, positive dude.

The psychedelic hippie scene in Israel, in my experience, is centered around electronic music. It is definitely much more of like a Goa, India, kind of vibe. It is more that kind of global traveler hippie vibe than a going-on-Phish-tour hippie vibe. There's a similar mindset, but it comes from a different place, and the music is definitely different.

In Israel, there are more Grateful Dead fans here who were on Dead tour, who got a whole spiritual bug and became religious and moved to Israel. They're not into Phish, or they don't know Phish because they've been here. So yeah, I don't think there's a large Phish community here. There is a small Facebook group that talks about bringing Phish to Israel, but it's never going to happen. I got outed in that Facebook group as being someone who lives in Israel.

OKZ AND AWG: You mention being "outed" on social media. Do you have concerns about people knowing that you live in Israel? Is that something you're trying to keep quiet?

JS: I don't advertise it, but I don't hide it. It's the truth. It's not something we're going to put on the SiriusXM website or something I put on my Facebook page for the average listener, but I have no problem with it being in a scholarly publication.

OKZ AND AWG: Thank you for sharing. Returning for a moment to the relationship between Phish and Jewishness, do you have particular memories that connect Phish with Jewish life or Jewish identity?

JS: It's funny because one of my best friends who I've seen well over fifty Phish shows with, this is his experience, but we joke about it at every show. I wasn't there, but Phish was playing at Shoreline.[18] He had an incredibly intense psychedelic experience where he was anointed "Prince of the Jewish Phishheads." And it's a great story. And so that's kind of our code. We're both *kohanim*, so we have this priestly joke between us.[19] After the show I asked him, "So, did you get anointed?" He'll be at a show, especially when I'm in Israel and he's there and he's going to shows and I'm here listening to them on LivePhish, and I'll be like, "So, how was Vegas? Did you get anointed?"[20]

We always joke about him being the Prince of the Jewish Phishheads. But I don't really have any Jewish moments at a Phish show. I've been at a couple of Phish festivals where I bumped into some Orthodox friends of mine and they've asked me if I would daven with them so they can have a minyan.[21] I've done that, but it wasn't really something that I particularly sought out.

I think there are a lot of Jewish people who go to Phish shows and the music and the community has a spiritual effect on them. I think people might have a newfound spiritual connection that they never experienced through organized religion before. And what do you do with that spirituality? Do you listen to Deepak Chopra podcasts? Do you start practicing yoga or do you maybe [explore] your own traditions and culture? It's almost like a spiritual sieve is opened up at a Phish show, and people start seeking answers. Once it's open, you need to find out how to nourish that. And I think for Jewish people that have this experience there are aspects of Judaism that help fill that void very nicely. Phish may open up the door, and I think they do it for not just for Jewish people. It happened for Christian Phish fans, for Muslim Phish fans, for Hindu Phish fans. There's just a lot of Jewish Phish fans for the reasons that we've talked about. I think Phish helps people tap into their Jewishness that they may not have been otherwise tapped into. Hebrew school may not have resonated with them. They may have been bored in synagogue, hearing someone speak some ancient language that they have no real connection with. Phish might open that door for some people.

In fact, I don't know if there's so many Jewish Phish fans, maybe it's just because we know a lot of Jewish people because we're Jewish people, and we're going to Phish. If you go to a show in Tennessee, how many Jews are there? That's a good question. If you're going to a show in Salt Lake City, how many Jews are there? Are there more Jews than if you saw Metallica in Salt Lake City? I don't know. It's a good question. I think we're kind of looking at it in a vacuum, almost. We're looking at how many Jews do we see on fall tour. Most of those shows are in the Northeast, so there are a lot of Jews there. Phish recently played "Avenu Malkenu" at Nassau Coliseum in Uniondale, New York. Do they play "Avenu Malkenu" because they're in Long Island where all the Jews are? Are they going to play "Avenu Malkenu" when they play in Lexington, Kentucky? I don't know. Do they say, "Hey, yeah, we're in Long Island, there are a lot of Jews. Let's play 'Avenu Malkenu tonight.'"

NOTES

1. Phish, "Esther," track 3 on *Junta* (Elektra, 1992).

2. Phish, "Icculus," track 14 on *Junta* (Elektra, 1992).

3. Phish, "Fluffhead," track 9 on *Junta* (Elektra, 1992).

4. A reference to the once-common fan practice of trading cassette recordings of live Phish concerts.

5. Sponsored by Hillel International, Hillel functions as a gathering place and center of Jewish life on college campuses across the world.

6. The Wetlands was a club owned by Pete Shapiro that hosted concerts from 1989 through 2001 in New York City's Tribeca neighborhood.

7. Shlomo Carlebach was a rabbi, spiritual leader, and composer.

8. A moshav is a cooperative agricultural community in Israel.

9. Motza'ei Shabbat, which translates as "the going out of Shabbat," refers to the Saturday evening immediately following the end of Shabbat.

10. Established in 1974, *Relix* is a popular magazine that covers the live music scene.

11. The 9:30 Club is located in Washington, DC.

12. A reference to the band's 1997 fall tour dubbed by fans "Phish Destroys America."

13. *Shul* translates as "synagogue," and B'nai B'rith is a Jewish organization focused on ensuring a voice for the global Jewish community.

14. A kosher house is one wherein residents adhere to the Jewish dietary laws.

15. Someone who is *shomer Shabbat* keeps the sabbath by honoring behavioral restrictions surrounding the Jewish day of rest.

16. To daven is to pray Jewishly.

17. Kiddush is a blessing made over wine that sanctifies Shabbat and holidays.

18. Shoreline Amphitheatre in Mountain View, California.

19. *Kohanim* share a priestly lineage as the descendants of Aaron.

20. The LivePhish website offers soundboard recordings of Phish concerts.

21. A minyan is a prayer group of at least ten adults.

17.

Mike's Corner Reprise

AN INTERVIEW WITH MIKE GORDON

MIKE GORDON is a musician and filmmaker who lives in the woods in Vermont. He is the bassist and cofounder of Phish and the leader of his own band, which tours under his name.

OREN KROLL-ZELDIN AND ARIELLA WERDEN-GREENFIELD: Can you give us an overview of your Jewish background?[1]

MIKE GORDON: From a young age I went to temple with my parents on Saturdays, which usually meant playing in the temple's backyard. But by kindergarten, I'd started at Solomon Schechter Day School in Newton, Massachusetts.[2] I went there for seven years before transferring to public school in seventh grade. The Solomon Schechter schools and [their] offshoots are rooted in the Conservative movement and my family's temple was Reform. I also knew many observant Jews while I was growing up. One of my best friends, Rebecca Kolodny, became quite religious. My father also attended an Orthodox temple for a while, so I was exposed to many forms of Jewish practice. My rabbi at the time was Lawrence Kushner. Kushner is now a notable writer and scholar of Kabbalah.[3] He was a very cool rabbi to grow up with.

At Solomon Schechter, full disclosure would be that I didn't really learn Hebrew that well compared to other kids. At the time I rebelled against it a little bit—learning Hebrew, studying the Tanakh.[4] The whole thing, to some degree, felt like something my parents were putting me through that I hadn't chosen.

However, I was also aware that the cultural parts of my education were very enriching, and I was developing a feeling of fondness for aspects of Jewish life. From learning melodies to cooking different kinds of foods and celebrating different holidays and stories, my experience at Solomon Schechter certainly fostered that sense of fondness. Yet I still rebelled. I think as I got older, I realized the significance of what I had gained through that chapter of my education. My familiarity with all of the Jewish customs and rituals that I didn't entirely relate to as a child later felt like [they] had prepared me to have my own kinds of religious and transcendent experiences through music.

Now, many years later, I just finished watching Joseph Campbell's 1988 Bill Moyer interviews.[5] Talk about someone who's putting it all together from not only Judaism but all the religions, all of the mythology and writings, and all of my peak experiences and transcendent experiences. He's just saying that it's all the same thing, and that's what I started to sense early on.

OKZ AND AWG: Can you tell us a bit about the transcendent experiences that you referenced? What do transcendent experiences look like for you?

MG: We all experience transcendence in different ways. When I was younger, there were some really momentous ones. Going to my first Grateful Dead concert is one that stands out. That was in 1982. Only three years later, in 1985, Phish played Goddard College.[6] A couple of my bandmates were already going to school there. There were five people in the band that night because Jeff Holdsworth was still playing with us.[7] It was the first snowfall of November. It was beautiful. The snow had stopped and it was dark. All the lights were off, and outside the moon was shining. I should have that date astrologically analyzed. I wonder if the moon was full.

By the second set of the show, there were only two people in the audience. We walked back onto the stage and formed a circle. In sound circles there is a focal point in the middle, and the five of us were aiming the sound inward and outside. I had a transcendent experience in that moment. I was jumping up and down the whole time. I'd had one hit off of a joint. It wasn't laced with anything, but I did feel very floaty and I became more myself than I'd ever been in my entire life, by far. I started jumping up and down with the beat, and I felt like if I got a little off the beat, the peak, the transcendence, came down a little bit. Staying with the beat was important.

I knew I looked stupid, but first of all, it was pitch dark, and second of all, who cared anyway? I didn't care. Not caring was important.

After that, my mind was blown. I felt like I really loved the four other guys in the band. I walked out into the woods and I hugged a tree. I set a goal for my life that night. I wanted to play music in different cities every night with these guys. I wanted to live in the woods. Here we are, thirty-six years from that moment, and that's what I did, more or less.

I didn't want to play another set that night because my experience of the sound circle was such a high. But the rest of the band wanted to play again, so I said okay, and then I experienced another peak. I kept testing, like if I played with a pick instead of my fingers, would it still be a peak? Oh yeah, it still was. Then the show ended and I sat at a table with those guys and I asked, "So, did you have the same experience as me?" They were like, "No, not really, but we're glad you did."

Anyway, I remember talking to Jeff Holdsworth, who, not too long after, left the band, telling him that I was going to dedicate all of my journals for the rest of my life, or at least a few years, to figuring out what had happened. That was the big one. Over the years, there were other experiences that were peak experiences, and maybe not quite like the first time, but definite peaks as well.

As I've gotten older, the dedication and my intentions have changed. I spend much of my time on my other musical endeavors. I also put a lot of time into my filmmaking career. My first movie took five thousand hours of work. I'm thinking of making my third feature-length film sometime, hopefully. I'm very excited about that.

OKZ AND AWG: Was there something specific about the set list that night at Goddard College that encouraged your transcendent experience?

MG: There were two kinds of gigs that we had had in 1985. One where everything was tight, all the endings were perfect and the beginnings were perfect, and the other, where we would jam and go through these flights of fancy for a long time, but they never were the same. A gig was either going to be type A or type B. From the first notes of the first set that night at Goddard College, which was not the transcendent set, I could tell that this was different and this was both. It was completely free and completely structured at the same time.

OKZ AND AWG: That marriage between structure, order, and creativity is certainly a hallmark of Phish's musical approach. Speaking of the band's music, how did Phish come to play "Avenu Malkenu" and "Yerushalayim Shel Zahav"?

MG: Well, I introduced them to the band. "Avenu Malkenu," for me, is a special song not because of what the lyrics mean but because of the melody. Now, I've been informed by Jewish friends recently, not to mention my wife's sister who is a cantor, that the classic melody [*sings the tune*] was actually taken from a folk song, and it is not the original.

Still, that melody was familiar and ever present for me. When I was growing up, if there was ever a lull in a service, Rabbi Kushner would begin to chant that melody. He would start singing that melody as the soundtrack—the score music—to my religious experience in temple, and notably, the Havdalah service.[8] Not many people would attend the Havdalah service. Maybe twenty-five people, and they weren't facing forward, they were in a circle or a square, facing inward. It's very communal, and then that melody comes, so that's a real heart place.

My appreciation for the melody started from something really meaningful stemming from the Jewish upbringing that I wasn't so sure about. I was sure about the emotion of that Havdalah moment and that chant. That melody was haunting in the best of ways for me, and so I really wanted to bring it to the guys and try it, as a lark. Anyway, then we put it in five and gave it the funk groove and sandwiched it within Trey's "The Man Who Stepped into Yesterday," but I believe that at least part of that was called "I'm Going to Get My Head Sharpened," even though that got truncated from the name.[9]

In two days, my daughter and I will be singing at a Havdalah service at a virtual "Havdalah coffee shop," with our two local temples, the Reform one and the Conservative one, together on one Zoom.[10] So it's still going. But anyway, a beautiful song.

OKZ AND AWG: Why did you decide to sandwich "Avenu Malkenu" within "The Man Who Stepped into Yesterday"?

MG: The decision probably came from Trey, as he's "Mr. Broadway." He knows how to be extra-dramatic. I don't remember the specific reason, but I can imagine that there's something about just playing it. Maybe it's a little too stark to just launch into it. Jewish prayer, funk groove. Maybe it works better to give it a ramp-up and a ramp-down.

OKZ AND AWG: How did audiences respond when you first started playing "Avenu Malkenu"?

MG: At the time, looking out into the crowd, it was easy to see who the Jews were because their eyes would light up when we went into it, and that was kind of fun. I loved the unexpectedness of it. It became different when Phish had a bigger following, but when we were playing in clubs and theaters and Jewish people wandered in having no idea that they were going to hear anything in Hebrew, there it was. A look of shock. I liked that part of it.

It's interesting that "Avenu Malkenu" ends up being something kitschy. It's in five. To some people, it could be sacrilegious. "Avenu Malkenu" is a holy prayer, so some people might find us playing it sacrilegious.

Then, we put it into a kitschy funk—maybe even cheesy—context. While this may bother some people, others understand where our rendition is coming from. Even though it might be sort of funny, there are actually some real parts of our identity, our heritage, our DNA, and our emotions that are finding this root through a strange context.

OKZ AND AWG: What about "Yerushalayim Shel Zahav"? Why did the band begin to play the song and why did it fall out of the rotation?[11]

MG: "Yerushalayim Shel Zahav" is another one that, for me, is really emotional. But, instead of conjuring memories of temple, I most associate "Yerushalayim Shel Zahav" with the break fast after Yom Kippur.[12] Everyone in my temple clique went to the Blechers' house, and Mari Blecher would sit with an acoustic guitar and strum the song. My parents also had the Naomi Shemer album.[13]

It's a very beautiful song and melody, and it's haunting. Not to get too technical, but the way that it goes back and forth between minor and major—first within the verse because it starts the verse on a major chord, A major, and then it comes back, maybe, to A minor at the end of the line—it's already kind of tragic-sounding. Then, for it to migrate to the relative major chord for the chorus, the song dancing from minor to major is very haunting. That would be a technical reason, but I love the overall package, including the line "In all your songs, I am a violin."

There are a few people from my Solomon Schechter class that I've been in touch with almost the whole time. Jill Goldman is one of them. When it was time for Phish to try the song out, I think I called her, and she helped me find this choral arrangement. I don't know what gave us the inspiration to go after that song with two people who had never spoken one word of Hebrew in their entire lives and somehow memorize it. That was very impressive. Even for us that had spoken Hebrew, it was still hard to memorize. I didn't know what the words meant. I didn't learn Hebrew. We learned the a cappella version, I don't know what gave us that idea, which ended up being a perfect song for *Hoist*.[14]

It was really hard. That's probably the reason we didn't keep doing it, because it was too hard to remember something like that. It's like me trying to remember

"Mock Song," which is never going to happen.[15] Before the Magnaball, I practiced it maybe two hundred times in a row on the tour bus, and I really thought I had it.[16] I got on stage and I only remembered one-third of it. Oh, and then I did it again with Abby, who works in Phish's production office. She held up the words on signs like Bob Dylan does with "Subterranean Homesick Blues," and I still couldn't do it, so never mind being able to remember a song in Hebrew with four verses.[17]

OKZ AND AWG: Since you mentioned Magnaball, we have to ask. There's a rumor that you played "Avenu Malkenu" on the first night of the festival because someone in the band spotted a Star of David flag among the fans. Is that true? And looking beyond Magnaball, what inspires the band to play "Avenu Malkenu"?

MG: I have no idea whether that was true then. Sometimes, we've played it because of some event, but it could be a number of things. Maybe there's been some historical event that went down, and the guys might say, "Oh, well maybe it'd be good to do 'Avenu Malkenu.'" That doesn't mean that there's a reason every time we play it. It might just be "Oh, we haven't done this one in a long time. I just heard it from '93, and it's a fun one. Let's throw it in."

It's really always Trey. I don't help decide. Trey very strongly encourages everyone to contribute to making up a song list, and I think Page does so more than anyone else. I just appreciate and respect that Trey spends hours each day, halfway between a science project and a religious ritual, creating the set list and then eventually veering from it. It's a lot to think about. What key? Do we want to stay in the same key and the same tempo? Do we want to build up to a certain thing by the end? I think a lot more about that kind of thing with my own band.

OKZ AND AWG: How did the non-Jewish members of Phish respond when you brought "Avenu Malkenu" and "Yerushalayim Shel Zahav" to the band?

MG: They were very respectful and into it. I think that we are each really good at respecting other people's identities. One of our secrets to success has been communicating so well over the years. With that understanding and that communication, I think there's a willingness to accept that we're different individuals with different upbringings and heritages, and not only to accept that but to want to encourage it. Let this person really be who they are, and let them bring that to the table. We respect that each one of us has a richness of character that comes from all kinds of different experiences and we really want to put that on a pedestal rather than ignoring it.

I think we realized we were going to be an eclectic band pretty early on. In my opinion, the shows work better when there's a flow and there's a consistency of vibe that goes through the sets rather than getting thrown from here to here to there, which I think, back in the earlier days, we did more. Some of the sets weren't so cohesive-feeling because they went so far all over the map, but in later years, it feels like whether we're playing a song in Hebrew or bluegrass or whatever, that it's more melded, integrated.

I mean, that's a big challenge for any artist. It's one of the biggest challenges: to be able to express and develop your own voice while not throwing out the influences, to be able to dissociate somewhat from your influences while not throwing them out completely. Also honoring the traditions at the same time. I think there's a sense that "Hey, if you want to bring something interesting, crazy, and unexpected to the table, then please do." There's always been that encouraging atmosphere.

OKZ AND AWG: Let's shift our focus from your Phish bandmates to the band's fans. Why do you think that so many Jews like Phish?

MG: I'm not sure that I know, but my gut feeling is that there's a certain energy. Fans of the Grateful Dead, and then Phish fans, created a culture around the bands and their music and, in some ways, a little way of life. Concerts served as a kind of religion and a kind of ritual for people in the way that organized religion used to. This is not a replacement, but there's a matching of a kind of vibe.

This is not specific to Phish, but the whole idea of thinking of someone dancing at a show as someone davening, moving back and forth, the movement and the chanting and facing different directions. Facing the front, thinking these thoughts, and having these transcendent experiences. It matches up.

The Grateful Dead being from the West Coast and from a certain generation, the 1960s, it seems like the kind of rebellion or separating from the status quo that happened with Deadheads is a West Coast cowboy sort of phenomenon, whereas, with Phish being from the Northeast, two of us being Jewish, it is different.

When I think about Jewish people getting together at a seder, during the meal, or just sitting around together, there's this kind of analytical mindset where, sometimes, I see Jewish people, including myself, having an intellectual, almost academic way of looking at a situation, describing it, reflecting on it, analyzing it, laughing about it.[18]

This is a silly tangent, but my mind went to meeting Sun Ra, who was such a big influence on Phish. Fishman had already met him the night before. There we were at three o'clock in the morning in his hotel room after his performance in Cambridge, Massachusetts. We're sitting there, me, Fish, and Sun Ra, and I became this one kid who you would expect to be the most annoying kid at the seder, who talked a little too loud, a little too fast, and so much in the head and not in the heart and body, saying "So, Sun Ra, when you said that, then did you mean that?" Just that whole sort of analytical thing.

That, sort of, for me matches some of the Phish experience, where the band members, we're so analytical that we had to develop the "No Analyze Rule."[19] The No Analyze Rule was the most beautiful thing. As we matured, I think we really cultivated this part of our being and realized how inferior the mind alone can be and moved toward getting the body involved with stuff that's more danceable, getting the spirit involved with stuff that's more transcendent, getting the heart involved with stuff that's more emotional, and not just mental.

Still, this kind of mindset leads to the creation of music that's sort of quirky—the way that there's a fugue here, there's a bluegrass song there, and there's a Hebrew prayer there—it's woven together with this incredible energy. Then, the fans in turn analyze that. "Why were these songs played and in what frequency?" and all of the analytics and all that kind of thing, there's something a little bit Jewish-seeming.

OKZ AND AWG: Do you often see expressions of Jewish identity at Phish shows?

MG: I mean, I hear about things. For example, when we've played at Deer Creek or somewhere like that, I have heard, "Oh, there's a Friday-night temple service set up in the parking lot, and it's actually in every town." I've heard of things like that.[20]

OKZ AND AWG: What's so remarkable about Phish shows and the Jewish experience is that there is a massive spectrum of Jewish people in attendance at shows, and people across that spectrum articulate their Jewish identity in numerous ways, some explicit and some much more subtle. There are some people who gather to pray at set breaks.

MG: Wow.

OKZ AND AWG: And of course, Jewish fans who, while at your concerts, connect with their Jewish identities in countless other ways.

MG: Also, if there are two people in the band, even if Fish didn't really have as strong of a religious upbringing, still, there's this cultural thing that's built in, and that's half the band, which might be a higher percentage than some bands. It's probably a higher percentage than the Grateful Dead. Is Mickey Hart Jewish? I can't remember.

OKZ AND AWG: Yes, he is.

MG: Well, there you have it, because even Mickey and I have a strange connection. There is a thing with some Jewish people. If you're at a cocktail party and there's another Jewish person that's on the other side of the room, you just know. When people are from a similar culture, there's a nonverbal thing that happens that connects them. And when I get in a room with someone who is Jewish, there's something where I'll just know and we will be connected. A connection is established and then there are extra channels of connection going on in the room that end up enhancing the cohesion of the entire room.

NOTES

1. The title of this interview is inspired by Gordon's column, titled "Mike's Corner," which appeared in the early Phish newsletter the *Doniac Schvice*.

2. Solomon Schechter Day School is a network of Jewish Day Schools affiliated with the Conservative movement.

3. Rabbi Lawrence Kushner was a rabbi at Congregation Beth-El in Sudbury, Massachusetts. He has published over twenty books on Jewish religion and spirituality.

4. *Tanakh* is an acronym for the Hebrew Bible that is derived from the names of its divisions, Torah, Nevi'im, and Ketuvim.

5. *Joseph Campbell and the Power of Myth* is a six-episode series of Moyers interviewing Campbell that aired on PBS in 1988.

6. On November 23, 1985.

7. Jeff Holdsworth is a founding member who left the band in 1986.

8. Havdalah is a traditional Jewish ceremony that marks the end of Shabbat.

9. In a 5/4 time signature. Trey Anastasio, "The Man Who Stepped into Yesterday," track 2 on *The Man Who Stepped into Yesterday* (senior thesis, Goddard College, 1987).

10. During the COVID-19 pandemic, Jewish services, rituals, and communal gatherings often convened on the virtual platform Zoom.

11. Phish last played "Yerushalayim Shel Zahav" on December 31, 1994, at the Boston Garden.

12. Yom Kippur is a fast day for Jews that ends with a communal break fast.

13. Shuli Natan, *Jerusalem of Gold* (Hed Arzi Music, 1967).

14. Phish, *Hoist* (Elektra, 1994).

15. Phish, "Mock Song," track 7 on *Round Room* (Elektra, 2002).

16. The Magnaball festival took place in Watkins Glen, New York, August 21–23, 2015.

17. Bob Dylan, "Subterranean Homesick Blues," track 1 on *Bringing It All Back Home* (Columbia, 1965).

18. A seder is a traditional ritual meal that commemorates the Passover story.

19. For a discussion on the "No Analyze Rule," which prohibits bandmates from commenting on one another's playing, see Patrick Doyle, "Phish's New Harmony: How America's Greatest Jam Band Learned to Get Along," *Rolling Stone*, October 21, 2016, https://www.rollingstone.com/music/music -features/phishs-new-harmony-how -americas-greatest-jam-band-learned-to-get -along-107239.

20. Deer Creek is a music venue in Noblesville, Indiana, where Phish has played twenty-four times since 1995.

Afterword

Dean Budnick

Why is this night different from all other nights?

When it comes to Phish that's actually a pretty easy question to answer given the fact that the quartet doesn't repeat set lists.

It is also the question that remained top of mind as I read all the essays and interviews in this volume.

Phish is a singular band and its audience is equally nonpareil. So what exactly is the full nature of the connection between the group and Jewish identity?

In contemplating my response to this query within the context of the preceding work, my thoughts turned to the Passover Haggadah. While the "Four Questions" may consist of one question and four responses, I've opted to formulate eighteen question prompts (*chai*!) that I hope will resonate with scholars as they continue to refine and nurture this burgeoning field.[1]

L'Shana haba'ah b'Yerushalayim (or failing that, Fish side, knish side).[2]

1. *Can Phish's appeal to Jews be framed in the context of multigenerational cultural assimilation?* In his essay "Why Are There So Many Jewish Deadheads?" Douglas

Gertner contends that "lacking both a strong *chevra* (a sense of community) and finding Judaism devoid of *ruach* or *neshama* (spiritual foundation or soul) third-generation American Jews were adrift in search of meaning, purpose, and roots."[3] Gertner then concludes that this personal exploration contributed to the disproportionate population of Jewish Grateful Dead fans going back to the late 1960s and 1970s. The current wave of Phish enthusiasts are fourth- and fifth-generation Jews. What are we to make of this?

2. *Has the percentage of Phish fans who self-identify as Jews changed over time and if so, what accounts for it?* In Mike Gordon's conversation with Oren Kroll-Zeldin and Ariella Werden-Greenfield, he notes the evolving crowd response to "Avenu Malkenu" over the course of the band's career. Gordon recalls, "Looking out into the crowd, it was easy to see who the Jews were because their eyes would light up when we went into it, and that was kind of fun. . . . When we were playing in clubs and theaters and Jewish people wandered in having no idea that they were going to hear anything in Hebrew, there it was. A look of shock. I liked that part of it."

Now that the element of surprise has dissipated (not in every instance, to be clear, as some concertgoers are still flabbergasted when "Avenu Malkenu" makes its rare appearance), it might be fruitful to consider whether Phish's appeal to Jewish fans has changed since the mid-'90s.[4]

Are there particular eras during the band's musical evolution that have resonated more deeply with Jewish Phish fans? Or is this more a product of the cultural institutions surrounding the group, such as the summer camps referenced in some of the prior chapters? Another consideration may well be that the band has become known for performing both "Avenu Malkenu" and "Yerushalayim Shel Zahav."

3. *Does Phish's musical assimilation correlate with Jewish cultural assimilation?* Phish has been celebrated for the range of its musical influences that transcend traditional genre boundaries, and the group has come to absorb and synthesize many of these styles over time. When Mike Gordon appeared on my *Long May They Run* podcast, he expressed some mild disapprobation with what he characterized as the band's early "Tour of the World gigs, where every style was used from one to the next to the next. I didn't like those gigs because they were too scattered for me. It just was kind of like watering down each genre by slamming it against another one." While speaking with Kroll-Zeldin and Werden-Greenfield he adds, "In later years, it feels like whether we're playing a song in Hebrew or bluegrass or whatever, that it's more melded, integrated." Salad bowl / melting pot

analogies aside, are there relevant parallels between the band's creative endeavors and the efforts of Jews to find a place of comfort within the surrounding society and culture?[5] Do the various eras of the band, which typically are described as 1.0, 2.0., 3.0, and 4.0, correspond in any manner with the generational demarcation of American Jewry?

4. *What can be gleaned from examining the band's lyrics?* Most of the preceding chapters reference two songs that Phish covers: "Avenu Malkenu" and "Yerushalayim Shel Zahav." But what about the group's original material? Are there particular compositions that reflect a Jewish sensibility or foster community (and are they vested with additional zest or nuance when a Jewish member of the band has written them)? Can one read Phish's music in a similar way as Seth Rogovoy does in his book *Bob Dylan: Prophet, Mystic, Poet*? Rogovoy has explained, "One of the most rewarding ways of approaching Bob Dylan's lyrics is to read them as the work of a poetic mind apparently steeped in Jewish texts—Torah, Talmud, liturgy, and works of mysticism, or kabbalah—and engaged in the age-old process of midrash, riffing on the texts in order to elucidate or elaborate upon their hidden meanings."[6]

Interjecting a personal anecdote, to my mind some of the most profound Phish lyrics appear in "Bug."[7] The song references God early on, which may put one in a certain frame of mind, but when I first heard the line "Nothing I see can be taken from me" my initial thought was of Holocaust survivors, who can forever testify to the horrors they've experienced. Those words hit me unlike any others in a Phish song, even if this was not the intent (I've asked, although applying reader response theory to musical reception diminishes the import of such an inquiry).[8] However, I would point out that I am a fourth-generation American Jew (culturally and mostly otherwise, although my mother's mother immigrated from Russia at an early age, which demonstrates how complicated it can be to define and circumscribe all of this) who has been exposed to a fair share of Holocaust accounts over the years, which certainly informs my reaction to the song.

Let me supply another analogue from Grateful Dead world. In the "No Shows on Shabbos" entry that appears in David Shenk and Steve Silberman's *Skeleton Key: A Dictionary for Deadheads*, Abby Mendelson comments on "Scarlet Begonias": "'*Once in a while* you get shown the light / In the strangest of places *if* you look at it right.' *Once in a while—if* you look at it right. That's classic Jewish thought: you don't know exactly where the message is coming from, and you've got to look for it." She later adds, "I know there are other subgroups among Deadheads. It's funny—I see these people and I wonder 'what do they see in these guys?' How do you get 'Stella Blue' if you're not *Shomer Shabbos*? How do they get 'Franklin's Tower'? For us it strikes a chord. The fragility of life is reflected in everything about the Dead."[9]

Again, what can one discover in the music of Phish?

5. *Do Trey Anastasio and Page McConnell share cultural affinities with the Jewish community that may foster a nexus with that community?* While Jon Fishman and Mike Gordon were raised in Jewish households, in thinking about the band's appeal to Jews one shouldn't necessarily overlook the group's other two members. Although the principal goal of this afterword is to propose subjects of analysis for others to explore, I will suggest a demographic consideration in this instance. As Jonathan Schwartz observes in his interview with Kroll-Zeldin and Werden-Greenfield, "Phish was a northeastern band and there are so many Jews in the Northeast, so I think that definitely plays a role."

Both Anastasio and McConnell grew up in New Jersey. What's more, in the context of the *Long May They Run* podcast, Anastasio told me, "New York is a huge influence. My mom grew up in New York and went to public school there in the '50s. I took my first guitar lessons in New York." I yield the floor to another scholar, whether at a conference or perhaps in a second volume, who can relate this to the matter at hand.

6. *How many Jewish members are required for a band to enter the "Challah Fame"?* In Kroll-Zeldin and Werden-Greenfield's conversation with Marc Brownstein, he reveals, "It meant a lot to me that the Beastie Boys were Jewish. It meant everything as a kid from Brooklyn." All three band members had Jewish affiliations and the group's music has been examined through this lens from a scholarly perspective.[10] However, this does beg the question regarding the constituency of other bands' rosters. Is Kiss Jewish? Blue Öyster Cult? Mountain? Anthrax? Twisted Sister? In the latter three instances I point you to VH1 Classic's *Matzo and Metal* from 2005, which featured Twisted Sister's Dee Snider and J. J. French alongside Anthrax's Scott Ian and Mountain's Leslie West.[11]

All of the aforementioned groups occupy a place of honor in the Challah Fame section of Jewsrock.org, a nonprofit organization from the mid-2000s "devoted to illuminating the intersection of rock and roll and Jewish culture." Still, is there a particular threshold before a musical act attains the status of "Jewish artist," or is this less important than the roles of certain figures in the group and/or the nature of a band's music and following?

7. *Has the music of Phish found its way into Jewish prayer?* In "Jewish Deadheads: A Cultural Demographic Story" Leora Lawton emphasizes, "Despite contemporary ignorance of Jewish rituals by the majority of American Jews, other Jews are very much connected to synagogue music as a vehicle for spirituality."[12] Kroll-Zeldin cites a survey by Rabbi Josh Ladon that examines the connections between Phish and Jewish identity, noting that 32 percent of respondents said that they first encountered Phish at Jewish summer camp. I'm going to conflate these two essays and draw on my own Jewish summer camp experience (which occurred before Phish left Burlington) while observing that my camp rabbi set "Adon Olam" to the music of two Simon and Garfunkel songs: "Scarborough Fair" and "The Sounds of Silence." The 2011 "Blues for Challah" weekend at the Isabella Freedman Jewish Retreat Center in Connecticut touted "Grateful Dead–inspired meditation and prayer, an examination of Jewish themes in Dead lyrics, and guest rabbis who will muse on their experiences straddling both worlds" including a version of "Adon Olam" performed to the tune of the Dead's "Ripple."[13] To what extent has the music of Phish made similar musical inroads and how can this be interpreted?

8. *What conclusions can be drawn from the presence of Jews in the Phish crew and fan networks?* Douglas Gertner identifies over two dozen Jewish *menschen* who served as "close collaborators, devoted chroniclers, and key constituents in the vast family tree of Grateful Dead genealogy."[14] Gertner compiles this list to underscore the connection between Jews and the band, asserting that the presence of these individuals reinforced that association. Is this a worthwhile line of inquiry when contemplating the relationship between Phish and Jewish identity?

9. *Can subsets of the Phish fan community be described as Reform, Conservative, and Orthodox?* I am intrigued by the prospect of a study that assigns Phish devotees to categories based on the nature of their devotion, akin to Jewish denominations. David Gans takes a different tack in his essay "Grateful Dead Concerts Are Like Baseball Games," which addresses the various ways that people engage with the music of the Dead.

10. *Jews are "the People of the Book," but what is the analogous Phish text?* While I think it's clever to suggest a parallel with the fictional "Helping Friendly Book" from Anastasio's Gamehendge saga, I also think there's value in defining the book of Phish in a different manner, encompassing the totality of the band's creative output that is read by an audience, as Werden-Greenfield does in her exploration of Phish's canon. However, if one wants to focus on a specific tome, then I would point to the collections of set lists and ephemera assembled by fans into such works as *The Phish Companion* or *The Pharmer's Almanac*. To bring this

full circle, I also think it's worth noting that the collection of set lists compiled in the early '90s by the folks who would launch Phish.net and, later, the Mockingbird Foundation, was called the *Helping Phriendly Book*.[15]

(While I've limited myself to eighteen sources of inquiry, since I mentioned the Mockingbird Foundation I'll drop a bonus one into this parenthetical, as I believe there is potential work to be done on the Jewish tradition of tzedakah [giving] and the charitable efforts initiated both by Phish [the WaterWheel Foundation] and the group's stalwart supporters [the Mockingbird Foundation]. The concept of fans gifting tickets to one another—"miracle tickets" in Grateful Dead argot after the song "I Need a Miracle"—also merits consideration.)[16]

11. *Can we characterize Phish tapers as scribes or scholars?* In Kroll-Zeldin's piece he cites the experience of a fan named Avi who recalls that "at camp we pass the music down from generation to generation, acting the way Jews are supposed to act when we pass down the teachings of the Torah from generation to generation." Back in the early days of Phish, this process was facilitated by the community of tapers who recorded the group's shows (and yes, some folks continue to do so). Is there a comparable place within Judaic tradition for these individuals? And what should we make of the fact that many of these people have found their roles (and status) disrupted by the LivePhish series while archival recordings/totems have become more accessible to the community?

12. *Does the expressive dancing by some Phish fans draw on Jewish tradition?* In Isaac Slone's essay he writes, "I, too, dance to Phish's music in a way that mimics the act of *shuckling*, a Yiddish word meaning 'to shake,' that refers to the way observant Jews sway back and forth when deep in prayer, a bodily method meant to foster total physical, mental, and spiritual immersion." In an interview with *The Forward*, Gertner shares a previous exchange with a Deadhead who told him, "If you saw my dad davening and what he did with his body and then you saw me dancing at shows, it's the same movement. I embody my father, I'm just davening differently than him."[17] So too, in Shenk and Silberman's *Skeleton Key: A Dictionary for Deadheads* the entry for "spacedancing" includes this observation: "It is very much like the loose-jointed bowing and swaying one sees in Orthodox Jewish synagogues."[18] I'd like to see additional exploration of this topic and whether the correlation described by Slone and others is directly referential or otherwise culturally based if not something else altogether.

13. *Do Jewish Phish fans experience shows in a manner that parallels the observance of Sabbath?* In my *Long May They Run* podcast Jon Fishman recounted a conversation

with Trey Anastasio regarding the photo on the back cover of the booklet that accompanies the Baker's Dozen three-CD set. Anastasio had declared, "This is my favorite picture of our crowd right now," then asked, "What do you notice?" Fishman told him, "I don't know. It's a lot of happy-looking people. That feels good." Anastasio responded, "No, there's not one cell phone in the air."

In "Why Are There So Many Jewish Deadheads?" Douglas Gertner likens Grateful Dead concerts to Shabbos: "A Dead show was a time for 'being' rather than 'doing,' for what Bill Graham [a German Jew who fled the country and escaped the Holocaust, unlike his mother and one of his sisters] once called a true 'time out' to celebrate in what for many was a truly sacred space."[19]

Is this sacred space being carved out at Phish shows, where fans jettison their phones and social media feeds to embrace the moment in a matter that corresponds with Jewish observance?

14. *What is it about the nature of Phish's music, community, and culture that leads fans to study the group with a volume and intensity that parallels Talmudic discourse?* As Mike Gordon explains to Kroll-Zeldin and Werden-Greenfield, the band is "so analytical that we had to develop the 'No Analyze Rule.'" The same is not true of the group's devotees, who debate and confabulate with a depth and richness that eclipses any other contemporary band. This is not a recent phenomenon, as one can trace it back to 1992, when the Usenet administrative board acknowledged Phish's ardent online following by approving the rec .music.phish newsgroup as only the fourth artist-focused forum on the platform, following three acts of much longer standing: the Grateful Dead, Bob Dylan, and the Beatles. More recently, even as active online deliberation and exchange continues, the third edition of the fan-produced *Phish Companion* extends to over eight hundred pages and includes a ribbon bookmark commonly found in Jewish prayer books.[20] How do these efforts correlate with the Jewish exegetical tradition?

15. *Do Phish name-drops in contemporary television programs echo Yiddish references on TV in the 1950s and '60s?* Leora Lawton states, "As is the case for many ethnic minorities, Jews follow accomplishments of Jews in different professions and cultural activities."[21] This is particularly true when it comes to entertainment figures, as Lawton observes in the context of Adam Sandler's "The Chanukah Song," which name-checks a number of Jewish celebrities. Werden-Greenfield similarly cites the song in this regard and also mentions the rapper Lil Dicky (Dave Burd) as someone who interjects "the same fusion of humor and Jewishness."

Over the past couple of decades, Phish increasingly has been mentioned in a humorous light on television programs such as *The Simpsons*, *Key and Peele*, *Parks and Recreation*, and *Broad City*, and the band's fans have taken pleasure in these reference points.

The situation is analogous to the early days of television when Jews made their initial appearances on the medium, typically in comedic settings. Sam Levenson was a Jewish pioneer who hosted a few iterations of his own variety show and also appeared on such programs as *Match Game* and *To Tell the Truth*.[22] In the process, he helped to pepper the airwaves with Yiddish words such as kvetch, chutzpah, and meshuga, which eventually found their way into common parlance. Since this typically occurred in humorous contexts, the same way that Phish has appeared, a comparison may well be in order, which also draws in both Phish and Yiddish memes.

16. *Is Phish like "Judaism for Newbies"?* 18Doors is an organization that helps people in interfaith relationships "engage in Jewish life and make Jewish choices, and encourages Jewish communities to welcome them." In a blog post on the 18Doors website titled "Phish Is Like Judaism for Newbies," a fan of the group suggested, "As someone who is not Jewish, but is married to a Jew, entering the Jewish world meant being exposed to a community who also have a shared past, common experiences, rituals, and intimate knowledge of the language, practices, and songs associated with religious gatherings. Like the person who is not a fan of Phish, these things would be unfamiliar to someone who is not Jewish and has never been exposed to that world."[23] The Phish live experience, particularly as the fan community has defined it, contains cues, rites, and jargon. Is it possible that absorbing these elements—knowing when to clap during "Stash" and chant during "Harry Hood"—can offer a structural primer for individuals entering the world of Judaism?[24] Or approaching this from a different perspective, since many modern American Jews experience nonmainstream reference points while growing up within their subculture, are they predisposed to embrace a band that occupies a similar social environment?

17. *What would non-Phish fans say about all this?* One element that recurs through this volume is the first-person pronoun. Although Oren Kroll-Zeldin and Ariella Werden-Greenfield issued a general call for contributors through a number of academic platforms, it is not surprising that every participant appears to be a Phish enthusiast, most of whom have interjected personal experiences into their pieces. As Phish studies in general, and the subject of this book in particular, continue to evolve, I hope to see the work of anthropologists, historians,

musicologists, and religious studies scholars with limited prior Phish engagement lending their voices to the discourse.[25]

18. *Why is this night different from all other nights?* Given our subject matter, this reprise/afikomen feels inevitable.[26]

I'd like to frame my query to address a recent disruption of the status quo. COVID-19 suspended live gatherings, from Phish concerts to High Holy Day services. As members of both the Jewish and Phish communities recalibrated and reconnected in the virtual world, were their responses analogous and/or complementary? Did one approach inform the other in any manner? What do these cumulative collective actions during tragedy and turmoil teach us about the people of the Helping Friendly Book?

NOTES

1. In Judaism, the number eighteen, or *chai*, is significant because it represents life.

2. This Hebrew phrase, meaning "next year in Jerusalem," closes the Passover Haggadah.

3. Gertner, "Why Are There So Many?" 71.

4. I can speak to my own experience when I brought a friend of mine with whom I had attended Hebrew school to his very first Phish show at Symphony Hall in Springfield, Massachusetts, on December 30, 1992. When the band performed "Avenu Malkenu" during the second set, I peeked over at him and watched his confusion give way to a perma-grin that remained through the ride home.

5. Gloor, "From the Melting Pot."

6. Rogovoy, "Talkin' Hava Nagilah Blues."

7. Phish, "Bug," track 3 on *Farmhouse* (Elektra, 2000).

8. Fish, *Is There a Text?*

9. Shenk and Silberman, *Skeleton Key*, 206.

10. Stratton, "Beastie Boys."

11. Blabbermouth.net, "Twisted Sister Frontman."

12. Lawton, "Jewish Deadheads," 77.

13. Goodwin, "Examining Links."

14. Gertner, "Why Are There So Many?" 69.

15. The Mockingbird Foundation is a nonprofit organization dedicated to improving access to music education for children in the United States.

16. Grateful Dead, "I Need a Miracle," track 6 on *Shakedown Street* (Arista, 1978).

17. Wall, "'We Are All a Bunch of Weirdos,'" 268.

18. Shenk and Silberman, *Skeleton Key*, 268.

19. Gertner, "Why Are There So Many?" 73.

20. Mockingbird Foundation, *Phish Companion.*

21. Lawton, "Jewish Deadheads," 69.

22. See, for instance, Herrmann, "Folk Humorist from Brooklyn."

23. Garnett-Cook, "Why Phish Is Like Judaism."

24. Phish, "Stash," track 5 on *A Picture of Nectar* (Elektra, 1992); Phish, "Harry Hood," track 11 on *A Live One* (Elektra, 1995).

25. On a lighter, related note, I would like to share what was for me the most

memorable letter to the Phish newsletter, the *Doniac Schvice*, which the band produced multiple times per year over the course of the 1990s. In the October–November 1994 edition, someone describes the experience of moving into a new apartment and reading a couple of issues of the *Schvice* that had been addressed to the prior tenant (after acknowledging "I know that it is wrong, illegal even, to tamper with the U.S. mail but I have opened and perused both newsletters"). The author goes on to describe a woman that he found attractive but chose never to meet because "she could never fulfill my expectations, never live up to the person I had created in my head, and I wanted to retain that person, perfect and pure," before the missive concludes, "Letter writers in your newsletter seemed disappointed in the prospect of possible fame and fortune for Phish. But they cannot know the purity of loving Phish having never heard Phish."

26. An afikomen is a ritually significant piece of matzoh consumed at the end of the Passover meal.

REFERENCES

Blabbermouth.net. "Twisted Sister Frontman Discusses 'Matzo and Metal' VH1 Classic Special." April 14, 2005. https://www.blabbermouth.net/news/twisted-sister-frontman-discusses-matzo-and-metal-vh1-classic-special.

Budnick, Dean, host. *Long May They Run*. Produced by C13Originals. Released September–November 2019. Podcast. https://shows.cadence13.com/long-may-they-run.

Fish, Stanley. *Is There a Text in This Class? The Authority of Interpretive Communities*. Cambridge, MA: Harvard University Press, 1982.

Gans, David. "Grateful Dead Concerts Are Like Baseball Games." *Levity*, http://www.levity.com/gans/baseball.html.

Garnett-Cook, Andrew. "Why Phish Is Like Judaism for Newbies." *18Doors*, https://18doors.org/why-phish-is-like-judaism-for-newbies.

Gertner, Douglas. "Why Are There So Many Jewish Deadheads?" In *Perspectives on the Grateful Dead: Critical Writings*, edited by Robert G. Weiner, 67–78. Westport, CT: Greenwood Press, 1999.

Gloor, Leana B. "From the Melting Pot to the Tossed Salad Metaphor: Why Coercive Assimilation Lacks the Flavors Americans Crave." *Hohonu: A Journal of Academic Writing* 4 (2006): 29–32.

Goodwin, Jeremy D. "Examining Links Between Judaism and the Grateful Dead." *Boston Globe*, December 9, 2011. https://www.bostonglobe.com/arts/2011/12/09/seminar-examines-unique-links-between-judaism-and-grateful-dead/YNIUvr5d2YVSq7bTaxjK0M/story.html.

Herrmann, Helen Markel. "Folk Humorist from Brooklyn; Sam Levenson, Former Schoolteacher, Finds a Rich Vein of Appealing Comedy in Everyday Hazards of Family Life." *New York Times*, December 17, 1950. https://www.nytimes.com/1950/12/17/archives/folk-humorist-from-brooklyn-sam-levenson-former-schoolteacher-finds.html.

Lawton, Leora. "Jewish Deadheads: A Cultural Demographic Story." *Journal of Popular Music Studies* 27, no. 1 (2015): 69–89.

Mockingbird Foundation. *The Phish Companion: A Guide to the Band and Their Music*. San Francisco: Miller Freeman Books, 2000.

Rogovoy, Seth. *Bob Dylan: Prophet, Mystic, Poet*. New York: Scribner, 2009.

———. "Talkin' Hava Nagilah Blues." Jewsrock.org. https://web.archive.org/web/20080111052415/http://www.jewsrock.org.

Shenk, David, and Steve Silberman. *Skeleton Key: A Dictionary for Deadheads*. New York: Doubleday, 1994.

Stratton, Jon. "The Beastie Boys: Jews in Whiteface." *Popular Music* 27, no. 3 (2008): 413–32.

Wall, Alix. "'We Are All a Bunch of Weirdos': Q&A with Doug Gertner, the Grateful Jewish Deadhead." *The Forward*, July 3, 2020. https://forward.com/news/450161/we-are-all-a-bunch-of-weirdos-q-a-with-doug-gertner-the-grateful-jewish.

CONTRIBUTORS

EVAN S. BENN is an award-winning food journalist and James Beard Foundation committee member. He is currently Director of Special Projects and Editorial Events at the *Philadelphia Inquirer*.

DEAN BUDNICK is editor in chief of *Relix* and the founder of Jambands.com. The debut season of his podcast *Long May They Run*, which focused on Phish, was selected as a top pick by the *New York Times* and reached number 1 on the Apple Podcasts charts. He is the coauthor of Blues Traveler frontman John Popper's memoir *Suck and Blow: And Other Stories I'm Not Supposed to Tell* as well as *Ticket Masters: The Rise of the Concert Industry and How the Public Got Scalped*. Budnick reports on the live entertainment business for *Billboard*, *Variety*, and the *Hollywood Reporter*. He directed the documentary *Wetlands Preserved: The Story of An Activist Rock Club*, which aired on the Sundance Channel. Budnick holds a JD from Columbia Law School and a PhD from Harvard's History of American Civilization program. He has taught at a variety of institutions including Harvard University, the Massachusetts College of Art and Design, Roger Williams University, and the University of Rhode Island.

JACOB A. COHEN is a scholar of music, place, and identity in both classical and popular music of the United States. He earned his PhD in musicology from the CUNY Graduate Center with a dissertation on constructions of New England identity in early twentieth-century American classical music. In 2020, Dr. Cohen was a Visiting Assistant Professor of Musicology at Oberlin College Conservatory of Music, and has previously taught at Baruch College, Lehman College, Rutgers University–Newark, Queens College, and the University of Washington. He has written and presented papers on topics ranging from the Grateful Dead, Phish, and Talking Heads to Charles Ives, Aaron Copland, and the MacDowell Colony. He is always hoping for a soaring "Reba" jam.

BENJAMIN DAVID is the Senior Rabbi of Adath Emanu-El in Mount Laurel, New Jersey. An avid reader, writer, and runner, he is also a longtime Phish fan. Rabbi David, a cancer survivor, is a proud supporter of the Leukemia Lymphoma Society, Planned Parenthood, and an array of Jewish causes.

JESSY DRESSIN, when asked why she became a rabbi, sometimes likes to tell people that "at some point, the decision felt more radical than going on Phish tour." She has a BA in history and Jewish studies from the University of Maryland, College Park, MAs in both Hebrew letters and Jewish education, as well as rabbinic ordination from the Hebrew Union College–Jewish Institute of Religion. In 2016, she was named one of *The Forward*'s most inspiring rabbis. She currently works as the Senior Director of Jewish Education for Repair the World. Dressin is happiest at the intersection of live music, nature, ritual, craft beer, and adventure, all the while hoping to help make the world a more just and equitable place for all its inhabitants.

JOSH FLEET is a writer, winemaker, and Hebrew scribal artist. He is compiler of *The Geulah Papyrus*, a Phish-inspired Haggadah that is part of his ongoing Phish Talmud book project. For his day job, Josh manages Hadar's Rising Song Institute, which cultivates Jewish spiritual life through music. He lives in Atlanta, Georgia, but his heart is in Jerusalem/Gamehendge.

MIKE GREENHAUS is a writer, blogger, and self-described "live music geek." He is the editor in chief of *Relix*, the longest-standing print magazine dedicated to improvisational and independent music. Additionally, he edits the daily newswire for Relix.com and its sister site Jambands.com and is the vice president and cofounder of Relix Media Group. A former college radio DJ, Mike has spoken on panels at the South by Southwest and CMJ music conferences, helps oversee *Relix*'s official video channels, cocurates the collaborative "Brooklyn Is Live" event series, and serves on the Young Patrons Board for City Parks Foundation. He has written for *Spin*, *Paste*, *American Songwriter*, and a variety of other outlets, and penned the introduction to noted music photographer Jay Blakesberg's book *Jam*.

OREN KROLL-ZELDIN is the Assistant Director of the Swig Program in Jewish Studies and Social Justice at the University of San Francisco, where he is also an Assistant Professor in the Department of Theology and Religious Studies. He holds a PhD in cultural anthropology and social change from the California Institute of Integral Studies. His primary research interests focus on Israel/Palestine, contemporary Jewish culture, and the complexity of Jewish identity. He is the cofounder and lead curator of Mapping Jewish San Francisco. Oren's writing has appeared in numerous academic journals, books, and online publications including *Jerusalem Quarterly*, *Tikkun*, *International Journal of Education for Social Justice*, *Peace Review*, *Truthout*, and *+972 Magazine*.

JOSHUA S. LADON is West Coast Director of Education for Shalom Hartman Institute of North America, where he oversees educational and programmatic activity in the San Francisco Bay Area. Joshua received a BA from Washington University in St. Louis and subsequently lived in Jerusalem for seven years, where he completed an MA in Jewish Thought at Tel Aviv University. He received rabbinic ordination from the Shalom Hartman Institute. He has a doctorate in Jewish Education from the Jewish Theological Seminary.

NOAH MUNRO LEHRMAN has seen almost four hundred Phish shows. He studied religion and graduated magna cum laude at Brown University, drumming at the Collective Conservatory, and Torah at Beis Midrash Chernobyl in Tzfat, Israel. His existential love songs use Jewish imagery to explore universal themes and universal metaphors to probe Jewish concepts. A descendant of the Baal Shem Tov, Noah has performed with members of moe., RatDog, and Phil Lesh and Friends, and studied with Talmidei Hachamim including Dovid Klein of Navordna, the Talner Rebbe, and Elimelech Kohn of Telze. Noah has also lectured on Phish and Judaism at the Blues for Challah Festival.

CAROLINE ROTHSTEIN is an internationally touring and acclaimed writer, poet, performer, and educator. Her work has appeared in *Cosmopolitan*, *Marie Claire*, *Narratively*, *The Guardian*, *BuzzFeed*, *nylon*, *The Forward*, the *New Yorker*, the *Chicago Tribune*, *Newsweek*, and on *MTV News* and *CBS Evening News*. She serves on faculty for the Foundation for Jewish Camp's annual Cornerstone Fellowship, acts as a youth mentor at Urban Word NYC, and is a facilitator for the Dialogue Arts Project.

ISAAC KANDALL SLONE is the development manager for ROOM: A Sketchbook for Analytic Action and a candidate at the Psychoanalytic Training Institute of the Contemporary Freudian Society. He received his BA and MA at the NYU Gallatin School of Individualized Study, where he studied the relationship between psychoanalysis, music, and literature.

ARIELLA WERDEN-GREENFIELD currently serves as the Associate Director of Temple University's Myer and Rosaline Feinstein Center for American Jewish History, where she also serves as Temple University's Special Advisor on Antisemitism. She holds a PhD in religion from Temple University. Ariella's primary scholarly interests include contemporary Jewish culture, American Jewish history, religion in the African Diaspora, and religion and popular music. Her writing appears in academic journals and edited volumes, including *Religion in Philadelphia: A Reader*, *Savoring Gotham: A Food Lover's Companion to New York City*, *Religion*, and *Journal of Contemporary Thought*.

INDEX